The Creation of iGiselle

The Creation of

iGiselle

NORA FOSTER STOVEL, *Editor*

Classical Ballet Meets
Contemporary Video Games

UNIVERSITY *of* **ALBERTA** PRESS

Published by

The University of Alberta Press
Ring House 2
Edmonton, Alberta, Canada T6G 2E1
www.uap.ualberta.ca

LIBRARY AND ARCHIVES CANADA
CATALOGUING IN PUBLICATION

The creation of iGiselle : classical ballet
meets contemporary video games / Nora Foster
Stovel, editor.

Includes bibliographical references and index.
Issued in print and electronic formats.
ISBN 978–1–77212–381–4 (softcover).—
ISBN 978–1–77212–441–5 (EPUB).—
ISBN 978–1–77212–442–2 (Kindle).—
ISBN 978–1–77212–443–9 (PDF)

1. Giselle (Choreographic work). 2. Ballet.
3. Video games. 4. Artificial intelligence.
I. Stovel, Nora Foster, 1942–, editor

GV1790.G5C74 2019   792.8'42   C2018–906055–7

First edition, first printing, 2019.
First printed and bound in Canada by Houghton
Boston Printers, Saskatoon, Saskatchewan.
Copyediting and proofreading by
Lesley Peterson.
Indexing by Stephen Ullstrom.

University of Alberta Press is committed to
protecting our natural environment. As part of
our efforts, this book is printed on Enviro Paper:
it contains 100% post-consumer recycled fibres
and is acid- and chlorine-free.

University of Alberta Press gratefully
acknowledges the support received for its
publishing program from the Government of
Canada, the Canada Council for the Arts, and
the Government of Alberta through the Alberta
Media Fund.

*Frontispiece: Alberta Ballet artist Mariko Kondo,
floating. Photo by Paul McGrath.*

Canada   Canada Council   Conseil des Arts
            for the Arts   du Canada

Alberta
Government

Contents

NORA FOSTER STOVEL

Preface

Revisioning Giselle *as the Video Game* iGiselle

THE CREATION OF iGISELLE: *Classical Ballet Meets Contemporary Video Games* is a collection of essays composed primarily by the members of the team that created the video game *iGiselle*, a contemporary response to the 1841 ballet *Giselle*. *iGiselle* is an innovative project that unites classical ballet and contemporary video games—unusual bedfellows—by uniting cross-disciplinary colleagues in a collaborative venture. Until recently, ballet has remained a relatively unexplored territory in the field of gaming, and video gaming has not played a very significant role in the world of ballet. This preface chronicles the inception and development of *iGiselle* from a personal perspective.

This project was initiated at a Canadian Association for Theatre Research meeting in 2012 when I presented a paper on *Giselle*, the quintessential Romantic ballet. Following my presentation, illustrated by video clips from a televised production featuring the National Ballet of Canada, starring Karen Kain as Giselle,[1] a production that ended, as always, with Giselle doomed to remain in the company of the Wilis—spirits of maidens, jilted by heartless lovers before their wedding day, who come alive at midnight at the summons of their Queen Myrtha to avenge themselves on men by dancing them to death—an audience member inquired whether I had ever seen any other productions of *Giselle*. I replied that I had seen several productions, with various dancers—including Alicia Markova with the Ballets Russes, Galina Ulanova with the Bolshoi Ballet, Natalia Makarova with Mikhail Baryshnikov and the American Ballet Theatre, Veronica Tennant and Karen Kain with the National Ballet of Canada, and Evelyn Hart with the Royal Winnipeg Ballet.

She asked if any of them ended differently. I replied that *Giselle* was considered sacrosanct, and directors did not dare to change the ending. I subsequently discovered that there have been some recent postmodernist revisions, as Laura Sydora explains in her chapter "(Re)creating *Giselle*: Narrative and the Ballerina." Most productions of *Giselle*, however, stick comparatively closely to the traditional production. For example, when the Alberta Ballet mounted its premiere of *Giselle* in 2014, they invited an expert from La Scala to stage it to ensure that their version was faithful to the original. Even daring postmodernist revisions end with Giselle relegated to the kingdom of the shades.

Much as I love these beautiful ballets, I began to critique them from a feminist perspective. Why does the ballerina always have to die, usually survived by her perfidious lover? American Romantic poet Edgar Allen Poe remarked, "The death of a beautiful woman is unquestionably the most poetical topic in the world."[2] Granted the nineteenth century's fascination with disease and death, why do contemporary audiences enjoy the spectacle of a woman's sacrifice? Why do ballets from two centuries past that portray female victimization still fill theatres today? I also became intrigued by the paradox of the nineteenth-century ballerina and began to wonder how that ethereal, asexual figure remains a sexual icon, despite contemporary gender theories. Why do these ballets still enrapture twenty-first-century audiences when their portrayal of women is so far from what we say we believe women to be? I began to wonder if we could revise these misogynistic librettos.

I began to think: Why not? Why can't we change the ending? Why must all these nineteenth-century ballets that still fill theatres today—including *La Sylphide*, *Giselle*, *La Bayadère*, and even *Swan Lake*—conclude with the death of the ballerina, paralleling the fate of the diva of opera—as we see in Donizetti's *Lucia di Lammermoor*; Verdi's *La Traviata* and *Rigoletto*; Puccini's *La Bohème*, *Manon*, and *Madama Butterfly*; and Bizet's *Carmen*, to name but a few? In fact, Puccini's first opera, *Le Villi*, composed in 1883, four decades after *Giselle* premiered, is a response to the ballet, in which Anna and the Villis take revenge on her perfidious love Robert by dancing him to death. Indeed, imitations began appearing mere weeks after the premiere of *Giselle*. After I discovered that Puccini's first opera was inspired by *Giselle*, I invited Mark Morris, an expert on opera, to contribute a chapter on the topic. His research led him to discover additional operas and plays that he explores in his chapter titled "The Other Giselles: Moncrieff's *Giselle; or, The Phantom Night Dancers*, Loder's *The Night Dancers*, and Puccini's *Le Villi*." Clearly, the desire to rewrite this tragic narrative, including the desire to keep Giselle alive, a desire that also inspired the creation of *iGiselle*, began almost immediately after its premiere and continues to this day.

Death, however, is not the end for the Romantic ballerina. In fact, death is just the beginning, because the so-called *"ballet blanc,"* or "White Act," following the heroine's death, features the ballerina as an ethereal spirit, enhanced by a diaphanous white tutu that seems to float when she is airborne in leaps and lifts in supported adagio, pointe shoes that allow her to skim the ground in *bourées*, and wings that make her resemble an angel—notably in Act II of *Giselle* and in Act III of *La Bayadère*, called "The Kingdom of the Shades."

As I considered revising *Giselle*, I recalled how some nineteenth-century ballets are being drastically revised: consider Matthew Bourne's 1995 *Swan Lake*, the longest-running ballet production in London or on Broadway, which was featured in the 2000 film *Billy Elliot*, with an all-male corps de ballet of swans; or Bourne's 2012 revision of *Sleeping Beauty*, in which the prince and the fairies are vampires; or Mats Ek's *Sleeping Beauty*, in which Aurora is a heroin addict, and her four courtiers, who support her in the Rose Adagio, are all drug addicts. In fact, much modern dance, as well as contemporary ballet, is a rebellion against such Romantic ballets as *Giselle*. In "Ballet as Ideology: 'Giselle,' Act II," Evan Alderson argues, "much of the tradition of modern dance can be seen as an ideologically grounded critique of the ideals of beauty embodied in ballet. The saints of modern dance from Isadora Duncan forward have characteristically harnessed some ideal of the 'natural'—that war-horse of ideological conflict—to ride against the dragon of artifice" (Alderson 291–92). And the same could be argued regarding recent choreography—as well as *iGiselle*.

Another serendipitous event catalyzed the inception of *iGiselle* when I met Vadim Bulitko, a computer science specialist with an interest in video games. As we compared notes on our various interests, I raised the possibility of creating video games that would allow the player to rewrite these tragic ballets to empower the heroines and keep them alive, rather than consigning them to death and defeat. He was intrigued by the challenging concept, especially because—even though choreographers, including Merce Cunningham, Bill T. Jones, and William Forsythe, have invested in computers and technology in their dance projects—video games have seldom incorporated ballet, and vice versa.[3]

Inspired by this collaboration, I assembled an interdisciplinary team of experts—Vadim Bulitko, Associate Professor of Computing Science; Pirkko Markula, Professor of Physical Education; and Christina Gier, Associate Professor of Music; assisted by graduate research assistants Emilie St. Hilaire from Art and Design, Sergio Poo Hernandez in Computing Science, and Laura Sydora, a doctoral candidate in the Department of English and Film Studies—all of whom have contributed fascinating chapters to this collection, along with Mark Morris and Wayne DeFehr, who joined the project at a later stage. I applied for and was awarded a Research Cluster Grant from the University of Alberta's Kule Institute for Advanced Study (KIAS) in June 2013, and we all set to work.

We met regularly for one and a half years. Everyone agreed the ballet video game was a great idea, but we had a problem: most members of the team had never seen a ballet. So I began to educate the group about ballet by showing them film versions of each of five ballets—*La Sylphide*, *Giselle*, *La Bayadère*, *Swan Lake*, and *Sleeping Beauty*—introducing each ballet and discussing it with the team members afterwards.

Giselle, known as the ballerina's *Hamlet* because of its dramatically challenging title role, particularly caught the imagination of the team—just as it has enraptured audiences for almost two centuries. It was a natural, because the situation of an innocent young peasant girl, deceived by an aristocrat disguised as a peasant and condemned to death by betrayal and heartbreak, was a narrative crying out to be rewritten. *Giselle* is the ballet we love to hate and hate to love because, even though we are cognizant of gender debates and feminist concerns, it never fails to move audiences.

I was pleased personally, because *Giselle* was my first ballet. My mother took me as a child to see the legendary ballerina Alicia Markova, born Alice Marks in England, dance *Giselle* at Toronto's Royal Alexandra Theatre. We sat in a box overlooking the stage, almost close enough to reach out and touch her. When she balanced in a *posé en arabesque* before vanishing into the wings, she looked straight at me, and I fell in love—with the dance. The fairy had touched me with her magic wand, and I was fascinated by the ballet. Productions of *Giselle* never fail to thrill me, and the ending always leaves me moved, though perplexed. My chapter in this collection, "The Creation of the Romantic Ballet *Giselle*: The Ballerina's *Hamlet*," chronicles the creation of this quintessential Romantic ballet.

Just as I introduced the team to ballet, so Vadim introduced us Artsies to video games. We sampled *Jade Empire* and were appalled by its sexist representation of female characters portrayed in skimpy, tight-fitting clothing and in suggestively vulnerable positions. The computing science members of the team, even the female ones, were surprised by our reaction, so accustomed were they to such gender construction in video games. But we found that, as Pirkko Markula discusses in her contribution to this collection, "The Ballet Body and Video Games: A Feminist Perspective," the representations of the female body in ballet and video games actually have much in common, in ways that have inspired feminist critiques from numerous dance scholars. Such insights inspired the creation of *iGiselle*, a project that empowers the female protagonist.

I wanted our video game to give the player the opportunity to rewrite this tragic narrative, to keep Giselle alive, and to give her agency, allowing for possible "feminine endings" (see McClary). We began to design a video game using artificial intelligence that Vadim had developed with his graduate students. Vadim, who headed the team developing the video game, suggested calling our video game *iGiselle*, as in iPhone or iPad. (We hope Apple appreciates the homage.) We met frequently to compose the narrative, discussing alternative fates for Giselle; she could live or die, seek revenge or prefer forgiveness; she could come back to life, or Albrecht, the faithless lover, could join her in death; the Wilis could defeat Albrecht, or the lovers could destroy the evil spirits. The possibilities were limitless.

I suggested a metanarrative, or meta-balletic scenario: Giselle is a young dancer who is in love with her artistic director and who longs for the starring role of Giselle but who is threatened by a heart condition that she has kept secret for fear of damaging her career and also by a rival who aspires to both the role *and* the director. Besides the likelihood that a contemporary setting would appeal more to today's audience, we hoped that this interface between centuries would heighten the contrast in attitudes towards women and encourage players to revise the heroine's fate. We employed names for the dramatis personae that would link them to *Giselle* but also connect them with the contemporary western world: thus Albrecht became "Albert," "Berthe" became "Betty," "Hilarion" became "Henry," and "Bathilde" became "Beatrice," but the eponymous heroine had to remain "Giselle."

I wanted a musical accompaniment that would evoke, but not replicate, Adolphe Adam's haunting score for *Giselle*. Because Adam's score, following principles of nineteenth-century opera, in effect dooms the heroine to death, I did not want to employ it for our game in its original form. However, I also wanted our score to echo *Giselle* as the Romantic background to our contemporary game. We invited our colleague Wayne DeFehr to compose a contemporary revision of Adam's score, which he did using an ensemble of software-based orchestral instruments filtered through a synthesizer. The sound was calculated to help players travel back to the mid-nineteenth-century setting of the original *Giselle* ballet, while the software simultaneously conveyed a contemporary atmosphere. In his chapter, "Renewing Adolphe Adam's Score: Creating the Music for *iGiselle*," Wayne chronicles the development of his score for *iGiselle*, reviewing his artistic choices, contextualizing his comments with reference to elements in Adam's score. The Romantic belief "that music was as crucial to a ballet's identity as the story" is as true now as it was then (Garafola 1).

Vadim decided to change *iGiselle* from a traditional video game to an interactive installation, an interface in which the player would select the desired narrative branching by performing balletic poses. This system has the added advantage of making *iGiselle* an exercise game, while reinforcing the balletic context. In creating *iGiselle*, the team employed a Microsoft Kinect featuring an infrared camera interface for pose recognition. They also employed an artificial intelligence (AI) experience manager that allowed the developers to anticipate players' choices. Thus the player, as well as the heroine, has options; and, in contrast to the passive spectatorship of a ballet audience, players can interact with their avatar, as Sergio and Vadim explain in their chapter, titled "Artificial Intelligence for Managing the Interactive Ballet Video Game, *iGiselle*."

Excited about *iGiselle*, but unfamiliar, as a literature specialist, with computerized gaming technology and the intersection of dance and technology, I referred to Sergio to contextualize *iGiselle* in relation to other computer games that involve ballet. In recent years, he explained, with the popularity of dancing video games, a few games, such as *Imagine: Ballet Star* and *My Ballet Studio*, have given players opportunities to imitate ballet dancers. While *iGiselle* shares a similar design with these games regarding the way they interact with the players—*My Ballet Studio* through the Wii Fit board and *iGiselle* through the Microsoft Kinect—the designers' motivations for doing so are quite different. The interaction is the core element in the design of games such as *My Ballet Studio*, while *iGiselle* uses it as an additional way to immerse the player, as the core of the design of *iGiselle* is its narrative, which allows the player agency while traversing it. Ballet-themed video games, such as *Imagine: Ballet Star* and *My Ballet Studio*, are constructed to make the player feel like a ballet dancer, but *iGiselle* focuses on exploring the narrative of ballet and allowing players to affect the outcome of the story through their decisions. Thus, *iGiselle* is unique, as there are no other ballet-themed games that focus on a ballet narrative. Moreover, *iGiselle* was the vehicle through which the research team tested new AI techniques to provide a more engaging narrative experience for the player. While there have been articles comparing, and finding similarities among, video games and ballet as art forms, there have not yet been any attempts to explore themes found in ballet through a video game as *iGiselle* does.

I also consulted Pirkko, a physical cultural studies scholar, who helped me to further contextualize *iGiselle*, since she researches the role of dance in popular culture, in relation to the interface of technology and dance. She had developed an interest in interactivity in improvised performance, where the dancers' movements are tracked through digital camera technologies, and discovered a vibrant community of scholars—including Johannes Birringer, Scott deLahunta, Susan Kozel, Tara Mullins, and Stamatia Portanova—who are immersed in experimentations with technology and dance that can be traced back to the 1940s. Dance has become influenced significantly by the development of digital technology ever since dance-on-film and video-dance attracted attention in th 1980s. Merce Cunningham, in his experimental works, and William Forsythe, working with the Frankfurt Ballet, have long incorporated technology in their choreography. Other artists experimenting with interactive digital media include Yacov Sharir, Ellen Bromerg, Suzan Kozel, Robert Wechsler, Lisa Naugle, Troika Ranch, Random Dance Company, Company in Space, Palindrome, and Chunky Move. Dance performances currently incorporate cameras, video projectors, microphones, sensors, synthesizer, computer software–designed motion tracking cameras, and wearable computers in dance performance. While Pirkko observes that much of this interactive work coming from the contemporary dance community focuses on performance, the *iGiselle* project, instead of focusing on performance alone, employs the dancing body/technology interface to create a prototype for a computer game playable by anyone interested in becoming involved in its narrative. Thus, *iGiselle* enables any player, not only dancers performing a piece, to experience the bidirectionality made possible by technological innovation.

Once the narrative options were developed, the team auditioned local dancers and held a photo shoot, with choreography by Nicole Papadopoulos, assisted by Laura, and photography by Vadim, with post-production led by Emilie. The visual element was followed by the auditory aspect, and the team auditioned local actors to record the voiceover for the narrative, again directed by Nicole, with Emilie editing the recordings, assisted by University of Alberta undergraduate students and Edmonton high school students participating in Summer Internships. Once the video game was completed, Wayne created the musical accompaniment for *iGiselle*, and Emilie advanced our appreciation of the theoretical implications of the project with an in-depth analysis of *iGiselle* within the context of computer interaction design and new media philosophy. Her chapter, "Re-playing *iGiselle*: Dance, Technology, and Interdisciplinary Creation," describes this process, explaining how *iGiselle* is unique in embodying ballet in interactive gaming. She considers *iGiselle* within the context of computer interaction design and new media philosophy, thus prompting reflection on ways of seeing beyond the default movements and viewpoints often adopted by game designers. Her analysis extends insights from *iGiselle* towards potential future projects that could explore further some of the valuable questions proposed by the *iGiselle* project.

On October 25, 2014, the interactive video game *iGiselle* was launched as part of a colloquium that included presentations by each of the team members—the origins of the chapters in this collection. A KIAS Dialogue Grant, awarded in 2016, enabled me to contribute to a number of symposia and book launches, in partnership with Alberta Ballet, the Association for Canadian College and University Teachers of English (ACCUTE), and other organizations. Although *iGiselle* was not made available for purchase, as the development and marketing of a video game costs vast amounts of money, the value of the prototype demonstrates the importance of multidisciplinary collaboration. *The Creation of* iGiselle: *Classical Ballet Meets Contemporary Video Games* provides possibilities to researchers in dance studies, game studies, AI studies, computer science, gender and women's studies, and sociology, and we hope that it may inspire future interdisciplinary and collaborative projects.

Notes

1. The production was filmed by the Canadian Broadcasting Corporation in 1976.

2. Poe includes this statement in his 1846 essay, "The Philosophy of Composition," which offers writers suggestions for composition, employing his own poem, "The Raven," as an example.

3. *Bounden,* "an indie dancing video game developed by" the "Dutch developer Game Oven in collaboration with the Dutch National Ballet," was released on IOS on May 21, 2014, and on Android on July 3, 2014, the same year that *iGiselle* was developed. (*Bounden*)

Works Cited

Alderson, Evan. "Ballet as Ideology: 'Giselle,' Act II." *Dance* Chronicle 10.3 (1987), 290–304.

"*Bounden.*" *Wikipedia.* en.wikipedia.org/wiki/Bounden.

Garafola, Lynn. Introduction. *Rethinking the Sylph: New Perspectives on the Romantic Ballet.* Studies in Dance History. Hanover, NH: Wesleyan U P, 1997. 1–10.

McClary, Susan. *Feminine Endings: Music, Gender and Sexuality.* 1991. Rev. with a new introd. Minneapolis and London: U of Minnesota P, 2002.

Poe, Edgar Allen. "The Philosophy of Composition." *Graham's Magazine,* April 1846: 163–67.

Acknowledgements

I WISH TO ACKNOWLEDGE the Kule Institute for Advanced Study (KIAS), the Natural Sciences and Engineering Research Council of Canada (NSERC), and the WISEST, HIP, and Science-without-Borders programs at the University of Alberta for their financial assistance that made the development of this project possible.

I wish to acknowledge all the people who developed this project: the KIAS team consisting of Vadim Bulitko, Christina Gier, Pirkko Markula, Sergio Poo Hernandez, Emilie St. Hilaire, and Laura Sydora. Special thanks go to Vadim Bulitko, who designed the artificial intelligence part (PACE) and directed the development of the video game iGiselle; Sergio Poo Hernandez, who, with Igor Pereira Machado, Renato Ribeiro, Sarah Beck, and Trevon Romanuik, developed the software; Emilie St. Hilaire, who developed the narrative, assisted by Laura Sydora, Sarah Beck, Nicole Papadopolous, Sergio Poo Hernandez, and Nora Foster Stovel; Nicole Papadopolous, who developed the choreography, assisted by Laura Sydora; Vadim Bulitko, who photographed the dancers; Emilie St. Hilaire, who photographed, composed, and edited the background images, assisted by Sergio Poo Hernandez,

Allyson Shewchuk, Luke Slevinsky, and Jesse Underwood, who edited all the photographs; Wayne DeFehr, who composed the soundtrack; dancers Aphra Sutherland, Andrea Ginter, Kandise Salerno, Nathan Lacombe, Charles Nokes, Kiera Keglowitsch, Tara Gaucher, Rachel Ginter, Karly Polkosnik, Sierra Lacombe, and Justin Kautz; voice actors Dawn Harvey, Jessica Watson, Jeanine Bonot, Grant Eidem, Yvonne Desjardins, Sarah Beck, Dale MacDonald, Leah Beaudry, Nicole Papadopolous, and Larissa Thompson, who read the script for the soundtrack; Nicole Papadopolous, Kevin Hoskin, Emilie St. Hilaire, Laura Sydora, Sergio Poo Hernandez, Allyson Shewchuk, Luke Slevinsky, and Jesse Underwood, who recorded and edited the voice-over soundtrack. Thanks also are due to Sarah Beck, Susan Howard, Sunrose Ko, Alejandro Ramirez, Mark Riedl, Geoffrey Rockwell, Oliver Rossier, and David Thue, who all supported the project in valuable ways. Finally, I wish to thank Jean Grand-Maître, Artistic Director of Alberta Ballet, and Hayna Gutierrez, principal ballerina, who danced the demanding dramatic role of Giselle in Alberta Ballet's 2014 production, for their assistance in promoting awareness of this interdisciplinary collaborative project.

Introduction

Recreating Giselle *for the Twenty-First Century*

THE CREATION OF iGISELLE: *Classical Ballet Meets Contemporary Video Games* is a collection of eight essays by the research team that created the video game *iGiselle* with funding from a Research Cluster Grant from the University of Alberta's Kule Institute for Advanced Study awarded in June 2013: Nora Foster Stovel, Professor of English and Film Studies; Vadim Bulitko, Associate Professor of Computing Science; Pirkko Markula, Professor of Physical Education; and Christina Gier, Associate Professor of Music; plus graduate research assistants Emilie St. Hilaire from Art and Design, Sergio Poo Hernandez in Computing Science, and Laura Sydora, a doctoral candidate in English and Film Studies. This multidisciplinary team, comprised of specialists from the humanities, fine arts, human sciences, and computer science, collaborated on an innovative project that joined classical ballet with contemporary video games to create *iGiselle*, a ballet-themed video game, inspired by the original 1841 ballet *Giselle. iGiselle* brings this tragic tale of a nobleman's betrayal of a peasant girl into the twenty-first century by allowing players to choose various options for the eponymous heroine that empower her and give her agency.

This collection of essays includes two elements. First, each member of the creative team—including specialists in narrative, music, and movement—addresses the origin and significance of the artistic elements of this project. Second, each member of the technical team that created *iGiselle*—including computer experts, a visual artist, and a composer of music—addresses a technical aspect of that creation: artificial intelligence (AI), narrative branching, and visual and musical accompaniment.

The Creation of iGiselle: *Classical Ballet Meets Contemporary Video Games* is therefore divided into two sections. The first section, "An Interdisciplinary Approach to *Giselle*," contains four chapters that provide historical background to the project by synthesizing research on the libretto, choreography, and musical score of the Romantic ballet *Giselle*, followed by accounts of revised versions of the 1841 ballet in nineteenth-century fiction, plays, and operas and in late twentieth-century and early twenty-first-century ballets.

In "The Creation of the Romantic Ballet *Giselle*: The Ballerina's *Hamlet*," I outline the history and distinguishing characteristics of Romantic ballet in general and *Giselle* in particular as the quintessential Romantic ballet. I explain the inspiration, inception, and development of the libretto, musical score, and choreography that combine to realize the dramatic conflicts dictated by the libretto, including the class and gender issues that doom Giselle. I also provide an overview of the reception and influence of *Giselle*, which became the most famous, popular, and long-lasting Romantic ballet—one that is still performed all over the world today. The following chapters by Mark Morris and Laura Sydora explain the influence of *Giselle* on subsequent novels, plays, operas, and ballets.

I explain how *Giselle* was responsible for the birth of the White Goddess, the ballerina, and the Golden Age of Romantic ballet, 1830–1845, because the development of pointe work and supported adagio, augmented by the costume of white tutu and wings, plus gas lighting and stage machinery, etherealized woman and inspired the *ballet blanc*, or White Act, wherein the heroine reappears after death as a spirit. In Act II of *Giselle*, the White Act,

Giselle is initiated into the Wilis, ghosts of brides who have been jilted before their wedding and come alive at midnight to avenge their doom on men by dancing them to death.

The following three chapters analyze the effects achieved by *Giselle*'s score and explain the influence of *Giselle* on subsequent novels, plays, operas, and ballets. In "'No Feminine Endings': Adolphe Adam's Musical Score for *Giselle*," Gier provides an historical overview of Adam's 1841 musical score for *Giselle*, explaining how it accompanies the choreography in reinforcing patriarchal attitudes to women prevalent in nineteenth-century Europe by following established musical principles that, in effect, doom the eponymous heroine to death and defeat, while allowing her lover, the perfidious Albrecht—a nobleman who disguised himself as a peasant to woo her—to survive and return to his aristocratic life of privilege. Gier interprets and contextualizes Adam's musical score, providing detailed close readings to highlight narrative and gender implications in the formal elements, such as key signatures, instrumentation, and orchestration. Specifically, she demonstrates how Adam utilizes particular musical techniques—including the symbolic role of instruments and harmonies to help convey characters and dramatic contexts, various harmonies and melodic gestures to convey ideas of gender, different orchestral textures to highlight relationships, and rhythmic characterizations to emphasize the narrative. Adam composes the ideal allegro and adagio accompaniments to the dancing of the lovers in the celebratory company of the medieval Rhineland villagers of Act I and the sinister sisterhood of the Wilis of Act II. To understand the need for a contemporary revision of Adam's score for *iGiselle*, and to comprehend DeFehr's essay on his musical accompaniment for *iGiselle*, it is necessary to consider Adam's original score.

Morris, in "The Other Giselles: Moncrieff's *Giselle; or, The Phantom Night Dancers*, Loder's *The Night Dancers*, and Puccini's *Le Villi*," explains how these three works, one play and two operas, respond to the 1841 ballet *Giselle*. W.T. Moncrieff's play, incorporating songs and a ballet to music adapted from Adolphe Adam's score for *Giselle* by J. Collins, was first performed in 1841, mere weeks after Moncrieff read a review of *Giselle*, and published in 1842.

Moncrieff departs from Gauthier's libretto for the ballet by introducing new characters, varying the incidents, and changing the dénouement. Edward Loder's *The Night Dancers* (1846), originally titled *The Wilis*, is cast in two acts, reflecting the structure of Adam's ballet, with two stage settings, but Loder deviates dramatically from Gauthier's libretto by casting the entire opera as a dream from which Giselle finally awakens, allowing for a happy ending. Loder drew the Giselle story not from the ballet, but from its original source, poet Heinrich Heine, via "Les Willis," an 1852 story by the French writer Alphonse Kerr. Giacomo Puccini's *Le Villi* (1883), originally composed as a one-act opera, titled *Le Willis*, includes dances—the opening village folk dance, the "Witches' Sabbath," and the Wilis' dance at the end—although ballets within operas were in the French, not the Italian, tradition. In Moncrieff's play and Loder's opera, as in Adam's ballet, Giselle is a victim; in Fontana's libretto, however, Puccini's Giselle takes her revenge. *iGiselle* allows the player a range of options in concluding the narrative.

In her chapter, "(Re)creating Giselle: Narrative and the Ballerina," Sydora discusses the importance of narrative to Romantic ballets and video games, examining notable contemporary adaptations of *Giselle*: Fergus Early and Jacky Lansley's 1980 production of *I, Giselle*; Mats Ek's twentieth-century *Giselle*, wherein Giselle is incarcerated in an insane asylum, staged by the Cullborg Ballet in Sweden in 1982; Frederic Franklin and Arthur Mitchell's 1984 American reproduction titled *Créole Giselle*, by the Dance Theatre of Harlem; Michael Keegan-Dolan's Irish retelling, combining theatre, opera and dance, premiered by Fabulous Beast Dance Theatre at Dublin's Samuel Beckett Theatre in 2003; and, finally and most recently, a version of *Giselle* portraying Albrecht and Hilarion as lovers in a Vancouver production by José Navas, Director of Compagnie Flak in Montreal and resident choreographer with Ballet BC. Sydora reflects on gender issues in *Giselle* and the choices made in developing the narrative of *iGiselle*, positioning them in the context of feminist historiography and gaming narratology.

The second section, "Creating *iGiselle*," also contains four chapters, beginning with "Artificial Intelligence for Managing the Interactive Ballet Video Game, *iGiselle*" by Sergio Poo Hernandez and Vadim Bulitko. In this chapter, the programmers explain their use of AI and a new computational model connecting play-style modelling to goal inference to emotion prediction to narrative selection, plus their implementation of the narrative planning module in an approach they call Player Appraisal Controlling Emotions, or PACE, which they applied in creating *iGiselle*. While AI techniques have been used in video games to control non-playable characters, including their movement patterns and how they react to the player's presence, there have been recent efforts to apply new AI techniques to other areas of video game design, such as narrative creation. Currently, most games involving narratives fall into two categories: either they include a single narrative, or they offer various possible narrative branches. In the first category the author has complete control and can create a complex narrative, but the player has no ability to influence the story and might feel disengaged as a result. In the second category players might feel they are influencing the story through their actions, but the story branches available are created by the author, limiting the number of options for the player and running the risk of creating storylines that are less amusing. The new narrative planning model PACE, described in their essay, addresses these potential weaknesses. PACE predicts the player's emotions in any given scenario and uses this prediction to adjust the narrative in order to keep the player close to an author-supplied target emotional curve. It thus offers players opportunities to influence the story through their actions, while creating engaging storylines. PACE was implemented in the creation of *iGiselle*, allowing for the gamer's satisfaction at giving Giselle the agency to act autonomously.

In "Re-playing *iGiselle*: Dance, Technology and Interdisciplinary Creation," St. Hilaire explores how embodied research such as the *iGiselle* project can provide opportunities for interdisciplinary collaborations. She describes the process of the creation of *iGiselle* as the team implemented emotion-modelling techniques to map player styles and explains how using a Microsoft Kinect as a game controller requires players to interact with the narrative via ballet-inspired, full-body poses. She then situates the project within a theoretical framework that highlights relevant intersections between *iGiselle* and current literature pertaining to the body in dance and the phenomenological experience of the body in technology. She provides an analysis and theoretical framing of the body in technology and the body in dance in relation to the most interesting aspects of the *iGiselle* project.

In "Renewing Adolphe Adam's Score: Creating the Music for *iGiselle*," DeFehr, composer of the video game's musical score, explains how he adapted the musical motifs of Adam's 1841 score for *Giselle* by using strings, woodwinds, and percussion, recreated with computer software and filtered through a synthesizer, to accompany the *iGiselle* video game in order to echo Adam's nineteenth-century style, while rooting the player's experience in the twenty-first century.

In the final chapter, "The Ballet Body and Video Games: A Feminist Perspective," Markula investigates the representation of women in the highly sexualized and frequently victimized female characters of twentieth- and twenty-first-century video games *and* of nineteenth-century ballets like *Giselle*, drawing parallels between these two apparently very different, but surprisingly similar, genres. While several studies have demonstrated connections between playing violent games and acting aggressively, some feminist critics consider ballet a potentially harmful, exploitative and oppressive practice for women, as the ideological construction of the image of the ballet body, associated with western upper-class ideologies of the female aesthetic, supports patriarchal hegemony. Some critics cite the concepts of the male gaze and the marriage plot to argue that ballet heroines, like female game characters, are often defined through their relation to male characters as mothers, lovers, daughters, wives or fiancées, and are divided dualistically into good and evil to support dominant, male-defined ideas of femininity, reflected in the eponymous heroine of the Romantic ballet *Giselle*. Markula also explores popular action heroines, such as Lara Croft, a postfeminist icon emphasizing female participation in traditional male spheres, combining an attractive female image with an active character. Recent feminist critics call for ballets and computer games that reflect and inspire real girls and women as sites of empowerment. Markula critically assesses the potential of *iGiselle* to marry these apparently different genres to empower feminist practice.

Ultimately, it is hoped that *The Creation of* iGiselle: *Classical Ballet Meets Contemporary Video Games* will help dance and video game scholars to imagine the possibilities for future innovation, and will, more generally, serve to promote scholarly and creative collaboration and interdisciplinarity.

I

An Interdisciplinary Approach to *Giselle*

1

The Creation of the Romantic Ballet *Giselle*

The Ballerina's Hamlet

The Golden Age of Romantic Ballet 1830–1845

Giselle is the quintessential Romantic ballet, the incarnation of the Romantic Movement in nineteenth-century European literature, music, and painting, which emphasized imagination over the rationality of the preceding Age of Reason. Romanticism, so vividly expressed by English poets—including Blake, Wordsworth, Coleridge, Keats, Shelley, and Byron—and German composers—including Beethoven, Brahms, Schubert, Schumann, Wagner, and Liszt—is well documented, but less is written about Romantic ballet, which was inspired by this movement and formed its apotheosis, an amalgam of the Romantic sister arts.

I would argue that ballet and Romanticism were inextricably interconnected. Romanticism liberated ballet from its subordination to opera, because, until 1832, ballets were performed as entr'actes in operas. For example, "The Ballet of the Nuns," in Giacomo Meyerbeer's 1831 opera *Robert le Diable*, introduced ballerina Marie Taglioni in the lead role of the Abbess Héléna. Subsequently, Taglioni starred in the first Romantic ballet,

La Sylphide, which premiered in 1832.[1] Moreover, ballet served as the ideal embodiment of the principles of Romanticism. Carol Lee explains the importance of ballet to the Romantic Movement as a whole:

> *Dancing, by its very nature, was uniquely suited to transmitting the ideas of the Romantic Movement. Because ballet production incorporated transcendentalist literary ideas, reinforced by visual and aural forces, theatrical dance was rendered a powerful medium of expression...While the Romantic ballet's peak years were brief, they possessed a creative intensity that served to synthesize the cumulative results of well over a century of dance experience and experimentation into a veritable golden age...While the Romantic ballet was formed by the accumulation of decades of technical knowledge, the art form triggered its unparalleled aesthetic synthesis by being grounded in the stimulating intellectual atmosphere of the epoch.* (138, 145–46)

The Golden Age of Romantic ballet, 1830–1845, featured the very ballets— *La Sylphide* (1832) and *Giselle* (1841), followed by the Classical ballets *Swan Lake* (1877), *La Bayadère* (1877), and *Sleeping Beauty* (1890)—that still fill theatres today. Although *La Sylphide* was the first Romantic ballet, *Giselle* best incarnates the spirit of the Romantic Movement and remains the most popular. "*Giselle*'s innovation is its summing up of what we know as the Romantic ballet," twentieth-century choreographer George Balanchine declares (Balanchine and Mason 194).

The Romantic era was distinguished by the collaboration of artists from diverse disciplines—literature, composition, design, and choreography. Nowhere was such collaboration more important than in ballet, as *Giselle* illustrates. Artists' imaginations were engaged by the idealized world of ballet, which portrayed exotic locales and supernatural fantasies. Poets wrote librettos for ballets:

> *Poets and novelists of the time were all interested in stories of the romantically supernatural, stories that told of lovely young girls whose love was never fulfilled because of intervening powers...The mysterious and supernatural*

powers that Romantic poetry invoked to secure its ideal soon became natural to
the theatre, where dancers attired in billowy white seemed part of the world and
also above it. (Balanchine and Mason 194)

English Romantic poet Percy Bysshe Shelley (1792–1822) declared in his
1821 *Defence of Poetry* that the literature of the age "has arisen as it were
from a new birth."[2] That birth was embodied by ballerina Marie Taglioni's
Sylphide—"that ghostly, uncanny female figure who has haunted the stages
and the classrooms of classical ballet since the early 19th century"—who best
epitomized the spirit of the age (Carter 115). Théophile Gautier (1811–1872)
proclaimed, "Taglioni is not a dancer, she is the embodiment of dancing" (69).
Ballet historian Mary Clarke affirms that Taglioni was "the visible expression
of the Romantic idea" (51). Taglioni established the phenomenon of the White
Goddess, the cultural icon of the Romantic ballerina, who "became a kind
of film star" (Chazin-Bennahum 218). As Clarke asserts, "The success of *La
Sylphide* and of Taglioni, the visible expression of the Romantic idea, was
absolute. The ballet and its star were the heralds of a golden age, a period of
supernatural and exotic creations that starred not only Taglioni, but a galaxy
of ballerinas during the next twenty years. *La Sylphide* altered the nature of
ballet in theme and decoration...throughout Europe" (51).

"With the Romantic era began the great feminization of ballet," declares
Lynn Garafola (7). The Romantic ballerina is an ethereal creature resembling
religious and romantic icons of angel and bride. According to Balanchine
and Mason, "the sylph became ballet's symbol for romantic love—the girl
who is so beautiful, so light, so pure that she is unattainable: touch her and
she vanishes" (194). Deirdre Kelly observes, "She floats on air, a swan, sylph,
or spirit haunting our imaginations from beyond the grave"; in Rayner
Heppenstall's words, "there is a kind of eternal virginity about her. She is
inaccessible. She remains unravished" (qtd. in Kelly 1). When the Romantic
ballet heroine tries to love, she dies, for she is not free to be sexual or even
human. Such ballets are based on poets' libretti, or scenarios, which draw on
folk tales and literature to depict femmes fatales reminiscent of Odysseus's
Sirens, such as the seductive but sinister Wilis in *Giselle*—ghosts of brides

jilted by heartless lovers before their wedding day who revenge themselves on men by dancing them to death.

Although the ballerina is the star of each ballet, she is a tragic figure much like the heroine of opera—Lucia di Lammermoor, Guilda, Violetta, Aïda, Mimi, Madama Butterfly, and Carmen, to name but a few—who dies, often survived by her lover. Many Romantic ballets, including *La Sylphide* and *Giselle*, are tragedies pivoting on love triangles that catalyze the heroine's death. Death divides the ballet into two dimensions: natural and supernatural. The heroine is transformed from woman to sylph or spirit in *Giselle* and *La Bayadère*, shown to her lover in a vision in *Sleeping Beauty*, or impersonated by another woman in *Swan Lake*. Many Romantic ballets include one act that features this transformation, known as the White Act, or *ballet blanc*, notably Act II of *Giselle* and the "Kingdom of the Shades" sequence in Act III of *La Bayadère*, which is often performed as an independent piece.

This dichotomy between woman and sylph allows the ballerina to display her expertise in both artistic arenas, the allegro and adagio, or fast and slow, musical modes. The dual aspects of the heroine may be danced by two dancers, each excelling in that style, such as the Sylphide and the mortal bride, Effie, in *La Sylphide*, where the hero, James, is "caught between duty to a flesh-and-blood fiancée and an obsession with an unattainable image of ideal perfection" (Cass 122). When both roles are danced by one dancer, as in the roles of Odette/Odile in *Swan Lake*—a dichotomy exploited by the 2010 film *Black Swan*—the ability to excel in both modes produces a virtuoso performance. In *Giselle* these dual roles combine in one woman, making *Giselle* Romantic ballet's most dramatically challenging role, because Giselle must appear "real and unreal at the same time" (Balanchine and Mason 195).

In such ballets the heroine's divided self is reflected in all artistic areas: choreography, music, costume and design. The choreography expresses the dichotomy by combining lively solos and duos before her death with ethereal variations and pas de deux after. The music reflects this duality, including allegro and adagio segments to represent the quick and the dead selves. Costume is crucial in creating this dichotomy: in Act I of some ballets, the heroine wears colourful costumes, such as peasant dresses in

Giselle or sensual saris in *La Bayadère*; in Act II, following her death, the ballerina's translucent white tutu conveys her spiritual state. Set design mirrors costumes, as the White Act is often set in a forest, a liminal union of natural and supernatural dimensions, creating a romantic sylvan atmosphere that is a traditional setting for mysterious metamorphoses, as in Shakespeare's *A Midsummer Night's Dream*. Some ballets, including *Giselle* and *Swan Lake*, may feature a pool or lake in the background—symbolizing death and the psyche—in which characters may drown. The development of stage machinery that enabled the Sylphide to fly or Giselle to arise from her grave allowed for haunting effects. The development of gas lighting in 1817, inspired by pioneer photographer Louis Daguerre, also contributed to the surreal illusion of Romantic ballet by creating the impression of spectral moonlight. Combined with the new practice of darkening the theatre, previously illuminated by a myriad of candles, and lowering the curtain before the performance, these new technologies enabled stage crews to prepare a striking set, allowing for the element of surprise.

Three elements are crucial to creating the ethereal figure of the White Goddess: the tutu, the pointe shoe, and wings. Many heroines, beginning with the Sylphide and Giselle, wear wings. In *Swan Lake*, Odette, the Swan Queen, simulates wings with her graceful *ports de bras*, or arm movements, as does the ballerina in the modern reflection of this tradition, *The Dying Swan* (1905). In *La Sylphide* Madge, the witch, offers James a magic scarf that will cause the Sylphide's wings to fall off so that he can embrace her and she can no longer fly away to evade his grasp; when he winds the scarf around her arms, her wings do fall off, but she dies as a result. Thus, a sylph cannot become human. Similarly, Giselle, after death, is given wings by Queen Myrtha when she is initiated into the band of Wilis.[3]

The tutu, first used in the ballet *La Péri* (1843), paradoxically creates an ethereal lightness while allowing the audience to view forbidden flesh—the dancer's legs. "She prays with her legs," wrote Gautier of Romantic ballerina Fanny Elssler as the Sylphide, (qtd. in Lee 155), and he referred elsewhere to Taglioni's "spiritual arms and aesthetic legs" (qtd. in Cass 124). "No single theatrical costume in the history of ballet is more important than that worn by Taglioni in *La Sylphide*," Chazin-Bennahum affirms, "for of it was born the tutu, which is to ballet as the ermine is to royalty" (214).

Pointe shoes encapsulate the contradiction that is ballet by demanding strength to convey effortlessness. They complete the illusion by allowing the ballerina to skim the stage in *bourrées en pointe* and to spin on her pointe like the doll atop a music box. Pointe shoes, as Lee observes, "enhanced the dancer's ability to defy gravity, to be the ethereal, never-to-be-attained ideal woman of the troubadour's passionate song or the fleeting, soulless creature of the forest" (142). Garafola calls pointe work "a uniquely female utterance" that became "a metaphor for femininity" (4). Although Taglioni (1804–1884) was not the first dancer to use pointe shoes, her expertise made them famous,[4] inspiring Russian balletomanes to cook her shoes and devour them. Dancers still place their pointe shoes on her Paris grave in tribute, as they constitute both a blessing and a curse.

Pointe shoes necessitate another method of etherealizing the ballerina: supported adagio, that relic of a medieval courtly tradition where the man serves the woman. Because balancing on pointe is so difficult, a partner is required to pivot, or promenade, the ballerina on her turning pointe. The illusion is completed by lifts that create the impression of flying. Although the heroine's lover survives, the choreography reduces him to the supporting role of a human crane, highlighting gender performance.

Thus, the Romantic ballet was dominated by the ballerina, while the male dancer became "a necessary evil" (Clarke 57). Poetry made flesh, the ballerina was the heart of Romantic ballet, displacing the male dancer such as Auguste Vestris (1760–1842), known as *"le dieu de la dance"*—both metaphorically and literally at centre stage.[5] So ascendant was the ballerina that men were discouraged from dancing to the point where male roles were danced by women *en travesti*. While most ballets feature a prince—Albrecht in *Giselle*, Siegfried in *Swan Lake*, and Florimund in *Sleeping Beauty*—they also often feature an evil wizard, such as Von Rothbart of *Swan Lake*, who enchants the heroine into a swan, forbidding her freedom to love—although the evil force in *Giselle* is Queen Myrtha.

"Ballet is woman," famously declared Balanchine. Nevertheless, ballets were still created by male librettists and choreographers, who portrayed woman in an idealized manner that appealed to men. The mystique of the White Goddess was intensified by the contrast between the virginal creature she impersonated and the reality of what Kelly terms the "ballerina-courtesan" (15): a titillating paradox that reflected the nineteenth-century male view of woman as virgin and whore, or as spiritual and sexual being—a paradox realized when Gautier seduced ballerina Carlotta Grisi away from her partner and choreographer, Jules Perrot.

The Creation of *Giselle*

Although *La Sylphide* was the earliest Romantic ballet, *Giselle* has remained the most popular. *Giselle* is widely regarded as "the first true Romantic ballet" as well as "the most celebrated ballet of the Romantic era" (Clarke 50, 60). Cyril W. Beaumont affirms, "That a ballet should have endured for over a hundred years, triumphantly surviving so many vicissitudes of taste and fashion, is a sufficient tribute to its popularity and wide appeal." He concludes, "*Giselle* was and remains the supreme achievement of the Romantic Ballet" (9). Indeed, *Giselle* was the perfect product of the Romantic Movement, being the brainchild of two European poets, Gautier and Heinrich Heine (1797–1856).[6] No wonder it is, arguably, the most poetic of the Romantic ballets!

Giselle was profoundly influenced by *La Sylphide*, the first ballet to epitomize the Romantic Movement in motion, thus effecting a revolution in dance and setting the stage for the Golden Age of Romantic ballet—thanks to the creations of artists such as librettist Gautier, composer Jean-Madeleine Schneitzhoeffer, designer Pierre-Luc Ciceri, costumier Alexandre-Evariste Fragonard, and choreographer August Bournonville. All the features of *La Sylphide*—scenario, choreography, music, design and costuming—were calculated to effect such a dramatic revolution. *La Sylphide* transferred from Paris to London in 1832, then to New York and St. Petersburg in 1835, spreading the image of the White Goddess. Its impact was profound. *Giselle*, however, best incarnates the spirit of the Romantic Movement.

How was this incarnation effected? Gautier, impressed by Taglioni's performance in *La Sylphide*, read German poet Heine's 1835 prose volume about Germany, in one part of which Heine describes the "elemental spirits" of German folklore, including the Wilis.[7] This description inspired Gautier's libretto for *Giselle, ou les Wilis*, especially the White Act. The Wilis, according to Heine, are betrothed maidens who have died on their wedding day. Frustrated because they have not been able to satisfy their *Tanzlust*, their passion for dance, during their lifetimes, they rise from their graves at night and lure young men to dance to death. Beaumont suggests that the name of the Wilis, who have a Slavic origin, originates in the word *vila*, or *vile* in the plural, the Slavic term for vampires, with *wilis* likely being a Teutonic form of *vile*. Meyer's *Konversations-Lexicon* defines Wilis as vampires[8]—in Heine, however, they are vengeful spirits of brides who have been jilted on their wedding day, which would explain their desire for vengeance on men. The Wilis do resemble vampires in their thirst for human blood. Gautier writes in *La Presse* in 1841, in the form of a letter to Heine, that, after reading about the Wilis, "I said to myself, 'What a lovely ballet that would make!' In a burst of enthusiasm I even took up a large sheet of fine white paper and wrote at the top, in superb rounded characters, 'Les Wilis, a ballet'" (Gautier 94).

So well does Miss Havisham of Charles Dickens's 1860 novel *Great Expectations* reflect the vengeful Wilis in her determination to mould Estella to avenge on the male sex her own devastation at being jilted on her wedding day that one may well wonder if Dickens was fortunate enough to see *Giselle*. As Molly Engelhardt says, Miss Havisham "seeks vengeance against men by trapping them in a cobwebbed circle of thwarted desire where they figuratively dance until their hearts break" (98).

In her chapter in this collection, "(Re)creating *Giselle*: Narrative and the Ballerina," Laura Sydora discusses other literary echoes of *Giselle*, as well as recent ballet adaptations. Echoes of *Giselle* appear not only in the literature of the nineteenth century but also in its opera and drama. Giacomo Puccini's first opera, *Le Villi*, composed in 1883, four decades after *Giselle* premiered, is a response to the ballet in which Giselle takes revenge on her perfidious love Albrecht. In his chapter in this collection, "The Other Giselles: Moncrieff's *Giselle; or, The Phantom Night Dancers*, Loder's *The Night Dancers*, and Puccini's *Le Villi*," Mark Morris explains how each of these three nineteenth-century works—a play and two operas—responds to the 1841 ballet *Giselle*. Domenico Ronzani's *Giselle* at Rome's Teatro Argentina, in 1845, added a third act and a conventionally happy ending to the ballet, with Giselle and "Alberto" "pledging their troth beyond the grave" (Garafola 5). *iGiselle* responds to the 1841 ballet by allowing players to keep Giselle alive and give her agency.

Heine's haunting vision of the Wilis provided Gautier's Act II of *Giselle*. Gautier had feared "that it was quite impossible to transpose onto the stage that misty, nocturnal poetry, that phantasmagoria that is so voluptuously sinister, all those makings of legend and ballad that have so little relevance to our present way of life" (94). The Wilis, with their spectral aura, were similar to the aerial sylphs of *La Sylphide* and equally suited to the new possibilities for dancing and staging. Heine describes these bitter brides in *Religion and Philosophy in Germany*:

> *Dressed in their wedding clothes, with garlands on their heads, and glittering rings on their pale hands, laughing horribly, irresistibly lovely, the Willis dance in the moonshine, and they dance ever more madly the more they feel that the hour of dancing, which has been granted them, is coming to an end, and that they must again descend to their cold graves.*[9]

Attired all in white, with gauzy tarlatan skirts, coronets of flowers, and mothlike wings, the Wilis were the ghostly sisters of the Sylphides. Clearly, *La Sylphide* influenced Gautier's creation greatly.

Giselle displays a similar structure to *La Sylphide*, which appealed to the Romantic sensibility through its juxtaposed dualities, as it presents two worlds—the actual and fantastic, or the natural and supernatural—divided between the two acts. Victor Hugo wrote,

> *Christianity told man "you have a double nature. You are composed of two beings, the one perishable, the other immortal; the one flesh, the other spirit." One is chained by appetites, needs and passions. The other is carried on the wings of ecstasy and vision. The former always falls towards the earth, its mother; the latter constantly shoots towards heaven, its father.*
> (qtd. in Cass 109)

Giselle embodies this duality perfectly.

The challenge for Gautier was to create an Act I that could account for Giselle's reappearance as a Wili in Act II. He found his concept in Hugo's poem, "Fantômes," from *Les Orientales* (1829). Hugo describes, in Part III, verse 3, the fate of a Spanish girl who loves to dance, but who lingers too long at a ball, catches a chill, and dies: "She was over fond of dancing and paid with her life" ("*Elle aimait trop le bal, c'est ce qui l'a tuée*"; qtd. and trans. Beaumont 20). Gautier describes to Heine his vision of the Wilis dancing in a beautiful ballroom, in hopes of attracting a new recruit, while the queen waves her magic wand to inspire the Wilis with an insatiable desire to dance, until the entrance of the ladies and gentlemen makes them fly away like insubstantial shadows. But "Giselle, having danced the whole night through... would be surprised by the cold of morning just like the young Spanish girl, and the pale Queen of the Wilis, invisible to all, would have placed her icy hand on her heart" (98).

Gautier realized that this opening act would not set the stage for his second act. So he consulted an opera librettist, Jules-Henri Vernoy, Marquis de Saint-Georges (1801–1875), who had created several scenarios for opera and would create several more for ballets. Initially Saint-Georges was skeptical, exclaiming, "How could a spectre exist in Paris?...How miserable a stray ghost would feel in that lively throng!" (qtd. in Gautier 51). But as Gautier explains to Heine, "I had only to take your pale and charming phantoms by their shadowy fingertips and present them, to ensure their receiving the most polite reception" (51). Together, Gautier and Saint-Georges crafted a scenario for *Giselle*, and Léon Pillet, director of the Paris Opera, accepted it just three days later. Gautier tells Heine, "The Director and the public offered not the slightest Voltairian objection. The wilis immediately received the freedom of the city...the few lines in which you speak of them being placed at the head of the scenario and serving as their passport" (qtd. in Beaumont 95). Gautier describes Act I of *Giselle* to Heine as "the story invented by M. de Saint-Georges to bring about the pretty death we needed" (Gautier 54).

The scenario was presented to composer Adolphe Adam, who, enthused by the project, completed a first draft of the score in a mere week. As he writes in his unpublished *Memoires*, "I enjoyed composing the music. I was in a hurry and that always stimulates my imagination. I was on very good terms with [Jules] Perrot, with Carlotta [Grisi], the work took shape as it were in my drawing-room" (qtd. in Beaumont 23). Gautier sums up triumphantly, "I told him the tradition of the Wilis. Three days later, the ballet of *Giselle* was accepted. At the end of the week Adolphe Adam had improvised the music, the scenery was nearly ready, and rehearsals were in full swing"—an ideal example of artistic collaboration (51).

Giselle ou les Wilis, advertised as a *"Ballet-Pantomime en deux actes,"* premiered at the *Théâtre de l'Académie Royale de Musique* in Paris on June 28, 1841, with libretto by Gautier, Saint-Georges, and Jean Coralli; choreography by Perrot and Coralli; music by Adam; scenery by Ciceri (the designer of *La Sylphide*), and costumes by Paul Lormier, with Carlotta Grisi as Giselle (fig. 1.1), Lucien Petipa as Albrecht, Adèle Dumilâtre as Myrtha, Queen of the Wilis, and Coralli as Hilarion. Gautier, a regular ballet reviewer for the Paris newspaper *La Presse*, wrote his own review of *Giselle* on July 5, 1841, ostensibly as a letter to Heine, whose Paris address he claimed not to know. He concludes his review triumphantly, "So your German *Wilis* have had a complete success at the French Opera. The newspapers will have already told you about it. I would have informed you sooner if I had known your address, but being without it, I am taking the liberty of writing to you in the form of a review in *La Presse*, which will no doubt reach you" (qtd. in Beaumont 102). As Balanchine and Mason record, "At its first performance...*Giselle ou les Wilis* was proclaimed the triumphant successor to *La Sylphide* and the greatest ballet of its time" (195). They explain:

> This story of the Wilis seemed to be ideal for ballet: it made the story of La
> Sylphide *look like merely the first step in the attainment of the romantic ideal.*
> *For the heroine of that ballet was purely a creature of the imagination, a figure*
> *in the hero's dream. We had admired her beauty and pitied her, but she was too*
> *illusory a character to make us feel deeply. What would accomplish this, what*
> *would make us care about such a character, would be to give her a basis in real*
> *life, to make her real and unreal at the same time—like the Wilis.* (194–95)

Figure 1.1: Carlotta Grisi as Giselle by Auguste Jules Bouvier c. 1841. [Wikimedia Commons]

Thus, nine years after *La Sylphide*, *Giselle* perfected the incarnation of the Romantic ideal. *Giselle* then transferred to Her Majesty's Theatre, London, on March 12, 1842, the Bolshoi Theatre in St. Petersburg on December 30, 1842, La Scala in Milan in January 1843, and the Howard Atheneum in Boston in January 1846, spreading Romantic ballet across the world.

The success of *Giselle* was confirmed subsequently by four adaptations: a comic parody and two serious reinterpretations in the 1840s—*Grise-Aile*, a comic parody by "Lorents," published in the satirical journal *Musée Philipon*;

W.T. Moncrieff's *Giselle; or, The Phantom Night Dancers* (1841), a play with music and dancing staged in London (Smith 71–74), and Edward Loder's *The Night Dancers* (1846)—followed by Puccini's *Le Villi* (1883), as Morris explains in his chapter, "The Other Giselles." Sydora describes postmodernist revisions of *Giselle* in her chapter, "(Re)creating *Giselle*."

The parallels between *Giselle* and *La Sylphide* are striking. The structure of Gautier's scenario is virtually identical to Taglioni's, divided, as each is, into two contrasting acts. Act I is set in a rural, agrarian locale, where realism and domesticity dominate. Act II, on the other hand, is set in a mysterious, moonlit forest glade, where supernatural creatures reign and where human beings are at the mercy of these exotic phantasms. The original scenery for *Giselle* was designed by Ciceri, chief set designer for the Paris Opera, 1815–1847, who designed the moonlit graveyard for the "Ballet of the Nuns" and the famous glade for Act II of *La Sylphide*, which, like his setting for Act II of *Giselle*, embodied a paradoxical union of picturesque spectacle and fantastical visions.

These similarities merely serve to highlight the crucial differences, however. Whereas *La Sylphide* presents two women who are rivals for James's love—the mortal bride, Effie, and the ethereal Sylphide—*Giselle* combines both natural and supernatural creatures in one woman, creating a challenge for the dancer. The Giselle of Act I parallels the mortal bride Effie, and the graceful shade of Act II parallels the Sylphide. *Giselle* enables the ballerina to demonstrate her versatility in both allegro and adagio modes in the two acts and also showcases her dramatic ability, especially in Giselle's mad scene.

Giselle is called the ballerina's *Hamlet* for good reason. The role of Giselle is especially challenging because of the contrast required between realism in Act I and fantasy in Act II. As Beaumont asserts, "There is no other ballet which in the short space of two acts offers such an immense range of expression to the *ballerina*, both as dancer and mime" (9). Giselle is a "complex being, paradoxically shy and simple, yet elusive and enigmatic, a restless, hypersensitive creature, introspective and essentially unworldly" (80). Never before had a character been explored so deeply in dance form, a triumph Perrot achieved by combining dancing with acting and contrasting the choreography between the two acts. Balanchine and Mason argue that "Giselle is probably the most deceptive role in all classical ballet since sheer dancing ability is simply not enough to make it work. The ballerina has to be totally convincing as a human and, later, as a supernatural being" (206).[10] This challenge to the dancer's artistry reflects the brilliance of *Giselle* itself; as Balanchine and Mason conclude,

> *Like* Hamlet, Giselle *is a classic: it is not only important historically, it also happens to be good. It is just as popular today as when it was first performed, more than 130 years ago. People go to see* Giselle *and to see new ballerinas dance it for the same reason we go to see new interpretations of* Hamlet: *the work is such a good one that we always discover something in it we hadn't seen before, some variation in performance that brings out an aspect that seemed previously concealed; we learn something new.* (193)

Giselle premiered with a strong cast of female dancers, including Grisi, Dumilâtre, and Mlle. Forester (called the "three Graces of the Opera" by Gautier) dancing the roles of Giselle, Myrtha, and Bathilde (Beaumont 70). Beaumont opines, "dancers of this quality are the very personification of the Romantic era, of the femme fatale, that elusive, fascinating, mocking vision, half woman, half goddess, which haunted the imaginations of so many poets, painters, writers, and musicians of the last century, and, becoming their muse, inspired some to achieve masterpieces" (134). Gautier praises Grisi's performance in *Giselle*: "Carlotta danced with a perfection, lightness, boldness, and a chaste and refined seductiveness, which place her in the front rank, between Elssler and Taglioni; as for pantomime, she exceeded all expectations; not a single conventional gesture, not one false moment; she was nature and artlessness personified" (qtd. in Beaumont 71). The critic of *Moniteur de Théâtres* enthused about the performance: in Act I, she "flies, bounds over the stage like an amorous gazelle," and in Act II, she "cleaves the air like a swallow" (qtd. in Beaumont 71). The gifted Lucien Petipa (1815–1898), brother of Marius Petipa (1818–1910)—choreographer, with Lev Ivanov (1834–1901), of the Tchaikovsky triptych *Swan Lake*, *The Sleeping Beauty*, and *The Nutcracker*—originated the role of Albrecht.

The choreography for *Giselle* was the product of two talented men: Coralli, appointed *maître de ballet en chef* to the Paris Opera, then under the direction of Dr. Vérnon, in 1831, and Jules Perrot, known as "Perrot the Aerial," distinguished dancer and partner of Grisi both on and off stage (Beaumont 58). Difficult as it is to determine who contributed which dances to *Giselle*, Beaumont believes Perrot, although he was not named in the program, "arranged all his wife's *pas* and scenes" (25), but suggests that Coralli, whose forte lay in corps dances and spectacle, planned the mimed scenes of Hilarion, Albrecht, Wilfrid, and Berthe in Act I and Hilarion's scene, the dances of Myrtha and the Wilis, and the scene (now omitted) between the peasants and the Wilis in Act II, while Perrot created the *pas seul* and *pas de deux*, *divertissements*, mass dances, and danced mime (Beaumont 35). Perrot's greatest contribution to the art of choreography was his creation of dance drama, combining acting with dancing to create a new, expressive ballet, because he believed dance should not be a mere display of virtuosity but should arise from a dramatic situation (Beaumont 35–36). Gautier admired the "exquisite elegance and novelty" of the Wilis' dances, while Adolphe Adam observed, "There has never been anything so pretty in choreography as the groups of women which Coralli has arranged with so superior a skill" (qtd. in Cass 129).

Giselle Act I

La Sylphide initiated a revolution in cultural sensibilities: "After *La Sylphide*, *Les Filets de Vulcain* and *Flore et Zéphire* were no longer possible; the Opera was given over to gnomes, undines, salamanders, elves, nixes, wilis, peris—to all that strange and mysterious folk who lend themselves so marvellously to the fantasies of the *maître de ballet*" (Gautier, qtd. in Adair 83). Ballet techniques had evolved from European court life and were influenced by the classical aesthetic sense of the ideal human form evident in Greek and Roman sculpture (Adair 92). Now, however, Romanticism involved the desire to overthrow those heroes of Greek and Roman mythology and history who had so long strutted the stage of the Paris Opera in favour of idealized worlds concerned with the supernatural and exotic (Beaumont 92).

Even stage sets reflected this cultural revolution: as Gautier records, "The twelve palaces in marble and gold of the Olympians were relegated to the dust of the store-rooms, and the scene-painters received orders only for romantic forests, valleys illuminated by the pretty German moonlight reminiscent of Heinrich Heine's ballads" (qtd. in Beaumont 14). Romanticism engendered a revolution in stage sets, transforming the Classical mode with both domestic and supernatural settings.

Act I of *Giselle* is set in Thuringia in the medieval Rhineland—an exotic locale for nineteenth-century Parisians, made famous by Madame de Staël's book *De l'Allemagne*, published in Paris in 1814, which became a bible for the Romantics (Fleming-Markarian 9).[11] Thus, *Giselle* combines European Gothicism with Nordic spiritism, reflecting the nineteenth century's romanticization of all things medieval. "We set the action in some mysterious corner of Germany, among hillocks weighed down with russet vines," Gautier records (qtd. in Brinson and Crisp 26). In the foreground is Giselle's humble thatched cottage, while in the background, "perched on the summit of a bare grey rock, so steep that grass has not grown on it, like an eagle's nest, with encircling walls, pepper-pot turrets and feudal weathercocks, is one of those castles that are so common in Germany" (qtd. in Beaumont 95). The class conflict that will create this love tragedy is apparent to the audience upon curtain rising. The cottage is Giselle's home, the hut opposite the dwelling of Loys, the newcomer with whom she is in love, and the castle the home of Duke Albrecht of Silesia, signalling the newcomer's true identity. Thus, the stage is set for heartbreak. The overture to Act I, with its agitated opening measures modulating into a romantic melody, sets the ominous tone for the fate governing this tragic love story.

Dramatic irony is also present from the curtain rising, as the audience sees "Loys" deferred to by his squire Wilfrid, whose obsequious behaviour is witnessed by Hilarion, a gamekeeper in love with Giselle. The audience realizes Loys is a nobleman impersonating a peasant. Consequently, his entire courtship of Giselle is suspect and given an ironic edge. Paul Lormier's original costumes for the rivals reflected their contrasting class, with Albrecht in a jerkin of purple, the colour of royalty, and Hilarion in a jerkin of green, appropriate for a forester, with a leather belt holding a hunting knife and horn (Beaumont 64).

Figure 1.2: *Jaciel Gomez as Hilarion, Hayna Gutierrez as Giselle, and Kelley McKinlay as Albrecht in Act I of* Giselle, *Alberta Ballet, 2014.* [Photo by Paul McGrath]

Albrecht hides, revealing his deceitful nature, when his knocking summons Giselle from her cottage. She is dressed in a pretty, feminine peasant's costume of blue and white, the colours of the Virgin Mary, the personification of purity, with a rose in her bodice.[12] Seeing no one, but assuming it is her suitor, she proceeds to dance for her unseen visitor. Her exuberant jumps to Adam's lively music—*ballonnés, ballottés, sauts de basques* and *grands jetés*—express her joy in being alive and in love—the "dance of life" of Act I, as opposed to the "dance of death" of Act II (Engelhardt 113).

Like the Sylphide, Giselle evades her lover's advances, eluding his grasp until, reaching heavenward, he promises eternal love and fidelity. Finally consenting to sit with him on a rustic bench, she plays the lovers' game—"He loves me. He loves me not"—pulling the petals off a Marguerite. The Romantic poets frequently employed flowers to symbolize emotion: for example, daisies were emblematic of purity, innocence, and simplicity

(Fleming-Markarian 15). Crushed by the flower's negative message, Giselle casts it down. Surreptitiously removing one petal, Albrecht shows her that the outcome is positive: "He loves me." Joyfully, they dance together, arms linked, performing the same energetic steps as in Giselle's solo and circling the stage with *grands jetés*. Suddenly she stops dancing, as if about to faint. Hilarion separates them, pleading his love, but is rejected.

Giselle loves to dance, and she is soon joined by the village maidens, but her mother, Berthe, whose name means "bright" or "clear" (Fleming-Markarian 18), suggesting common sense, warns her that dancing could prove fatal to her because she has a weak heart. This echo of Hugo's maiden lends Giselle's dancing a tension that renders it especially effective. In the original ballet, according to Marion Smith, Berthe warns her daughter that she will grow wings, and Giselle retorts that she will ignore them. In Berthe's lengthy mime scene (later omitted) she explains to the rapt village girls about the Wilis and her fear that her daughter could die and turn into a Wili—a prophecy realized in Act II (Smith 180–82).[13]

Giselle begins to dance a waltz with graceful *balancés*, drawing Albrecht into her dance, as he lifts her high while, like the first Sylphide, she executes *entrechats*. Giselle's six friends join them in a line as they circle to a lively waltz. Giselle and Albrecht are at opposite ends of the line, suggesting their subsequent division. Fleming observes, "this circular manoeuver could be interpreted symbolically, as a microcosm of the world spinning on its axis, with Giselle, whose person embodies innocence, at the opposite end of Albrecht, whose person embodies deceit" (Fleming-Markarian 18). As Giselle and Albrecht dance, joined by the villagers, Hilarion tears them apart. When he draws a knife, Albrecht reaches for the sword that is normally at his side in a visual clue that is understood by the audience, but not the characters— at least, not yet. Albrecht drives him off. After Berthe draws Giselle into the cottage, Albrecht, hearing a distant hunting horn, runs off. Hilarion, hiding in Albrecht's hut, discovers Albrecht's sword.

A hunting party of the Prince of Courland and his daughter Bathilde enters the village. Giselle graciously sets a table before them. Attracted by Bathilde's finery, originally a green velvet riding habit, Giselle approaches to feel her garments. Bathilde, whose name means "heroine" (Fleming-Markarian 22), asks Giselle about herself. Giselle mimes that she weaves and spins but loves to dance. She performs a virtuosic solo for Bathilde and then presents her with a bouquet of flowers. Touched by Giselle's youthful charm, Bathilde removes her gold chain and puts it around Giselle's neck.[14] The effect of the costly necklace on the peasant costume is incongruous. Moreover, it suggests the fate that is soon to engulf Giselle and choke her life. Giselle's mother invites the prince and princess to retire into her cottage. Wilfrid hangs the hunting horn outside the cottage.

The villagers gather to celebrate a bountiful harvest and perform the lively peasant dance that distinguishes many nineteenth-century ballets. Giselle is named Queen of the Vintage. Crowned with a wreath of vine leaves and holding a floral distaff, she resembles a Flora figure, goddess of the harvest. She performs a virtuosic solo filled with precise pointe work and poses in arabesque, which climaxes with a series of *ronds de jambe en pointe* and a frenzy of *soutenu*, *posé*, and *chaînés* turns circling the stage, while her six friends perform a lively dance filled with fast footwork. At the apex of Giselle's triumph, Hilarion, who hid in the hut where Albrecht's equerry stowed the insignia of his rank, interrupts the revellers. Bearing a ducal cloak and sword and making an ironic obeisance to Albrecht, he accuses "Loys" of being an imposter and seducer. Albrecht rushes at Hilarion with the sword but is intercepted by his squire. Hilarion blows the horn, summoning the hunting party, which emerges from the cottage. Bathilde is bewildered at seeing Albrecht dressed in peasant's costume. When Giselle, distraught, interposes, Bathilde mimes that she is engaged to marry Albrecht. When Albrecht kisses Bathilde's hand, Giselle goes mad with shock and grief. She tears off Bathilde's necklace and, in so doing, removes her headdress, causing her hair to cascade over her shoulders. If not exactly an example of *le droit de seigneur*, Giselle certainly suffers here the exploitation of a peasant girl by a nobleman.

In the most dramatic scene in Romantic ballet, Giselle reprises her dance motifs with Albrecht, miming the Marguerite petal play, but in a somnambulistic mode, accompanied by a haunting violin and oboe, while the appalled villagers observe helplessly. Giselle accidentally stumbles upon Albrecht's sword, and, before he can wrest it from her, she impales herself on it in a scene that predates Freudian phallic theory by several decades. Ambiguity reigns, however, for it is unclear whether she has died from the sword wound or from a broken heart.[15] Of Giselle's madness, Gautier wrote to Heine, "Women's minds are in their hearts; if the heart is wounded, the sanity is lost" (94). The heart may be our culture's primary metaphor for representing love and loss, but in this ballet's libretto, Giselle's heart attack transcends metaphor to resonate medically as the primary cause of her death (Engelhardt 131–32). In "What Killed Giselle?" Smith debates the "Broken Heart Theory" versus the "Suicide Theory," quoting Gautier as describing the former in his libretto and the latter in his published "Letter to Heine." Smith concludes that the original Giselle "died of a broken heart" (77). Gautier clearly, however, tells Heine that Giselle "seizes the fatal sword brought by Hilarion and would have fallen on its point if Albrecht had not turned it aside...Alas, the precaution is in vain; the blow has struck home; her heart is pierced and Giselle dies" (54). Thus, the "Suicide Theory" cannot be discounted.

As Albrecht and Hilarion grieve over Giselle's prostrate body, her mother claims her right as chief mourner. Albrecht attempts to stab Hilarion with the fateful sword but is drawn forcibly away by his faithful squire. The Act I curtain falls on Albrecht and Hilarion grieving over Giselle's dead body. Tragedies, including operas, usually end there, with the death of the heroine, but death is just the beginning for Romantic ballets.

Giselle Act II

Gautier explains, "The heart of our ballet lay in its second act. There is the poetry. It is where I began...A world of which the German poet speaks, where maidens who have died before their wedding day, because of faithless lovers, return as Wilis to dance by night" (qtd. in Brinson and Crisp 28). Gautier describes the set vividly in his libretto: "The stage represents a forest on the banks of a pool...At the foot of a willow, asleep and concealed beneath the flowers, lies poor Giselle. From the marble cross which indicates her grave is suspended, still fresh, the garland of vine branches with which she had been crowned at the harvest festival" (Gautier 55).[16] The set conveys the poignancy eloquently.

As the curtain rises on Act II, revealing the moonlit forest glade, a bell tolls twelve, the witching hour. Hilarion is revealed kneeling by the cross that marks Giselle's grave, but the ghostly apparitions of Wilis frighten him off. Adam's expressive music ushers in Myrtha, Queen of the Wilis, who dances a solo echoing the first Sylphide, which sets the stage for this phantasmagoric scene. Performed by a dancer with rare authority, poise, and control, the demanding role of Myrtha requires excellent technique, extension and balance, as well as exceptional elevation, plus the strength to make the dancing appear effortless. Attired all in white,[17] with a coronet of verbena and white flowers, a veil, and silver wings, Myrtha traverses the stage *en pointe*, seeming to skim the earth with *bourrées*. Beaumont cites Escudier's admiration of the orchestral effect as, over arpeggios on the harp, four muted first violins play in their highest register a four-part melody for strings to accompany her entrance. Escudier finds the effect magical, transporting the audience to the realm of fairyland: "It is the first time we have seen the fantastic treated with due regard to grace and charm," he exults, "and perhaps it never will be more happily achieved" (qtd. in Beaumont).[18]

Myrtha removes her veil and executes a slow *développé* into an *arabesque penchée*, like the first Sylphide. Then she begins a virtuosic solo, or *pas seul*, traversing the stage with *faillis*, *assemblés*, *pas de basques*, and *grands jetés*— all in a coldly controlled manner. As Balanchine and Mason explain, "Her movements are confident, controlled, beautiful, but they possess no warmth. The supernatural powers Myrtha possesses allow for nothing but perfection. She moves more rapidly now; the quickness of her dancing is brilliant and hard, like a diamond" (202). Beaumont considers Myrtha an unhappy phantom, a female vampire filled with an insatiable lust for revenge, which causes her to frequent the mystic glade in order to lure any male wayfarer into the web of her fellow vampires, who force the unhappy man to dance until, reduced to exhaustion, he can be driven to death in the marshy pool (82).[19] Adam describes Dumilâtre's performance as Myrtha as a "noble and cold style of dancing which would suit Minerva in a merry mood" (qtd. in Beaumont 74). Holding in each hand a branch of rosemary, symbolizing remembrance, and having both funerary and bridal associations, Myrtha tosses them into the wings to summon her band of Wilis.[20] Like automatons, the veiled dead brides enter and make their obeisance to their queen, their white tutus contrasting with the dark forest. Like a puppet-master, she controls them, as they bend and sway at her command. Their bridal veils have become shrouds, just as the magical scarf the sorceress gave James to make the Sylphide his bride becomes her shroud. Myrtha motions them to remove their veils, and they obey. They dance gracefully, with beautiful arabesques, graceful *développés*, charming *ports de bras*, and ethereal pointe work. Elegant, but anonymous, the corps de ballet dances in patterns with military precision. Nineteenth-century audiences, in the grip of the Gothic, thrilled to these zombie-like creatures. The arabesque, that elegant posture suggesting aspiration, is their signature pose, becoming, as Beaumont notes, "their choreographic sign manual" (88).

Myrtha summons Giselle to rise from her grave. She removes Giselle's veil, and Giselle, as if freed from her coffin, explodes into motion, whirling like a dervish in arabesque and circling the stage with bounding *enchaînements* combining *faillis and assemblés*. Gautier writes that Myrtha crowns Giselle with "the magic garland of asphodel and verbena. At a touch of her wand, two little wings, as restless and quivering as those of Psyche, suddenly grow from the shoulders of the youthful shade" (56).

After the Wilis depart, having welcomed Giselle into their ghostly sister-hood, Albrecht ventures into their haunts. He enters, grieving, onto an empty stage. Dressed in princely mourning and shrouded in a black cloak, he carries white lilies, emblematic of purity and death. Kneeling by Giselle's grave, marked with a cross, he lets them fall to the earth, accompanied by the lugubrious strains of a solo oboe that express his lamentation. Beaumont suggests that Albrecht, who began Act I as a perfidious seducer, has himself been seduced by Giselle and that his love for her is so strong that he has risked visiting her grave in the haunted forest (qtd. in Fleming-Markarian 41). That his black costume is relieved by a peacock feather in his cap— which, because peacocks renew themselves each spring, are symbols of resurrection—may suggest that Albrecht is experiencing a transformation (Fleming-Markarian 66).

Giselle flickers across the stage and disappears, reappears and vanishes. Like James with his Sylphide, Albrecht attempts to capture her, as if she were a butterfly that alights on a flower, as Beaumont observes, but she evades him. "The hero," Levinson writes, "struck by this diaphanous and mournful vision, by the beating of wings which have brushed past him, throws himself, too late, onto the path of the impassioned shade" (qtd. in Smith 177). If Myrtha resembles a diamond in her hard brilliance, Giselle is a pearl in her glowing warmth. Albrecht kneels, waiting, and she comes and places her hand on his shoulder. They proceed to dance a beautiful pas de deux in which he lifts her in poses that simulate floating or flight. They pass each other in simultaneous series of leaps diagonally across the stage.[21] Giselle leaps, tossing her flowers, and Albrecht leaps to gather them.[22] Beaumont admires her *grands jetés*, saying, "this soaring step is used to suggest Giselle's phantom-like swiftness and lightness, and when the throwing of the flower coincides with the highest point of the leap, an extraordinary effect of ecstasy is achieved" (86). As he maintains, in no other ballet are the intermingled themes of love of man for woman and the conflict between inexorable duty and the power of love treated with such refinement, lyricism, and delicate appreciation of the issues involved.

Giselle's ecstatic outbursts of dance characterize the Romantic ideal, defined by Levinson as "exalted spirituality" and "mystical love stronger than death" (qtd. in Fleming-Markarian 22). Another of Giselle's solos is notable for the brilliant *enchaînement* that concludes it—a series of sixteen *entrechats quatre en diagonal* that suggest the dancer is skimming, bird-like, just above the ground. There are also several pas de deux in Act II: the most beautiful is that danced by Giselle when supported by Albrecht, a duet expressing the strength of their love, despite the efforts of the Wilis to part them. Beaumont judges that this long pas de deux, "surcharged with an infinity of emotions,... in which the dance continually reflects the changing situations, is a superb example of Perrot's application of his theories"; he claims that few dances in the history of ballet equal it for sustained poetic expressiveness (36).

Just as Adam's score is deceptively simple, so Giselle's poses and steps are familiar to any student of classical ballet, including poses in arabesque and attitude; *pas de bourrée, développés, grands ronds de jambe*, and *glissande* steps in adagio sections; *pas de basques, ballonnés, ballottés, temps levés, entrechats, sisonnes, cabrioles, jetés, grands jetés*, and *soubresaut* steps in allegro sections;

and turning steps including *pirouettes, tours en l'air, posés tours* and *petits tours* (Beaumont 85–86). Although such steps are simple and familiar, they require great strength and balance, technique and elevation to execute gracefully.

The Wilis reenter with their prey—Hilarion. They proceed to dance him to exhaustion and death. Mercilessly, they reject his appeals, until, forming a diagonal line, they drive him through their "choreographed gauntlet" into the lake where he drowns, thus "achieving their perverse version of the *petite mort*" (Engelhardt 94). He is forced to dance with each Wili in turn, until "the last two Wilis make a gesture of seizing him and pushing him into the fatal pool, to meet his death by drowning" (Fleming-Markarian 44). According to the libretto, however, Hilarion, "arriving at the edge of the lake, at the last loop in the chain of waltzers, opens his arms, and thinking himself about to receive a new partner, falls into the abyss [of the lake]," clearly suggesting that Hilarion, demented, propels *himself* to his doom (Fleming-Markarian 44). Is this dance of death the punishment for Hilarion, labelled "Giselle's assassin" by Gautier in his published "Letter to Heine," for inadvertently causing the death of Giselle? If so, Albrecht is equally guilty. And he will be their next victim.

Adam's music is ideally suited to this tragic narrative and to the simple, but effective, dancing. Beaumont observes that Adam employs the *cantilena* style of simple, sustained melody made popular by operas by Bellini and Donizetti, including flowing melodies and lively dance rhythms. He also incorporates motifs, melodic themes connected with particular characters or contexts, often associated with the operas of Richard Wagner (1813–1883). Beaumont also claims that Hilarion's theme, which marks his every entrance, is a quotation of the Fate theme from Beethoven's *Fifth Symphony*. Giselle has multiple motifs to accompany her quick and dead selves, themes that are reprised, in modulated or distorted variations, to convey her joy at being in love and her madness at being betrayed, her grief at loss and her ultimate eternal love. Gautier judges, "M. Adam's music is superior to the usual run of ballet music, it abounds in tunes and orchestral effects; it even includes a touching attention for lovers of difficult music, a very well-produced fugue. The second act solves the musical problem of graceful fantasy and is full of melody" (58). Beaumont, decades later, agrees: "The music of *Giselle* still exerts its magic. It is no less potent than the Wilis in its power to captivate and enchant those members of the audience willing to surrender to its mood" (58).

Adam's music, while not considered great, was nevertheless ideally suited to *Giselle*, as Christina Gier demonstrates in her chapter in this collection, "'No Feminine Endings': Adolphe Adam's Musical Score for *Giselle*." Ballet-pantomimes involved more narrative, conveyed through mime and action, with less abstract dancing than today's ballets, and music was expected to be programmatic, to help convey the emotions, relationships, and action of the story. Adam also composed numerous dances, or *divertissements*, each with its own key, mood, and tempo. Smith compares his score to opera, quoting Adam as saying that he treated the finale of Act I of *Giselle* "like a finale of an opera" (170).[23] Indeed, the solos parallel arias, the duos parallel duets or dialogues, and the mime parallels recitatives. Smith expresses eloquently the effect Adam achieves:

> *The dance instead of being subservient to expressive gesture, itself became the interpreter of the emotions and their symbolic equivalent...In a constant approach to a geometric purity of design, making a pattern in space of straight lines and sweeping perfect curves, idealizing the dancer's body and dematerializing her costume, the* ballet blanc *is able to transmute the formal poses of the slow dance movement—the* Arabesques *of the Adagio—as well as those aerial parabolas outlined by seemingly imponderable bodies...into a mysterious and poetic language.* (177)

Myrtha condemns Albrecht, like Hilarion, to the dance of death. Giselle draws him to the cross over her grave and, posing in cruciform, shields him from Myrtha's malice, causing her branch of rosemary to break. The queen's evil force is overwhelmed by the power of Giselle's love and the Christian symbolism. Although Myrtha has no power over Albrecht, protected, as he is, by Giselle and by the cross, she does have power over her initiate, and she resorts to the "infernal and feminine device" of commanding Giselle to dance in order to inveigle Albrecht away from the protection of the cross and into joining her in the dance to death (Gautier 57). Giselle displays ethereal grace in sustained *développés*, *grands ronds de jambe*, and *promenades en arabesque*. Albrecht is drawn to join her, and together they dance a tender adagio with gravity-defying lifts. "Exquisitely erotic, this adagio is also profoundly disconcerting," argues Jody Brumer (111). In fact, it is the first time in the ballet that Giselle and Albrecht actually dance together. But their appeals are rejected by the merciless Wilis. Albrecht must dance until he is dead.

This dance of death motif lends Giselle and Albrecht's dancing dramatic power—recalling the power of music to overcome evil in Mozart's opera *The Magic Flute*. In *Giselle*, however, the mainspring of this power is dance itself; as Beaumont observes, the many strange and varied incidents that compose the story of the ballet are the outcome of Giselle's passion for dancing (23). Albrecht's *enchaînements*, filled with *entrechats six*, *grands jetés*, *cabrioles*, and *tours en l'air*, constitute a tour de force, concluding with his collapse. Tenderly, Giselle helps him to rise, and the cycle is repeated. As they dance, the melodic theme of their Marguerite mime is reprised. After he collapses again, Giselle cradles him in her arms, supporting him (fig. 1.3). But, before the cycle can be repeated again, we hear the bell toll four times: it is dawn, and the new gas lighting signals sunrise—daylight symbolizing goodness vanquishing darkness and evil—and the power of the Wilis, like that of vampires, is vitiated. Giselle draws Albrecht to the cross, and, as she descends into the earth, he is left to grieve alone.

Giselle Apotheosis

Romantic ballets such as *La Sylphide* and *Giselle* continue to fill theatres to the present day. The question is: Why do these nineteenth-century ballets, which appear to contradict current views of gender construction and performance, continue to be so popular? In Romantic ballets, as in so many nineteenth-century operas—such as Verdi's *Rigoletto* and *La Traviata*; Puccini's *La Bohème*, *Manon*, and *Madama Butterfly*; or Bizet's *Carmen*—the heroine dies, to be survived by the man she loves. Why do audiences like to see the woman sacrificed? American Romantic poet Edgar Allen Poe declared, "The death of

Figure 1.3: Mariko Kondo as Giselle and Dayron Vera as Albrecht in Act II of Giselle, Alberta Ballet, 2014. [Photo by Paul McGrath]

a beautiful woman is unquestionably the most poetical topic in the world."[24] Yet recent critics have begun to question "the aesthetic of death" (Carter 124).

The National Ballet of Canada's former prima ballerina Karen Kain, herself a lovely Giselle and now artistic director of the company, remarked to me in an interview:

> I think there is some deep human fascination with death and power, and exotic romanticism. There are some things that we tap into when we're listening to fairy tales or watching fairy tales, and we can either care about the characters or be fascinated by their darkness. There's some part of us, some part of ancient memory, that still can connect or we wouldn't be fascinated. The other thing that keeps people watching is the beauty of the actual choreography and the beauty of the music. If it just becomes an exercise in technique, it isn't powerful;

it becomes powerful when it taps into something else. Despite knowing too much about technique and everything, I want to be swept away, emotionally, by a performance.[25]

Innumerable moving performances prove that *Giselle* still has the power to enchant over one and a half centuries later. Cass concludes, "Here once more is the dreamy face of the Romantic ballet, the image that keeps returning to haunt our theaters, dissolving like a drifting cloud and yet remaining in our memories" (122).

Is *Giselle* the tragedy of an innocent young peasant girl betrayed by an aristocratic lover, or is it Albrecht's coming-of-age story as he develops from a selfish youth to a mature man? In comparing Albrecht with James, the hero of *La Sylphide*, *premier danseur* Erik Bruhn (1928–1986) concludes, "Unlike James, Albrecht in *Giselle* is on the point of entering maturity. He realizes that he has done something terrible and that he must suffer. If he can survive his night of remorse he will come out the better for it. He pays the price as James never did. Therefore he can live" (qtd. in Balanchine and Mason 472). Bruhn, who considers the Wilis a figment of Albrecht's imagination, created by his guilt, believes that Albrecht "realizes some sincerity in life that he might not otherwise have known," as his "awareness of guilt makes him mature."[26] He concludes, "Albrecht survives because he can admit guilt and realize his responsibility" (qtd. in Balanchine and Mason 208). Indeed, although Giselle is the eponymous character, Albrecht frames the action, appearing on stage first and last, and he develops, perhaps to be redeemed.

But is Giselle a victim, or is she triumphant in the power of her love to transcend death? Evan Alderson records his epiphanic experience on witnessing a performance of *Giselle* by the Royal Winnipeg Ballet starring the transcendant Evelyn Hart: "Criticism fell away; I was for that time seized by beauty" (93). Alderson identifies with the perfidious prince:

I had been "let in" through Albrecht's longing for the absolutely faithful, abso-
lutely unattainable woman whose death he had occasioned because I share with
much of nineteenth-century culture an attraction to what is sexually charged

yet somehow pristine...The adagio was for me the time of transformation of
Albrecht's burden from guilt to sorrow, from the bearing of blame to an endless
forgiveness, the time when I knew *he was loved, and that his own longing was*
justified. The dematerialization of the object of his desire seemed a small cost to
pay for such a beautiful redemption. (293–94)

Evelyn Hart believes *Giselle* promotes forgiveness; in her view, "Giselle is the
most passionate, open-minded, trusting, loyal person that you could ever
know, and she has a great capacity, a spiritual capacity, for forgiveness and
love."[27] Nevertheless, as Alderson observes, the ballet perpetuates a patriarchal model wherein the woman is subservient to the man: "The fullest
mark of her love is that she denies her own power in helping him to survive,"
he argues, as "her femininity remains in the service of the male" (294). That
is precisely why the research team that produced the interactive ballet video
game *iGiselle* for a twenty-first-century audience elected to keep Giselle alive
and give her agency as a contemporary woman.

Notes

1. See Stovel, "The Birth of the Ballerina."
2. Shelley's *Defence of Poetry* was written in 1821, but published posthumously in 1840, one
    year before the premiere of *Giselle*.
3. Jennifer Homans similarly declares, "It is the wings that matter." She quotes
    Sophocles in Plato's *Phaedra*: "The function of a wing is to take what is heavy and raise
    it up into the region above, where the gods dwell; of all things connected with the body
    it has the greatest affinity with the divine" (Homans xxii).
4. Amalia Brugnoli created a sensation in 1822 by rising to her pointes by making wind-
    mill motions of the arms. Later, pointe shoes were developed with steel shanks and
    stiffened blocks to provide greater support for the dancer. Taglioni perfected pointe
    work.
5. Homans records that, heretofore, "men were the virtuosos and leaders of the art," as
    "*la belle danse* was unequivocally masculine...: it was, quite literally, the dance of kings"
    (20).
6. Gautier created the libretto for *La Péri* (1843), which presents the ballerina as a sylph,
    as well as for *Giselle* (1841).

7. In Part 7 of *De L'Allemagne*, Heine offers two folk songs about mysterious maidens who dance to death young men they find in the forest, and explains the legend of the *Wilis*.

8. Band 20. Leipzig 1909, S. 653. www.zeno.org/nid/200769699X.

9. This image recalls the "Ballet of the Nuns," in which the dead nuns dance a bacchanale, starring Taglioni as the Abbess Héléna, in Joseph Myerbeer's opera, *Robert Le Diable*, which inspired *La Sylphide*. Heine's words are available online through Project Gutenberg.

10. Evelyn Hart, who danced Giselle brilliantly, similarly comments, "The great thing about being able to do these big classical ballets is that it gives you a chance as a dancer to be a character, to be an actor." In conversation with Nora Foster Stovel, Toronto, June 6, 2013.

11. Thuringia was a part of Germany renowned for its troubadours during the Medieval era (Fleming-Markarian 9).

12. Beaumont says Giselle's costume, designed by Lormier, featured a blue wimple, bodice of light-brown velvet, skirt of buttercup yellow, and narrow white apron (63).

13. This scene is omitted from recent productions, as the version of *Giselle* that we know now is derived from Marius Petipa's revival for the 1884 Russian production (Homans xx). The original production ended with Albrecht's union with Bathilde in a restoration of the social order (Brumer 109)—a happy ending for Albrecht, but a tragic one for Giselle.

14. Fleming-Markarian offers an alternative analysis of the chain's symbolism: "In Antiquity, a golden chain (in Latin, *catena aurea*) was thought of as linking heaven and earth," and it may therefore symbolize "Giselle's receipt of the capacity to link herself between the two worlds of heaven and earth" (22).

15. Felicia McCarren argues that *Giselle* represented medical ambiguity rather than resolved it, with the mad scene serving as a symptomatic expression of the culture's unease about the relationship of sex and health (cited by Engelhardt 131).

16. Fleming-Markarian says Gautier's conception of the spirit world is almost certainly derived from of the works of the Swedish writer Emanuel Swedenborg (32).

17. Beaumont reports that Lormier's original costume design for Myrtha included a silver star worn above the centre of the forehead (63), perhaps suggesting a connection with Mozart's Queen of the Night. Gautier says in his letter to Heine that the Wilis have "stars on their foreheads and moth-like wings on their shoulders" (56).

18. Escudier's July 4, 1841, review in *La France Musicale* (qtd. in Beaumont 56).

19. Beaumont explains that the name *Myrtha* contains a biblical reference, for *Myrtha* is a variant of *Martha*, the name of one who was, with her sister Mary and brother Lazarus, a friend of Jesus (Luke 10; John 11). The name means "lady," as in "lady of the house,"

and depictions of St. Martha usually show her holding a ladle or having a large bunch of keys attached to her girdle. Although these domestic attributes are completely out of keeping with the wild moonlit forest here, Myrtha, nonetheless, proves that she is a formidable mistress (Beaumont 31).

20. Rosemary is an attribute of the Greek god Ares, who personified bloodlust and slaughter. In the Middle Ages, when the ballet is supposed to take place, rosemary was associated with wedding ceremonies and was worn by the bride as a love charm (Beaumont 34).

21. Stage machinery allowed Giselle to "fly" across the stage, but the machinery stuck during the second performance (Smith 68).

22. Edward Villella, a former baseball player transformed into a *danseur noble* in Balanchine's New York City Ballet, would, to the delight of appreciative audiences, leap in a *grand jeté* and catch the flowers in mid-air.

23. Smith suggests Donizetti's *Lucia di Lammermoor* may have inspired Adam's mad scene for *Giselle*.

24. Poe includes this statement in his 1846 essay, "The Philosophy of Composition," published in *Graham's Magazine* in April 1846, which offers writers suggestions for composition, employing his own poem, "The Raven," as an example.

25. Karen Kain in conversation with Nora Foster Stovel in her office at the National Ballet of Canada in Toronto on June 6, 2013.

26. Bruhn's comments were first published in his essay *Beyond Technique*.

27. Evelyn Hart, in conversation with Nora Foster Stovel, June 6, 2013.

Works Cited

Alderson, Evan. "Ballet as Ideology: 'Giselle,' Act II." *Dance Chronicle* 10.3 (1987): 290–304.

Balanchine, George, and Francis Mason. *101 Stories of the Great Ballets: The Scene-by-Scene Stories of the Most Popular Ballets, Old and New*. New York: Anchor, 1975.

Banes, Sally. *Dancing Women: Female Bodies on Stage*. London and New York: Routledge, 1998.

Beaumont, Cyril W. *The Ballet Called Giselle*. 2nd ed. New York: Dance Horizons, 1969.

Brinson, Peter, and Clement Crisp. *The International Book of Ballet*. New York: Stein and Day, 1971.

Bruhn, Erik. *Beyond Technique*. New York: Dance Perspectives Foundation, 1968. Dance Perspectives 36.

Brumer, Jody. "Redeeming *Giselle*: Making a Case for the Ballet We Love to Hate." *Rethinking the Sylph: New Perspectives on the Romantic Ballet*. Ed. Lynn Garafola. Studies in Dance History. Hanover, NH: Wesleyan UP, 1997. 107–20.

Carter, Keryn Lavinia. "Constructing the Balletic Body: The 'Look,' the Sylph and the
Performance of Gendered Identity." *Reframing the Body: Explorations in Sociology*. Ed.
Nick Watson and Sarah Cunningham-Burley. New York: Palgrave, 2001. 113–27.

Cass, Joan. *Dancing Through History*. Englewood Cliffs, NJ: Prentice-Hall, 1993.

Chazin-Bennahum, Judith. *The Lure of Perfection: Fashion and Ballet, 1780–1830*. New York:
Routledge, 2005.

Clarke, Mary. *Ballet: An Illustrated History*. London: Hamish Hamilton, 1992.

Clément, Catherine. *Opera, or the Undoing of Women [L'opéra ou le défait des femmes]*. 1979.
Trans. Betsy Wing. Minneapolis: U of Minnesota P, 1988.

Engelhardt, Molly. *Dancing Out of Line: Ballrooms, Ballets, and Mobility in Victorian Fiction and
Culture*. Athens, OH: Ohio U P, 2009.

Fleming-Markarian, Margaret. *Symbolism in Nineteenth-Century Ballet: Giselle, Coppélia, The
Sleeping Beauty and Swan Lake*. Bern, Switzerland: Peter Lang, 2012.

Garafola, Lynn. Introduction. *Rethinking the Sylph: New Perspectives on the Romantic Ballet*.
Studies in Dance History. Hanover, NH: Wesleyan U P, 1997. 1–10.

Gautier, Théophile. *The Romantic Ballet as Seen by Théophile Gautier*. Trans. Cyril W.
Beaumont. New York: Arno Press, 1980.

Heine, Heinrich. *Religion and Philosophy in Germany [excerpt of De l'Allemagne, 1835]*. Trans.
Fleischman. *The Prose Writings of Henrich Heine*. Ed. with introd. Havelock Ellis.
London: Walter Scott, 1887. *Project Gutenberg*. www.gutenberg.org.

Homans, Jennifer. *Apollo's Angels*. London: Granta, 2010.

Jowitt, Deborah. "In Pursuit of the Sylph: Ballet in the Romantic Period." *Routledge Dance
Studies Reader*. Abingdon, NY: Routledge, 2010. 209–19.

Kelly, Deirdre. *Ballerina: Sex, Scandal, and Suffering Behind the Symbol of Perfection*. Vancouver:
Greystone, 2012.

Lee, Carol. "The Foundations of Romantic Ballet." *Ballet in Western Culture: A History of Its
Origins and Evolution*. New York: Routledge, 2002. 133–63.

McClary, Susan. *Feminine Endings: Music, Gender and Sexuality*. 1991. Rev. with a new introd.
Minneapolis and London: U of Minnesota P, 2002.

Smith, Marion. *Ballet and Opera in the Age of Giselle*. Princeton and Oxford: Princeton U P,
2000.

Shelley, Percy Bysshe. *Defence of Poetry. Essays, Letters from Abroad, Translations, and Fragments*.
Ed. Mary Shelley. Vol. 1. Philadelphia: Lea and Blanchard, 1840. 25–62. books.google.
com.

Stovel, Nora Foster. "The Birth of the Ballerina in *La Sylphide*: Sylph or Self?" *W W R Magazine*
2.2 (2008), 13–18. www.crcstudio.org/wwr_magazine/mags/WWRMag_5.pdf.

2

"No Feminine Endings"

Adolphe Adam's Musical Score for Giselle

THE CREATION OF *iGISELLE* was inspired, as Nora Foster Stovel has
pointed out in her preface to this collection, by the desire to liberate the
eponymous heroine from her fate. What I would add is that this fate is a
doom decreed by Adolphe Adam's score for the ballet, which followed the
musical principles of early nineteenth-century opera. Opera and ballet
were inextricably intertwined in this period, as ballets were incorporated
into operas: the "Ballet of the Nuns" in *Robert le Diable*, for example, led by
Marie Taglioni as the Abbess, inspired the first Romantic ballet, *La Sylphide*
(1832), starring Taglioni as the Sylphide, which was soon followed by the
greatest Romantic ballet, *Giselle*, in 1841.[1] Henceforth, ballets were staged
as independent performances, equivalent to operas, as Marian Smith
explains in *Ballet and Opera in the Age of* Giselle (xviii). Because of these
origins, however, ballet music developed into an atypical musical genre as it
complemented a libretto or narrative composed in the embodied gesture of
dance. Adam's score for *Giselle* draws on the principles established in these
Romantic works to skilfully convey this narrative of supernatural doom.

Romanticism in opera and ballet was marked by a fascination with the supernatural, as Stovel explains in this collection's opening chapter. Numerous operas and song cycles composed in the Romantic era depict supernatural characters, including the Elf King in the song "Erlkönig" (1815), by Franz Schubert in Vienna; the opera *Der Freischütz* (1821), by Carl Maria von Weber in Berlin; the nuns in Giacomo Meyerbeer's opera *Robert le Diable* (1831), first produced at the Paris Opera; and the madness of *Lucia di Lammermoor* (1835), by Gaetano Donizetti in Rome. Paris productions of the Weber and Donizetti operas in the 1830s may also have inspired interest in creating ballets on similar supernatural themes (Smith 67–68). Romanticism's fundamental metaphysical concept of the spirit world is an integral part of this ballet narrative as well.

Character and narrative are conveyed through costume, gesture, action *and* music. In early nineteenth-century France, balletomanes would purchase ballet librettos with detailed descriptions of the plot and "dialogue" of the dancers, accompanied by "*parlante* music" or "talking music" (Smith 36). The dancers' mime was closely coordinated with the music, a method rooted in operatic recitative (Smith 170). Ballets at the Paris Opera, including *Giselle*, were called "ballet pantomimes," and "the composer was expected to hew to the action, tailoring the music to fit the choreography" (Smith 3–4). Thus, the music not only accompanied the dancing but also helped narrate the story of the ballet (Smith 167). In the ballet performance, then, the music, in addition to guiding the steps of the dancer, plays an important role in establishing the characters and shaping the narrative through its orchestration, harmonies, and themes. Orchestration helps to create both character and atmosphere, while the composer's harmonic key choices connect separate sections of the ballet aurally to help create audience anticipation and foreshadow the action; musical themes in the ballet attach to the characters by their placement, and their recurrence helps convey the narrative through musical depiction.

Adam, originally known as a composer of *opéra comique*, was commissioned to compose the score for the ballet *Giselle*—a task he completed in a mere three weeks (Forbes). Yet, despite its hasty composition, the score became Adam's most famous work. A musical stylistic interpretation and contextualization of the ideological threads of gender discourse in this dance about the woman Giselle, the Wilis, and the men who love her demonstrates Adam's success while illuminating the discourse at the foundation of the work.

Adam uses musical techniques specific to the ballet, including instrumentation, harmonies, and rhythms with symbolic force to help convey the idea of the Wilis, the personalities and relationships of the main characters, and the fateful events of the story.[2] For instance, the sound of the horn is symbolic of the hunting aristocracy. Adam also takes advantage of the symbolic power of the harmonic movement in tonal music between the dominant chord (the chord based on the fifth scale degree) to the tonic chord (the chord based on the first scale degree), also known as a perfect cadence, which is one of the most affective of all chord motions; in *Giselle*, this cadence symbolizes the impetus towards social harmony. As another instance, themes that share the same key of G major symbolize the connection between Giselle and Hilarion. Adam also uses harmonic motion, moving between harmonic areas to give the ballet narrative urgency and dramatic momentum in both Act I and Act II of *Giselle*. Harmonic motion between different chords on the various scale degrees moves the music from and to basic chords, including not only the dominant and tonic but also the subdominant (built on the fourth scale degree), and, less frequently, moves the music to minor areas (such as chords built on the second, third, and sixth scale degrees). The harmonic movement from dominant to tonic provides a particular directionality to the music; the listener feels the need for resolution. Within the context of this harmonic motion, the dancers' steps are related to the musical rhythm and the melodic themes, and their mime and acting are synchronized with the musical gestures.

The libretto, choreography, and music for *Giselle* all illustrate the patriarchal attitude to women prevalent in nineteenth-century Europe. Adam's score reflects gender instability in the story, reflecting the Romantic division of woman into the *femme fatale*, represented by the Wilis—spirits of brides jilted on their wedding day who come to life at midnight to avenge themselves on men by dancing them to death—and the ingénue, or *femme gentile*, represented by Giselle—a contrast that musically finds representation in the shifts between the major mode and minor mode and in the contrast between higher melodic figures and lower figures, as well as in the harmonic and thematic changes mentioned above. *Giselle* also presents a critique of the class system, since class is the initial hindrance to Albrecht and Giselle's love. More significantly, it can be read as a portrait of gender norms, where the virtuous woman is powerless, and the anger of wrathful women overrides male desire. The dynamic between the male protagonist, Albrecht, and the two types of woman, the ingénue Giselle and the vengeful Wilis, creates the fundamental tension of *Giselle*, and Adam's music is essential to creating and conveying this tension.

Giselle Act I

Adam's score for *Giselle* uses an abundance of themes and styles for the characters and settings, changing melodies and themes for each dance to convey the story of the ballet.[3] Act I opens with the drones of a folk dance, as we see a rustic country village, a scene that changes suddenly with the arrival of the forester Hilarion, who is in love with Giselle. His musical signature of double eighth notes followed by quarter notes in G major marks his entrance as he seeks out Giselle. When Duke Albrecht enters, disguised as the peasant Loys, the music is in C major with a more confident sound at *fortissimo*, with grace notes decorating the repeated notes and two rapid upward scales. The grace notes and dynamics indicate this is an important character (fig. 2.1). Giselle is an innocent young girl, and her first theme, with dotted rhythms in the key of G major (like Hilarion's) and a triangle joining with the strings, conveys her happy, carefree nature. This theme is marked by an eighth-note upbeat figure and speedy descending sixteenth notes at the end of the phrase (fig. 2.2). When Albrecht and Giselle encounter one another, the harmony is in G major (the "folk" key area, since it is both Giselle's and Hilarion's harmonic territory), which suggests his deception and foreshadows the future conflict between the rival men. When a pas de deux between "Loys" and Giselle ensues, Giselle's second theme is stated in G major as she falls in love (fig. 2.3). When they are interrupted by the entrance of Hilarion, the key, while

Figure 2.1: Albrecht enters in Act I (Stern 13).

Figure 2.2: Giselle's first theme (Stern 15).

still G major at first, modulates to B minor, which, as a minor key, heralds trouble. When Hilarion tries unsuccessfully to convince Giselle that Albrecht is a fraud, the section ends with repeated B-major chords (dominant to E) and then a final E-minor chord, the relative minor of G major. E minor is a key that will return as a signal of Giselle's troubles, and here it leaves no sense of resolution.[4]

Figure 2.3: Giselle's second theme (Stern 17).

In a sudden transformation, the folk music theme returns in G major
with accented drones in the bass on G and D. More villagers arrive as "Loys"
comforts Giselle. The music modulates to D major (the dominant of G
major), and Giselle's third theme is in waltz time, with weak beats on each
second and third beat, creating the sense of lightness (fig. 2.4).[5] Albrecht's
theme now alternates with the folk music theme, as Albrecht joins Giselle in
the group and they begin a pas de deux. The folk music theme soon begins
to crescendo and accelerate, as indicated by the score direction *più mosso*
(more motion), depicting the excitement of the dancing but also its danger
for her weak heart. The music soon slows to match the calmer pas de deux,
as the couple begins on a new theme in A major, and these sections repeat
to show the couple's growing love. Change occurs at the entrance of Giselle's
worried mother, Berthe, who looks for her daughter in the crowd of revellers.
Her music shifts to F minor and moves quickly to match the urgency of
her actions with its clipped rising figures in the woodwinds and upbeat

VALSE

Figure 2.4: *Giselle's third theme (Bolshoi, transcribed Gier).*

articulations in the bass. Giselle's third theme returns as she runs to Berthe, who dabs her forehead with concern. After a great deal of modulation, the section ends on a B-major chord (the dominant of E), and Giselle re-enters her cottage.

Hilarion enters with his signature call in G major, and then spells out his suspicions in gestures to long-held half notes, until he discovers Albrecht's hidden sword. This discovery foreshadows the arrival of the hunting party of the Prince of Courland, and the horn call on E and A (a fourth, as in a hunting call) signals their importance. Giselle enjoys the visit of the nobility and dances for them to musical accompaniment in B-flat major, after which she accepts the gift of a necklace from Bathilde, daughter of the Prince of Courland. Musically, this gift moves the orchestra briefly to E minor to emphasize Giselle's delight at Bathilde's generosity as she shows the necklace to Berthe. This is the first return of this key, giving an indication that something may arise from this meeting with the nobles. The hunting party then hangs a horn outside the house, and they depart to music in the key of E major.

The next scenes involve the peasant dances accompanied by music in A major, at which Giselle is a spectator initially. Giselle's variation follows, as she dances to a violin melody in the key of E major, with the time signature of 6/8 (recalling her happy time with the visitors). The keys throughout this section remain in the major mode and move steadily through the circle of fifths—from G to its dominant D major, then A major, and finally E major—before Hilarion re-enters.

Hilarion inserts himself between Albrecht and Giselle to reveal to Giselle that Albrecht is not a peasant but an aristocrat. Horns foreshadow his news with open fifths, and a striking A-sharp diminished chord marks the moment when he brings Albrecht's sword to show to Giselle. Giselle's distress is emphasized musically with a move to E minor again, and the music, now marked *Allegro mosso* (fast-moving), in the low brass and high wind and string figurations, underscores her emotional reaction to the news. The juxtaposition of low and high instruments introduces tension into the aural and psychological landscape. Giselle tries to intervene, but the men are determined to fight, and Hilarion's horn call sets the stage. Their conflict is interrupted by the return of the hunting party, and now urgency in the string lines helps paint the response of the villagers to their arrival. The nobility greet Albrecht, who blends into the crowd as he tries to explain himself. Giselle is horrified when Bathilde mimes that she is betrothed to marry Albrecht. Rushing string lines in E minor at *Allegro* with brass and percussion punctuations convey the agitation of the moment and relate Giselle's escalating distress.

The innocent ingénue realizes she has been deceived, and, desperate, she runs from one person to another for help and finally collapses. *Pianissimo* (very soft) strings segue to her rising in tears, and soon the strings and flutes bring in a variation of Giselle's second theme. The theme plays slowly in the strings in a call-and-response fashion, as she remembers how happy she felt before, emphasizing her current weakened condition. Albrecht comes to her aid, but she appears distracted. She dances to her second theme in

E-flat major and threatens to commit suicide with Albrecht's sword as she runs back and forth, urgently, seeking an answer. (The key of E-flat major is the key of the Wilis' dance in Act II, so the use of that key here foreshadows her fate.) As the music modulates to A-flat major, the instruments play only partial runs from her theme, and we know she is desperate. Marked *più animato* (more animated), the music suggests a gradual mental decline into madness, as she cannot keep her dancing or her theme straight. The theme starts and stops and then returns in the clarinet as she gets up again, truly distracted. Now, the low strings articulate a figure in E minor, with warning calls from the winds, and timpani rolls lead to her final collapse. The strings and brass bring in repeated descending lines, and the orchestra presents a tragic conclusion to Act I in E minor. Giselle has succumbed to heartbreak.

Giselle Act II

The orchestral introduction to Act II, including a timpani roll that reminds audiences of Giselle's fate, begins in D major, alternating with G minor chords, or a minor plagal relationship (iv–I), and then A major chords finally bring the music to a perfect cadence (V–I).[6] The plagal motion, reminiscent of church music, gives the opening a religious quality, honouring Giselle's death, with the B-flat (the minor third above G) emphasized in the wind melody. Bells toll in the first scene, and strings and winds play descending chords that do not resolve. As Hilarion enters to visit Giselle's grave, low brass and strings play rising figures in A minor, alternating with quick runs in the winds. At the grave, Hilarion encounters the Wilis, who frighten him away as the music ends in G minor (the parallel minor to G major, his key from the first act).

Myrtha, Queen of the Wilis, performs a solo variation, with music in B-flat major (the dominant of E-flat), to a harp and violin duet, with the strings as a gentle accompaniment. Her music continues with a different melody, similar to Giselle's themes, now in A-flat major, adding new melodies as it modulates from A-flat major to E-flat major. She acknowledges Giselle's grave, accompanied by an oboe melody in A-flat major, and summons the Wilis. They dance to the Wilis' theme, previously introduced by Myrtha, in E-flat major, marked

Figure 2.5: Wilis' Theme (Stern 105).

Figure 2.6: Giselle as Wili (Bolshoi, transcribed Gier).

by a high descending melodic line from G to B-flat and triplet eighth-note arpeggios in the harp (fig. 2.5). Heralded by quick violin figurations alternating with rising bass eighth notes, Myrtha draws Giselle from the grave to join them, and the key changes to B major as Giselle's role as a Wili begins. This key is the dominant of E major, the key of the hunting party, indicating

Figure 2.7: Albrecht's oboe theme, Act II (Stern 134).

Figure 2.8: Giselle as Wili, solo (Stern 140).

that she has now moved into a dominant world—that is, a world beyond them. Giselle, now with wings, starts to spin, accompanied by a new musical theme in D major in 6/8 time and at *Allegro* tempo (fig. 2.6).

A change to D minor announces the entrance of the grieving Albrecht. With a plaintive oboe solo, his sadness resonates with the music in this moving lament (fig. 2.7). As Smith observes, the oboe solo acts like an operatic aria to convey the depth of his sorrow (168). Giselle flutters by while quick trills in the strings sound on F. Albrecht attempts to grasp her, but she eludes him, as the flutes suggest with short two-note calls. Giselle finally stops and begins a slow variation accompanied by music in D major with the tempo marking *Larghetto* (fig. 2.8). The *Wilis* then chase Hilarion onto the stage, accompanied by music in B minor, and *fortissimo* trills on F-sharp (the dominant of B) mark their response. The brass and strings modulate to B major at the end of this scene, as the Wilis demonstrate their terrible power musically in the Wilis' second theme, with rapid string gestures and loud brass calls.

Albrecht approaches Myrtha, as chromatic modulation brings the Wilis' angry music back to B minor, now marked *Allegro feroce* (fiercely fast). They temper their hostility towards him because Giselle, now one of them, still loves him. Myrtha, however, remains implacable as Giselle pleads for him to be released, accompanied by a viola solo in A-flat major at *Andante moderato* (moderately slow), and Albrecht beseeches them for mercy. He and Giselle engage in a pas de deux to a waltz that modulates to E-flat major, with an ensemble of viola, flute and clarinet, cadencing on a cascade of descending A-flat major arpeggios in the viola. They both then engage in progressively faster and grander solos, individually striving to impress Myrtha. One sequence sets the tempo in the viola at *Andantino* (slow), with emphasis on the off-beats, imparting a sense of urgency to the dancing. The dances continue in this style until Albrecht, exhausted, appeals to Myrtha, accompanied by the low brass playing the off-beats. In a coda set to a waltz led by the flute, Albrecht and Giselle make a final plea to Myrtha as Giselle's second theme returns. Giselle dances to this theme now set in triple metre, and Albrecht re-enters to a melody with urgent repeated string patterns and wind responses.[7] He is then overcome by the Wilis' force. Harp arpeggios and a clanging bell return the scene musically to the Wilis' world. They allow Giselle to raise him up one last time, accompanied by a melody in the strings, harp and solo violin in F major. She revives him in time for him to see her depart; then a solo violin, clarinet, and finally a flute play in succession—the same ensemble of instruments they had just danced to together—and Albrecht realizes she is gone forever.

Giselle Apotheosis

Adam's score for *Giselle* reflects nineteenth-century class and gender attitudes by musically narrating Giselle's transformation from a lively young girl to an insubstantial phantom. As Susan McClary explains in her introduction to Catherine Clément's *Opera, or the Undoing of Women*, a typical nineteenth-century opera plot "demands the submission or death of the woman for the sake of narrative closure" (xi), and this principle is true of musical closure as well. *Giselle* tells a nuanced version of this standard plot with the death of the heroine and the failure of the hero to save his beloved. Albrecht's failure is palpable, while Giselle calmly accepts her fate. Success for Albrecht is impossible because the Wilis are too powerful for him in their supernatural realm.

Thus, the musical score of *Giselle* reinforces the libretto and choreography in conveying the patriarchal attitude to women prevalent in nineteenth-century Europe, as the male principle dominates even the musical resolution. As McClary explains, "in the world of traditional [musical] narrative there are no feminine endings" (*Feminine* 16). Musical principles determine the fate of the characters in a gendered sense. Giselle, the *femme gentile*, begins her story in G major and ends in F major. Albrecht, the hero, enters in C major, unsullied by any chromatics. Giselle then becomes one of the Wilis by virtue of her broken heart, but she cannot remain in their E-flat major mode while she still loves Albrecht. Instead, she wanders through various keys: she arrives in Act II in B major, moves through F major and into A-flat major. The solo violin melody in F major at the end solidifies the sadness of Giselle and Albrecht's fate. F major, or the subdominant of Albrecht's initial key of C major, is the key on the fifth scale degree *below* middle C, a key that represents the tragedy of the conclusion, even if it is not a minor key. Albrecht's sorrow seals the ending because Giselle is lost to him forever.

Adam's score aurally depicts the phantom world of the Wilis vividly and reveals how their power holds the key to the narrative of *Giselle*. Their musical world is introduced in E-flat major, traditionally symbolic of the holy, given its three flats. McClary explains how the codes of gender narrative in western tonal practice parallel those of western literary narrative, concluding that "the masculine protagonist makes contact with but must eventually subjugate...the designated [feminine] Other in order for identity to be consolidated" and to achieve "narrative closure" (*Feminine* 14). In *Giselle*,

Albrecht returns to his world of aristocratic privilege as a "consolidated" identity, while he mourns, in what we might term a *deflated* key, the subdominant of C, the death of his beloved.

Because *iGiselle* was developed with the aim of allowing Giselle to live and have agency and to situate her in a contemporary setting, the director of the project, Nora Foster Stovel, decided not to use Adam's score to accompany the video game. Instead she invited Wayne DeFehr to compose a new score that would evoke the music of the Romantic ballet as a touchstone, but would also contextualize the heroine in a twenty-first-century situation that would allow for the possibility of "feminine endings." As DeFehr explains in Chapter 7 of this volume, *iGiselle*'s updated story of a young woman conveys a new emotional journey for the empowered heroine, with free choices within the game world's adventures, for dance and love.

Notes

1. See also Stovel, "The Birth of the Ballerina."

2. My discussion and analysis are based on a specific performance by the Bolshoi Ballet recorded on a DVD produced in 2012 and on the piano score edited by Daniel Stern in 1974.

3. The Bolshoi production's conclusion returns to themes to which the piano score by Daniel Stern does not. Stern's score presents other variations as possibilities.

4. "Relative minor" refers to the minor key that shares the key signature of a major key.

5. In tonal harmonic theory, the dominant chord wants to move to the tonic chord, which offers the sense of resolution so important to tonal harmony. Often larger harmonic areas with diverse chords suggest this motion by moving to the dominant before the music resolves, adding a sense of progression that tells the story through music.

6. The plagal cadence, or IV–I, is also known as the "Amen" cadence, as it frequently concludes religious ceremonies.

7. In contrast to the piano score, the Bolshoi production switches to the music from Act I for Hilarion's challenge to Albrecht, confirming that Albrecht's conflict with the Wilis is the same as Hilarion's: it is over Giselle.

Works Cited

Adam, Adolphe. *"Giselle: Ballet en deux actes* (Piano)." Ed. and arr. Daniel Stern. Paris: Éditions Mario Bois, 1978.

Adam, Adolphe, composer. *Giselle.* Perf. Bolshoi Ballet. Bel Air Classiques, 2012. DVD.

Bolshoi Theatre Orchestra, perf. *Giselle.* Comp. Adolphe Adam. Bel Air Classiques, 2012. DVD.

Clément, Catherine. *Opera, or the Undoing of Women* (*L'opéra ou le défait des femmes*). Trans. Betsy Wing, foreword Marion Smith. Minneapolis: U of Minnesota P, 1988.

Forbes, Elizabeth. "Adolphe Adam." *Oxford Music Online.* www.oxfordmusiconline.com.

Jowitt, Deborah. "In Pursuit of the Sylph: Ballet in the Romantic Period." *Routledge Dance Studies Reader.* Ed. Alexandra Carter and Janet O'Shea. 2nd ed. London and New York: Routledge, 2010. 209–19.

McClary, Susan. *Feminine Endings: Music, Gender and Sexuality.* 1991. Rev. with a new introduction. Minneapolis and London: U of Minnesota P, 2002.

———. "The Undoing of Opera: Toward a Feminist Criticism of Music." Foreword to Clément, ix–xviii.

Smith, Marion. *Ballet and Opera in the Age of Giselle.* Princeton and Oxford: Princeton UP, 2000.

Stern, Daniel, ed. and arr. *"Giselle: Ballet en deux actes* (Piano)." By Adolphe Adam. Paris: Éditions Mario Bois, 1978.

Stovel, Nora Foster. "The Birth of the Ballerina in *La Sylphide*: Sylph or Self?" *WWR Magazine* 2.2 (2008), 13–18. www.crcstudio.org/wwr_magazine/mags/WWRMag_5.pdf.

3

The Other Giselles

Moncrieff's Giselle; *or,* The Phantom Night Dancers,
Loder's The Night Dancers, *and Puccini's* Le Villi

SAY THE NAME "GISELLE," and almost every music lover will immediately
think of Adolphe Adam's much-loved score for the 1841 ballet. But the Wilis,
whom Adam and his librettists Jules-Henri Vernoy de Saint-Georges and
Théophile Gautier—via Heinrich Heine—brought out of their Serbian folk
obscurity into a European mythical parlance, spread their crepuscular arms
far beyond the stage of the Paris Opera and into a wider nineteenth-century
European musical sensibility. After 1841, they appear in an English stage play,
W.T. Moncrieff's *Giselle; or, The Phantom Night Dancers* (1841); they are invoked
in Ophelia's aria in Ambroise Thomas's opera *Hamlet*; and they are central to
two nineteenth-century operas: Edward Loder's *The Night Dancers* (1846) and
Giacomo Puccini's *Le Villi* (1883).

Moncrieff's play was based directly on the scenario by Saint-Georges and
Gautier for Adam's ballet; Loder's opera combines elements of the Adam
scenario with ideas from Moncrieff; Puccini's opera has a distant nod to Heine,
but the primary source is a French short story by Alphonse Karr, published in

1856 (four years after Adam's ballet was revived in Paris), and has all the main traits of the Wilis legend. Neither of the operas is well known: Loder's has fallen almost completely into whatever operatic graveyard the Wilis prepare for such things, and while Puccini's opera may be recognized by name, few opera lovers have ever actually heard it.

Yet both operas are emblematic of the age and cultures in which they were written, and both say something about how the story of Giselle and the Wilis infiltrated the nineteenth-century consciousness. The importance of Puccini's opera, indeed, goes beyond that. Not only is it of great interest to Puccini scholars, as it was the first opera that Puccini wrote, but it also occupies a germinal place in the history of opera in Italy. It did not quite take Italian opera on a new course—that was left to Pietro Mascagni's *Cavalleria rusticana* of 1890—but it did herald that new course, influence Mascagni, and introduce the composer who was going to become the greatest Italian opera figure in that new era.

Moncrieff's *Giselle*; or, *The Phantom Night Dancers* (1841)

The story really starts with a now totally obscure British play, by the prolific playwright and theatre manager William Moncrieff (1794–1857). Usually known as W.T. Moncrieff, he wrote musical dramas, burlesques, plays, and extravaganzas. His *Cataract of the Ganges* (1823), a hit in New York as well as in London, concluded with the hero on horseback riding up the cataract, with the cross-dressing heroine draped over the saddle and fires raging all around (Rotter 519). Moncrieff's work was hugely popular, and he was cheeky enough to produce a play, *Sam Weller* (1837), before Dickens had actually finished serializing *Pickwick Papers*, on which the play was based (Stephens).

On July 9, 1841, Moncrieff read in the *Morning Post* a detailed account of the premiere of Adam's ballet in Paris, complete with synopsis (McCarren 232 n. 27). Never one to hesitate (or worry about plagiarism), he immediately wrote a play based on that newspaper synopsis, titled *Giselle; or, The Phantom Night Dancers: A Domestic, Melo-dramatic, Choreographic, Fantastique, Traditionary Tale of Superstition in Two Acts*, which, according to the 1842 publication of the play, was produced on August 23 (only six weeks later) at the Theatre Royal,

Sadler's Wells (Moncrieff). The play includes songs and a ballet; Moncrieff's introductory "advertisement" in the 1842 publication of the play states that the music used was an adaptation of Adam's music by J. Collins (xv). If so, Collins did his arrangements with extraordinary speed, and it must have been the first time that Adam's music, albeit in a truncated form, had been heard on a London stage. That one could write and organize the play (and the settings are quite complicated) and then acquire Adam's score and arrange it, all in the space of just over six weeks, boggles the mind.

It was a success, with H. Honner's "transcending" acting as Giselle "for some weeks the theme of universal admiration." That quotation is from a playbill for the opening of the play at another theatre, the Royal Pavilion Theatre in Whitechapel, to where the entire cast, including the Proprietor of Sadler's Wells, Robert Horner (who played Aloise), and presumably the production, subsequently transferred (Pavilion Theatre).[1] It opened there on October 18, 1841, complete with a complex water system (proudly announced in another playbill in huge letters as "Fountains of Real Water") for the second act. An anonymous local critic wrote, "The exquisite acting of Mrs. H. Honner, backed with that of the talented company, together with the well-selected set pieces, draws nightly together a crowded audience, who fail not to testify their approbation" (Pavilion Theatre).[2] With productions in two London theatres, the capital's audiences were primed for the main themes of the ballet when that reached Her Majesty's Theatre on March 12, 1842.

Moncrieff outlines his method in his "advertisement": "In fact, without losing sight of my original, I was obliged to depart very widely from most of its incidents. The dénouement is entirely different; many new characters have been added; and the whole conduct of the story has been altered, in many instances, to suit the more dramatic nature of my piece" (xi). He also suggests that his sources on the Wilis extended further than Heine and Gautier, citing John Bowring's "Vila Song" from his "poetry of the 'Magyars,'" William J. Thoms's *Lays and Legends*, and especially Thomas Keightley's influential *Fairy Mythology*, published in 1828. He is a little disingenuous in this, as Keightley has no reference to what he calls the Vilas being jilted women who ensnare men. Rather, he describes them as "mountain nymphs, young and beautiful, clad in white, with long flowing hair," though they are well known for their dancing (492–94).[3]

Moncrieff opens the play with a scene between Giselle and Bertha (here Giselle's grandmother) that sets some of the background and introduces the Wilis' story. The recurrent idea of the waltz is also introduced in this scene, as Giselle dances a snatch of the "Witching Waltz" (3). The first main change Moncrieff makes to the Adam ballet scenario is to introduce a self-important village bailiff, Baillie Otto von Fustenwig, who acts as a general factotum to the first-act plot, as well as to the village, and whose surname indicates his gently comic pomposity. Act I centres around a rather English village fête, with Giselle as fête queen, where the essential events follow the ballet story. Giselle ends the act by dancing the fatal "Wili Waltz" (35) before fainting into the arms of her fiancé Aloise (as the ballet's Albrecht is called).

Moncrieff's main addition to the central story is a religious element. A hermit, Father Christoph, appears in Act I, living in a suitably Gothic grotto cave. In Act II St. Walburg (Walpurga), the local saint, is introduced, and we learn that Giselle wears a rosary of the saint around her neck (Moncrieff 45). As Moncrieff proudly tells the reader in the "advertisement" (he enjoys showing off his research), Walpurga was a real person, and indeed she is an apposite character for his play. The daughter of "the King of the West Saxons,"[4] she presided over a nunnery in Serbia from 760 to 779, and was "a powerful patroness of chastity, having continued a virgin all her life; and her guardianship was especially held to extend to all young maidens by whom it was invoked" (Moncrieff xiv). She is also, of course, the origin of the name of Walpurgis Night, as her feast-day (April 30) coincides with it. Walpurgis Night is the night of witches, and it had appeared in both parts of Goethe's *Faust*.[5]

The ruins of the saint's nunnery are actually seen at the end of the play, where both Father Christoph and Hilarion (whose role follows that in the ballet quite closely) invoke her to save Giselle. It almost seems to work, but Giselle, now almost completely transformed into a Wili, disappears, and Hilarion falls in a faint. Not everything is lost, however: as the moon disappears, demons are seen ready to seize Hilarion, the stained glass windows of the nunnery's chapel suddenly become illuminated, the "solemn sounds of the organ proclaim the Matin Chant of the Holy Sisterhood," and Father Christoph literally has a final trick up the sleeve of his habit: the powerful amaranth branch,[6] the symbol of the saint's power (Moncrieff 59–60). Unfortunately, the queen of the Wilis gets hold of it, but it is no match for the little statuette of St. Walburg that Father Christoph also has about his person. The amaranth branch shatters, the queen is struck dead by a thunderbolt, Hilarion and Giselle are restored, and Father Christoph speaks the last words: "Hence with the shades of night, lost spirits, while we, to earth restored—to light and virtue—exhult [sic] once more in rapturous joy and love" (Moncrieff 62–63).

It's all heady Victorian (and Gothic) melodramatic stuff. As was necessary in British theatre at the time (for reasons discussed below), music and dance add to the *mise-en-scène*, reflecting not only the subject matter but also the expectations of the audiences. The stage directions indicate music for many of the entrances and exits, as well as at the beginning and ending of scenes. Slightly surprisingly, there are no general dances at the village fête, though Giselle dances wildly "for some time" to the "Wili Waltz" when she discovers that Aloise is actually a nobleman (Moncrieff 35). When the Wilis appear in the second act, there is a major "*Bal Fantastique*," with the dances specified; this is a set showpiece. Each is danced by a different individual Wili: a "wild *Alamande*," a "fanciful *Pas Odalisque*," a "*Bayadère Pas*," a "quick Gipsy Dance," "a Mazy Waltz," and finally a "Bizarre Minuet" (41). The waltz reappears shortly afterwards as the Wilis try to ensnare Peter (one of the villagers, who is saved by invoking St. Walburg), just after they have succeeded in drowning one of the villagers, Caspar, to a "rapid *Galoppe*" (42–43).

The waltz is combined with another fantastical element that was a favourite of early nineteenth-century Romanticism—a sleepwalking scene. After becoming slightly deranged by the news that her fiancé is actually a nobleman, Giselle wanders around her house in a sleepwalking trance, attired as if she were playing Ophelia or sitting for a Pre-Raphaelite painting:

She is simply dressed in white, her crossed hands folded on her breast, her long hair hanging loosely over her shoulders; the Rosary of St. Walburg suspended

round her neck, and resting on her bosom; a Chaplet of White Lilies is on her
head, her countenance is pale, and her look fixed... (Moncrieff 46)

Eventually the Wilis themselves enter the house (while she is still in the
trance), dance, and spirit her away. There is a final glimpse of the Wilis
dancing in the penultimate scene, as the sun rises and they disappear, but
not at the end, perhaps to avoid distracting from the extravagant set piece.

The other aspect of Moncrieff's play that so reflects the tastes of the time
involves the elaborate and complex semi-supernatural stage settings—
decidedly spectacle over substance. Myrtha, Queen of the Wilis, appears
from a "Tuft of Water-Lilies" rising out of a lake (39–40), and (like all the
Wilis), wears wings. She then touches various clusters of flowers with her
wand (Moncrieff's stage directions make her sound visually something like
a Disney fairy-godmother), and out of each appears a different Wili. Caspar
is drowned in the lake onstage. Doors and windows in Giselle's house fly
open of their own accord so that the Wilis can enter, and "a blue silvery light"
spreads over the room. The nunnery and its lighting effects have already
been noted. (There are constant references to lighting effects in the stage
directions; it is surprising how much could be realized in a pre-electric
theatre.) Giselle disappears into a tuft of flowers in a dell, amid a rising mist.

The most extravagant setting is reserved for the end. It is set beneath
"Wili Lake" in "the Palace of a Thousand Fountains," and the onstage appearance of at least some of the fountains was a major draw, as that Royal
Pavilion Theatre poster shows. The stage directions read: "MYRTHA appears
from the back in a magnificent Car, which expands as it advances; she is
surrounded by playing fountains of real water, brilliantly illuminated with
variegated fires.—GISELLE, in chains, is lying at her feet" (Moncrieff 62).
Almost immediately the queen, still in her car, is struck dead by a great light-
ning bolt. It could be a scene out of an H. Rider Haggard novel, and the Royal
Pavilion playbill proudly announced that the machinery of the car and the
fountains alone had cost 150 guineas.

Moncrieff's play, then, is very much of its London theatrical time,
including music and dance, revelling in melodramatic scenery and effects.

The first half of the play is essentially straight theatre, but, once the Wilis themselves are introduced, the stage effects build up to the grand finale that has relatively little text: the audience was there for the spectacle. While there are plenty of melodramatic situations, there is relatively little character development (though the characters are quite strongly drawn) and essentially little dramatic, as opposed to melodramatic, conflict. The action is propelled by set pieces (for example, Giselle's sleepwalking, her recounting of a dream, Peter's seeing Caspar drowned) and by reactions to events rather than any psychological interactions. But, with the undercurrent of the supernatural, be it a religious relic or the Wilis themselves, Gothic settings, or elaborate stage effects, that is what the audiences of the period expected, and they were given it by Moncrieff's play in good measure.

Edward Loder's *The Night Dancers* (1846)

In 1846, five years after Moncrieff's play and four after the British premiere of Adam's ballet, the first opera on the Wilis subject appeared. Its prolific, if now forgotten, English composer, Edward Loder (1809–1865), was one of a group of British composers who were, in the 1840s, establishing home-grown works alongside their continental counterparts, in an outpouring of British Romantic operas. They included Michael Balfe (1808–1870), perhaps the most talented and certainly the most successful of these composers, William Wallace (1812–1865), George MacFarren (1813–1887), John Barnett (1802–1890), and Julius Benedict (1804–1885). For a short-lived period of some twenty years, they were not only prolific but also exceedingly popular.[7] From 1834, when Loder's *Nourjahad* opened the new English Opera House (a rebuilding of the old Lyceum Theatre), to 1861, ninety-three new operas by twenty-nine British composers were premiered in Britain, mostly in London (White, *Register* 71–80).

These composers' tasks, however, were difficult, because of the rather convoluted history of British theatre in the early nineteenth century and the resultant effect on the tastes of audiences. Until 1843, only three theatres (including Covent Garden but not Sadler's Wells) had a licence to perform straight, purely spoken, theatre. As a consequence, other theatres had to include music in their plays to get around this restriction (as can be seen in Moncrieff's play), and the British theatre public got used to theatrical presentations that combined speech and music. Ballads in popular styles were a staple of such fare. By the early decades of the nineteenth century, the "ballad opera" (the most famous of which is Gay's *Beggar's Opera*, 1738) had long been the mainstay British genre; alongside, Italian opera became established, with Rossini and Donizetti well represented in productions, and in 1847 Verdi was commissioned to write *I masnadieri* for His Majesty's Theatre in London. But it was the triumphal success of Weber's *Oberon*, commissioned by Covent Garden and premiered there on April 12, 1826,[8] that introduced British composers and audiences to the new German school of Romanticism. As Nicholas Temperley succinctly states,

> It is no coincidence that several of the most successful English operas after
> 1830 were about fairies or nymphs, notably Barnett's The Mountain Sylph,
> Loder's The Night Dancers, Balfe's Keolanthe, and Wallace's Lurline. In all
> these the fairy music pays an obvious debt to Oberon; and generally, in most
> English Romantic operas the rich, warm glow which distinguishes them from
> their predecessors comes from Weber more than any other single influence.
> ("English" 297–98)

There was considerable support for home-grown operas from the new urban intellectual classes that were among the offshoots of the young Industrial Revolution and from royal support and interest: the first opera Queen Victoria saw after her succession in 1837 was Balfe's *The Siege of Rochelle*. That support increased when she married Albert, the Prince Consort, in 1840, as he was far more an aficionado of the theatre and opera than his wife. The budding operatic movement was also given impetus by the extraordinary singer Maria Malibran (1808–1836), a mezzo-soprano who could happily encompass high soprano and low contralto roles. She started appearing in London in Italian operas in 1834, but Balfe wrote for her *The Maid of Artois*, premiered at Drury Lane on May 26. She was a huge draw, and the opera was one of Balfe's great successes; her death that September, at the age of

28 (of complications following a fall from a horse), left contemporary critics judging her successors against her and propelled her into operatic legend (Cox 27–28).

But British opera was a precarious milieu, especially for impresarios, as Balfe himself discovered when he tried his hand at management and took the lease of the Lyceum in 1841 (White, *History* 276–77). New opera houses were created, or re-formed from older theatres, but they could fold equally easily. It was financial considerations, too, that partly dictated the forms of British Romantic operas. The British public, thanks to the ballad operas and the necessity of music in plays, were used to both dialogue and ballads— and popular songs—in their theatrical works. There was, too, a huge British demand for ballads and songs that could be sung and played on their own in the drawing-rooms of the burgeoning middle-class—which also meant that they could not be too complex or difficult to perform. Balfe's fees eventually became so great that he could afford to ignore that demand, but, for most other British composers, the financial necessity of including within their operas ballads that would then be sold separately partly dictated the material they created.

Thus, whereas composed operas with recitative but no dialogue were rare (Balfe's *Catherine Grey* is an example), most British operas still included more dialogue than recitative, and most still included ballad numbers. That format is actually familiar to most opera lovers through the works of Gilbert and Sullivan, since they used the general forms of British Romantic opera in their satirical works, partly to satirize the genre. All too often, these operas can therefore appear facile; however, their current almost complete neglect is somewhat inexplicable. The best of them, if not on the level of Donizetti or Rossini (or indeed Weber), are not only attractive in themselves, as the occasional revival and recording has shown (and as the original success of some of them in Europe should have suggested), but also reflect an important period in the history of British opera.

Loder's Giselle opera, the grand opera *The Night Dancers*, is included in that number by almost all commenters, whether nineteenth-century writers or modern critics and scholars. Loder had a checkered career.[9] His opera

Nourjahad, written when he was twenty-four, to all intents and purposes started off the British Romantic opera movement and broke away from the ballad opera tradition of simply putting together ballads and songs. But poverty led him to hack work, both in his subsequent stage dramas, which followed the old popular ballad and song format, and in churning out popular music; at one point he was contracted to a publisher to write one composition every week (Temperley, "Edward James Loder"). He became manager of the Princess's Theatre in 1846, and *The Night Dancers* marked his return to serious opera. Once again, subsequent works were of a lower standard, until his masterpiece, *Raymond and Agnes*, was produced (unsuccessfully) in 1855. Shortly after that, he was afflicted by a brain disease and became paralyzed; his last stage work was an operetta in 1859.

The Night Dancers seems to have originally been called *The Wilis*, but it almost immediately became known by its subtitle, *The Night Dancers* ("Occasional Notes" 243); on the title page of an 1847 American publication of a "melange" (so called) of its waltzes, it is titled *Giselle, Or the Night Dancers*. Its premiere at London's Princess Theatre on October 28, 1846, was a great success, although that performance also became celebrated for Giselle's costume catching fire.[10] The opera then ran for three consecutive seasons and was soon seen in other British theatres, in New York in 1847, and in Sydney. There were successful revivals at the Princess's Theatre in 1850 and in Covent Garden in 1860 (White, *History* 287), and it was revived in London as late as 1906 ("Occasional Notes").

The libretto—an induction and two acts—was by the writer and dramatist George Soane (1790–1860).[11] The *Fine Arts Journal*, reviewing the first performance, stated that "the story is taken from the ballet *La Giselle*, though altered considerably in its adaptation for an opera, and is of a much better description than those with which we have lately been favoured" ("Music" 27). The notice in *The Mirror* also stated that it was based on the ballet (St. John 416). The scenario indeed shows that the direct source was Adam's work;[12] however, a number of features seem to have been taken from Moncrieff's play, which would almost certainly have been known, or at least available, to both composer and librettist. The whole of the main action is framed as a dream of Giselle's, a major departure from Adam's ballet. This was probably suggested by Moncrieff, as his Giselle, having been rescued from the Wilis, says, "From what a fearful dream have I awakened" (Moncrieff 63)—exactly the kind of thing a librettist might pick up on when working out a scenario. The character of Peterkin, or Peter, appears in both play and opera but not in the ballet. The inclusion of a procession of monks also suggests the religious additions of Moncrieff's play, though the theme is not nearly so developed in the opera. The Wilis' haunt is a lake—the forest of the ballet appears directly in neither play nor opera. Last, but certainly not least, Baillie Otto Von Fustenwig of the play is clearly translated into the village bailiff Fridolin of the opera. He has a similarly pompous nature but is developed into a more central character who provides a thread of comedy throughout the opera, one that would seem out of place in Weber or Donizetti (but not in a Rossini comic opera), and which again reflects the origins of British Romantic opera in the ballad opera tradition. His conversation with his niece Gretchen is typical:

Gretchen: *Oh uncle! Uncle!*
Fridolin: *And oh, niece, niece! Whose house is on fire now?*
Gretchen: *The Herr Burgomaster is calling and bawling for his wig.*
Fridolin: *Tell him, child—tell him, it's in concoction!*
Gretchen: *In what?*
Fridolin: *Tell him, I say, his wig's in pontificabilis!*
Gretchen: *I don't understand.*
Fridolin: *Nor I, either; so fly, and don't forget pontificabilis!* (15)

In the induction, Giselle, who is to be married to Albert the next day, sings and dances in the company of her niece Mary and her father Godfrey, thinking of the coming day, and hears her fiancé Albert and a chorus serenade her from a nearby lake. Eventually she falls asleep and starts dreaming.

Act I introduces the theme of wine that recurs throughout the act (the villagers are vintners), and the spying activities of the bailiff Fridolin. Giselle tells Albert of the dream she has had: the Wilis appeared just as she was about to be married at the altar of the church, and she danced with them. Godfrey appears to tell them that the priest has been delayed and the marriage must be postponed a day. The Duke, his daughter Bertha, and their companions enter (following the ballet plot), which gives the opportunity for a rousing huntsmen's chorus before they leave. Fridolin, who has climbed through a window into Albert's house, finds objects there that show that Albert is, in fact, a nobleman. Albert and Giselle sing a love-duet, centred on Giselle plucking leaves in the "He loves me, he loves me not" game.[13] In a dramatic scene, Fridolin denounces Albert to the villagers and Giselle, and the Duke and his company appear. The Duke points out that Albert is betrothed to his daughter Bertha. Bertha magnanimously gives her ring to Giselle and blesses Giselle's marriage, but Giselle falls lifeless into Albert's arms, dying as the Abbey bells sounds, and the monks process in and join the final chorus of the act.

Act II is set beside a lake fringed with "lotuses"; to one side is Giselle's grave. Albert and Bertha (who is clearly now going to be his wife) pray at the grave. The villagers appear, and Mary points out to Albert that it is nearly the hour when the Wilis appear. Albert is left on his own, and he sleeps on the lake bank as the moon comes out. Myrtha, the Wilis' queen, rises from a bed of roses. She touches each of the lotuses with her wand, and the individual Wilis appear. At the end of their chorus, Giselle herself rises from the bed of flowers on her grave, and Myrtha transforms her into a Wili, complete with wings. Her reaction is not at all what one might expect, as she sings in an air:

What delightful being's this?
What rapture fills me!
What transport thrills me!
'Tis such wild ecstasy of bliss,
That only things of air
Could live and bear:
And I am air—all air and fire!
The dross of earth is spent,
Leaving the purer element,
That hardly needs these wings to lift it higher. (24)

They dance in a set-piece ballet until a footfall is heard, and all disappear.

The intruder is Fridolin, intent on seeing the beautiful Wilis. He summons them, and they do indeed appear, minus Giselle, and tease him rather in the manner of the Rhinemaidens and Albericht, eventually pulling him down to his death in the lake. Albert, being awakened, has witnessed this and hears Giselle singing "beneath the earth." She rises from the roses, and they sing a duet, in which Albert asks her to dance him into death to be with her. She rushes into his arms, and the Wilis reappear and dance a second ballet. They force Albert towards the lake, but the sun starts rising, and they all disappear into the mists of the morning. Giselle is left alone, singing of how she will "melt in light." Clouds cover the whole scene, horns and huntsmen are heard, the clouds lift, and Giselle is seen on the couch where she fell asleep in the induction. Albert sings an Ave Maria of thanks, the wedding bells are heard, the wedding party arrives, and the work ends entirely happily.

The opera is a mixture of elements, reflecting both its antecedents and the attempt to produce British Romantic opera. There are none of the extravagant stage effects of Moncrieff's play; instead, the work is quite succinctly cast into two acts, paralleling Adam's ballet, with two main stage settings. The lack of separate scenes means that, although there are a lot of individual numbers, there is a unity and flow to the work. It is of the type known as a numbers opera; the musical numbers are separated primarily by often very lengthy spoken passages (longer than would be expected from a continental opera) and occasionally by recitative (one recitative section quickly alternates between sung recitative and spoken word). There are generic choruses, such as the Huntsmen's, and Bacchanalian choruses. But there are also more complex set pieces that take the work beyond ballad opera—notably the plethora of changing emotions of the Act I ending, which begins with that Bacchanalian chorus, is followed by a general waltz, and continues through Fridolin exposing Albert as a nobleman, the Duke pointing out to Albert that he is engaged, Bertha giving up the ring, and so to the monks' procession and Giselle's death. As George Biddlecombe suggests, Giselle's death does not have "an equal in any other English opera of the period."

In contrast with such powerful set pieces, the purely stand-alone ballad songs have the least effective texts, as this excerpt from an aria by Albert demonstrates:

I've so often dreamed in stilly night
Of angels clothed in robes of light,
And, while I slumbered, deem'd they were
Beyond what earth could show me fair
But ever, when I wake, I see
There's nothing can compare with thee. (10)

The writing for other set pieces, such as Giselle's recounting of the dream, is more distinguished, especially when the metre is not so rigidly consistent. Sections, such as Albert's Act II recitative and air as he is beside Giselle's grave, go well beyond stereotypical ballad songs, with the dark orchestral harmonies of the recitative ("'Tis madness! Here alone") and the rather beautiful tune of the air.

Temperley has described Loder's music in *The Night Dancers* as containing "several reminders of Weber's *Oberon*, the obvious model of a number of the earlier English Romantic operas. It is in the evocative fairy music that Loder's talents are uppermost. The ordinary songs—and there are many of them—still have a tendency to be written for the music-shop rather than the stage" ("Edward James Loder" 308). The anonymous reviewer for the *Fine Arts Journal* was more prosaic: "The musical merits of the opera were certainly considerable. There was a great deal of music very good, though much of it indifferent; it is worked up with skill, but in general deficient in melody. The orchestral accomplishments were really written in a masterful manner, Mr. Loder showing that he perfectly understood the powers and capabilities of the different instruments" ("Music" 27).

Three features mitigate against the opera—and, indeed, other contemporary British operas—for modern audiences. The first is the extensive use of spoken word, which modern audiences are not used to in the majority of repertoire operas. The second are those ballad affiliations: the types of tunes and the cast of the songs are all too easily associated with the familiar kind of Victorian sentimental salon song, another genre little found in repertoire opera. Finally, the similarities between this type of opera and the familiar satirical operas of Gilbert and Sullivan are noticeable, and the latter are not normally associated with serious works. Such barriers would perhaps evaporate if more British operas of the period were regularly heard and the idiom became more familiar.

The structure of a dream-opera within an opera in *The Night Dancers* is also of interest: if Giselle is dreaming such a dream, *why* is she dreaming it? Clearly, for librettist Sloane it is a device that allows a happy ending, but that does not preclude a number of speculations about other, perhaps subconscious, motivations, suggested by plot details that in themselves reflect the period: Giselle's dream that her humble fiancé is actually a nobleman, the ease with which her rival Bertha gives up Albert to her, the repressed sexuality in the very idea of the Wilis (from both a male and a female perspective) and especially in their dances, and the interesting idea that Giselle is actually pleased when she discovers she is a Wili, to name but a few. In Adam's ballet, it is quite clear that Giselle can never marry Albrecht. In this opera she can, and, in a most English way, she actually does, when she wakes up; her fantasy has been fulfilled, yet social harmony has been restored. As Dorothy says, in not dissimilar circumstances in *The Wizard of Oz,* "There's no place like home." With such a scenario, and with its echoes of not only Weber but also Mendelssohn and Johann Strauss the senior, Loder's *Night Dancers* does deserve to be better known.[14]

Giacomo Puccini's *Le Villi* (1884)

Some three decades after the premiere of *The Night Dancers,* Italian opera itself was undergoing its own crisis of national operatic identity. Italian opera had dominated Europe in the first half of the nineteenth century, and if the French—Meyerbeer, and more recently Bizet and Massenet—had staked their claims by the 1880s, and if Wagner was making most conservative opera lovers despair of what the world was coming to, the greatest operatic figure of the age was Verdi (1813–1901). He was more than just the greatest Italian composer of the century: he was an Italian icon, inextricably associated with the very self-identity of the young country, socially and politically as well as musically.

But the grand old man, approaching his seventies, had, to all intents and purposes, retired to a comfortable old age in his estate at Sant'Agata. He had been composing for so long that one of the librettists he had worked with had written for one of Balfe's earlier operas.[15] His last completely new opera had been *Aïda* in 1871, and, since then (apart from revisions), only the extensive rewriting of *Simon Boccanegra* in collaboration with Arrigo Boito had appeared in 1881. His composing days, as he himself suggested, appeared to be over, and no one could have anticipated the final flowering of *Otello* in 1887 and *Falstaff* in 1893.

It is difficult, perhaps, for modern readers to comprehend fully how all-pervasive opera was in the cultural life of the country in the late nineteenth century: it was the popular entertainment of the Italian masses and remained that until the First World War. Even the smallest of towns had its opera house, and, in a very different era, there still are 49 in Italy; an official register in the 1890s listed 1,055 theatres and opera houses in 775 Italian towns and cities (Mallach 153). Opera music was heard everywhere—in municipal bands, in private houses, in amateur choruses, in the organ-grinders' tunes. The major opera composers were themselves superstars, not just in Italy, but in the other great centres of Italian opera as well, such as Buenos Aires and New York. When Mascagni arrived in New York in 1902, the Italian community marched up Broadway with him, complete with brass band; when he landed in Buenos Aires in 1911, some 50,000 people were waiting at the dock to greet him (Mallach 154, 193).

One of the singular features of Italian opera of the time—singular to modern sensibilities, at least—was the emphasis on a constant stream of new operas. These were required to maintain the tradition, as well as to appeal to audiences who expected new works. But in 1883 Mascagni was still unknown, and, with Verdi apparently in retirement, the burning question was who was going to be the next great Italian opera composer. Composers such as Ponchielli (then in his late forties), Boito himself (then in his early forties), or the young Catalani (then in his late twenties) had written important operas, but none of them had shown the consistent genius that could enable him to take up the mantle of Verdi. And few sought that great new Italian composer more assiduously than the major Italian publishing houses.

By the early 1880s, there were three major Italian music publishing houses engaged in a bitter—and often very public—rivalry. The oldest and the mightiest was the house of Ricordi, which had built its empire on Italian opera composers (notably Verdi), and was now run by Tito Ricordi, the son of the founder. The rival Casa Lucca was founded in 1841 and had published some of Verdi's early operas; after the death of Francesco Lucca in 1872, it was run with great success by his widow Giovannina. Casa Lucca introduced Italy to much French grand opera, including works by Meyerbeer, Gounod, and Flotow; and, in a far-sighted business coup in 1868, Giovannina bought exclusive Italian rights for the entire works of Wagner.[16] The newcomer was an old book-publishing house, Casa Sonzogno, which started publishing music only in 1874, at the instigation of Edoardo Sonzogno, the grandson of the founder. Since most of the Italian opera composers and the major international names were already firmly in the grip of Ricordi and Lucca, Sonzogno turned to French *opéra comique*, including works by Massenet, Offenbach, and Gounod, and scored a coup with Bizet's *Carmen*, introduced in Naples in 1880. Its much more realistic scenario, its raw emotions, and its very direct music imagery—such a contrast to the prevailing grand opera—were soon heard all across Italy.

These three great publishing houses battled each other through an extensive impresario and business network. In addition to persuading opera houses to take their works, they also either owned opera theatres themselves or had close ties to them. Ricordi was closely associated with La Scala; Sonzogno owned opera houses in Milan, and he was later to restore the city's Teatro Lirico to its former glories. The publishers also went head-to-head in often vitriolic and partisan music criticism and comment in the widely read publications they owned, in which they promoted their composers and their works. Ricordi published the well-established *La Gazzetta musicale di Milano*, as well as a number of other influential musical journals and magazines.

Lucca published the music journal *L'Italia libera*. Sonzogno was perhaps the most aware of the power of the press: in 1866 Edoardo founded Italy's first mass-circulation newspaper, *Il Secolo*, and in 1881 he launched the music magazine *Il theatro musicale* to counter the influence of *La Gazzetta musicale di Milano* (Mallach 81).

It was Casa Sonzogno, too, which took the initiative to find the new great young Italian composer, better recognizing, perhaps, the new tenor of the country: the growing, literate middle-class (the readers of *Il Secolo*), eager for new experiences in literature—such as the new, raw realism of Giovanni Verga, who used the lives of ordinary Italians as subject matter—and in opera, as the relevance of the grand subjects of Romanticism waned. There was, of course, a purely practical business motive: quite apart from the attendant publicity, Sonzogno needed to find new Italian composers to counter the dominance of Ricordi in Italy's native opera world.

In April 1883, the publishing house therefore announced in another of its publications, *Il teatro illustrato*, a new competition for a one-act opera, with a prize of 2,000 lire, and a performance, paid for by the journal, in a Milan opera house. The very idea of a competition was novel: usually publishing houses waited for a new composer to prove himself in a minor provincial opera house before approaching him with an offer to be published by their firms (Mallach 81).[17] Even more novel was the idea of an Italian one-act opera. Donizetti and Rossini had both written one-act operas in the early years of the nineteenth century, but by the 1880s large-scale grand opera ruled the opera houses. A one-act opera, however, would not only be more manageable for a new composer but would also reflect the vogue in Italian theatre for one-act, realistic plays (Carner 38).

The twenty-four-year-old Puccini had long known that he wanted to write opera. Giovannina Lucca had bought the rights to his first orchestral success, the *Capriccio Sinfonico*, but Puccini had failed to interest her in an opera; in fact, when he tried to visit her, he usually found her not at home. Such a competition was ideal, but, as a letter to his mother in July showed, he was "uncertain," especially as time was short, as the deadline was the end of the year (Puccini 42). What decided him was that he found both a librettist and a subject. That summer, Puccini and the poet Ferdinando Fontana, who had come across each other briefly before, both stayed at the *pensione*-cum-retreat of Antonio Ghislanzoni, the poet and librettist of *Aïda*. There musicians and artists gathered, and it was Ponchielli, Puccini's teacher at the Milan Conservatory, where Puccini was finishing his studies, who told Fontana of Puccini's desire to enter the competition and suggested that Fontana write the libretto. Fontana put forward the story of the Wilis, and Puccini agreed. The libretto was ready at the beginning of September (Puccini 36–37), although the terms had not been settled until August, when Fontana agreed to a greatly reduced fee, the reduction to be made up if Puccini won the competition (Carner 39).

Fontana (1850–1919) was an interesting character—a journalist, poet, and dramatist. He was one of the last of the Scapigliati, a group of artists who believed in socialist ideals, a hedonist lifestyle (immortalized in 1896 by Puccini himself in the opera *La Bohème*), and the rejection of outworn Romantic sensibilities—not to mention the dominance of the Catholic Church. In the field of music, the Scapigliati advocated breaking down the insularity of Italy by introducing wider European ideas. The group was instrumental in introducing Wagner to Italian audiences, and the composer (and the librettist of Verdi's last operas) Boito was among their number. They were widely influential while regularly scandalizing more conservative Italians, and perhaps their greatest legacy was the newspaper *Corriere della Sera*, still one of Italy's most widely read.

Fontana was politically active: indeed, he eventually had to flee to Switzerland, where he died. He had recently spent two years, 1878–1879, in Berlin as a foreign correspondent. By the time he met Puccini, he had written eight libretti—all for operas now long forgotten.[18] He had strong views on opera: in *In teatro*, published in 1884, he decried operas based on historical drama, and suggested that opera would move closer to symphonic music, in a *"poema sinfonico scenio"* (qtd. in Budden, *Puccini* 40–41). All the elements of the opera, from scenery to singers, would be melded into the symphonic whole, equivalent to individual instruments (Budden, *Puccini* 40–41). This, of course, has echoes of Wagner, but also reflects the fusion of the arts that some Scapigliati advocated.

Fontana himself claimed that he had sketched the basis of *Le Villi* when in Berlin (Burton 112). He had originally promised the libretto to the composer Francesco Quaranta, who renounced the rights when Fontana made his agreement with Puccini (Burton 111). Indeed, the libretto must have been at least partly written, as Puccini had set Anna's main aria and played it to Giulio Ricordi by August 30 (Ashbrook 9). The immediate inspiration was not, as has often been supposed, Adam's ballet, since the ballet had long since dropped out of the European repertoire (Budden, "Genesis" 81).[19] As with the ballet, the distant origins were in Heine's *Über Deutschland: Elementargeister und Dämonen* (1834),[20] but the immediate source was a short story entitled "Les Willis," published in 1856 in a collection of stories, *Contes et nouvelles*, by the French critic, novelist, and floriculturist Alphonse Karr.

This terse but effective tale is written in a compressed and symbolic fairy-tale style. It opens in the Black Forest, where Henry joins in a dance to a waltz tune composed by himself and played by his friend Conrad. He takes Conrad's sister, Anna, into his arms, much to her delight as she is in love with him. As their families have long hoped they will marry, the pair receive her father's blessing. Henry then receives a letter to go to his dying uncle in Mayence (Mainz), and he hangs "a white crown" of flowers at Anna's window before he leaves, as a token of his love. He initially writes regularly, but the letters stop, and Conrad goes to see what has happened to him. Conrad returns, wounded, and tells of Henry's fate.

Conrad, we learn, arrived in Mayence on the day of Henry's wedding to the beautiful daughter of his rich, and not-so-ill, uncle—a marriage set up by the uncle. Henry had earlier written to his mother begging her not to give her consent to the marriage, but his mother had written back pointing out all the advantages of such a match. The combination of the beautiful daughter, the wealth, the pleasures of the city, and his mother's comments had led him to forget Anna. At the wedding Conrad fought a duel with Henry; he dies from his wound shortly after returning home, soon followed by the grief-stricken Anna.

A year later, the uncle has also died. The now-wealthy Henry has bought a mansion in the Black Forest so his wife and newborn child can enjoy the countryside. One day, out hunting, he gets lost, but recognizes the area where the cottage of Anna's family is situated. He walks past the cottage where her father is cursing him, and in the woods he has morbid thoughts about his wife and child—and about Anna. He then hears the waltz that he and Conrad often played, and he makes the sign of the cross. The waltz is now sung to words he himself had thought up on his journey to Mayence. He eventually sees beautiful girls, singing and dancing, dressed in white and lit by moonlight, and he remembers the story of the Wilis. One of them looks like Anna, and he sees on her head the garland of flowers that he had left by her window. He is made to dance, initially with her, and then changing partners, faster and faster. The seventh partner is Anna again—only now she is a skeleton: "*il ne vit plus qu'une hideuse tête de mort toujours couronnée de bruyères blanches*" ("he could see nothing but a hideous death's head crowned with white heather"). Henry is found dead the next day (Karr).

Karr's story—and thus Puccini's opera—therefore parallels that of the *Giselle* ballet rather than directly emulating it: a different development of a common source. The basic events—the death of a disappointed bride who has been deceived by her lover, her transformation into a Wili, the ensnarement of the faithless groom, his death by dancing—and the basic setting of the German village surrounded by forest are the same. The major difference is a kind of inversion: instead of the nobility coming to the village, and Giselle discovering that her fiancé is both a nobleman and already engaged, the fiancé leaves the village, marries another, becomes rich, and does not return until some time later, when the Giselle-figure is already dead.

Such a story suited the current vogue in Italy for rather Gothic northern European tales, stretching back beyond Wagner and *Der fliegende Holländer* (*The Flying Dutchman*, 1843) to Weber's *Der Freischütz* (1821). Catalani's *Elda*, for example, is based on another Heine tale, the story of the Loreli, with its tale of a woman who, in return for the help of the spirits of the sea, becomes the bride of the Baltic. It was influenced by Wagner, published by Casa Lucca, and successfully produced in Turin in January, 1880, and in turn influenced the new generation of Italian composers.

Fontana's libretto on Karr's story was well summarized in the *Musical Times* of December 1, 1909, by an anonymous reviewer who had seen a revival at Milan's Teatro dal Verme:

The scene of "Le Villi" is laid in the Black Forest, and the story is founded on a
local legend, according to which the unfaithful lover of a village maiden, who
dies in despair, is, on his return to his native valley, enticed and killed by the
spirits of the forest, called the "Villi." The lover in this case is a young villager,
Robert [Roberto] who, on the eve of his marriage with Anna, the daughter of
a sturdy old peasant, is suddenly called away to Mayence [Mainz] to receive
the legacy of a relative. Although Robert vows that he will return to make his
bride both happy and rich, she is full of sinister forebodings; and these prove
only too true, for at Mayence Robert falls a victim to the charms of a wicked
siren, who not only despoils him of his money, but makes him forget his love in
the Black Forest. In the meantime the poor village maiden dies in despair; and
when Robert at last returns to the valley in the depth of winter, poor, and full of
remorse, she appears to him as a spirit, not of love but of retribution, and lures
him away to the spirits of the forest, who surround him, and in their mad dance
whirl him to death, while Anna is carried aloft. (C.P.S.)

Karr's story essentially falls into three sections: the opening, with the dance
and Henry leaving for Mainz, Conrad's tale (given by the story-teller rather
than Conrad himself), and Henry's encounter with the Wilis in the forest. To
fit it into a one-act length, Fontana reduced this to two main contrasting
sections: the opening dance and Roberto's departure, and Roberto's return
when he encounters the Wilis. The events in Mainz are related, spoken, by a
narrator. The uncle is replaced by an aunt, who, to simplify the story, has died
and left Roberto an inheritance (the reason for his departure to the city).
Conrad is omitted completely: instead, the story told is that Roberto had come
under the debauched influence of *"una sirena"* ("a siren") in Mainz. She is a
seducer of young and old, and *"Ella trasse Roberto all'orgia oscena"* ("she lured
Roberto into an obscene orgy"), with the implication that she was a cour-
tesan. He eventually returned home destitute, abandoned by the Mainz siren.

Fontana's main innovation was to join the two sections with an extended
intermezzo, with verses explaining what had happened to Roberto in Mainz,
followed by a mainly instrumental tableau, *"L'Abbandono"* ("The Desertion"),
depicting Anna's funeral, with offstage voices of the mourners. This leads

to a second set of verses telling the legend of the Wilis, *"La Tregenda"* ("The Spectre"), and another purely orchestral passage where the Wilis appear and dance their Witches' Sabbath. The verses were apparently not designed to be narrated, but read by the audience separately, in accordance with Fontana's views on the fusion of the arts. There is no mention of them in early reviews, although modern practice is to relate them from the stage (Carner 336).[21]

The one-act opera, originally titled *Le Willis*, and described as "A Legend in one act and two parts," was ready only just in time. Puccini must have been optimistic, as two of the five judges were his teachers at the Conservatory: Ponchielli and Faccio. However, his opera was not given even an honourable mention: the joint winners were Luigi Mapelli's *Anna e Gualberto* and Guglielmo Zuelli's *La fata del Nord* (another opera with a northern, fairy-tale theme), and three others were deemed worthy of note. The general reason given for this failure is that the manuscript was written so hastily that it was very difficult to read, as Puccini himself admitted (Carner 40). Ponchielli had earlier said about Puccini's handwriting, "Puccini brings me every lesson such a vile scrawl, that I confess, up to the present, I do no more than stare at it in despair" (qtd. in "Work" 2). Fontana, however, was not to be denied hearing his new opera and gathered support from his influential artistic friends. Puccini was invited to play excerpts from the opera at the celebrated salon of Marco Salo early in 1884, and among the guests was one of the most influential of the Scapigliati, Boito himself, who was then working on the libretto for Verdi's *Otello*. Boito was impressed; a successful appeal was made to fund a performance of the work, and Giulio Ricordi agreed to print copies of the libretto free (Carner 42). The opera received its premiere at the Teatro dal Verme on May 31, in a triple bill with a then-popular 1858 opera, *Jone*, by Errico Petrella (set in the last days of Pompei),[22] and a ballet.

Le Willis caused something of a sensation. The intermezzo was repeated three times, and Puccini took eighteen curtain calls (Mallach, *Autumn* 67). The critics were fulsome in their praise, Antonio Gramola writing in the *Corriere della Sera*, "In short we believe that in Puccini we may have the composer for whom Italy has been waiting for a long time" (Budden, *Puccini* 44). The results were immediate: on June 8, Ricordi announced in the *Gazzetta Musicale* that the publishing house had bought world-wide rights to the opera and had commissioned a new opera from Puccini and Fontana, to be performed at La Scala. The involvement of Ricordi—from that early playing of Anna's aria, through the printing of the libretto, to the purchase of the rights—has led to the suggestion that Puccini's exclusion from mention in the Sonzogno competition was intentional (Ponchielli was a friend of, and published by, Ricordi), part of a plan to secure the young composer for Casa Ricordi. While that is not beyond the bounds of possibility, given the intense publishing rivalries, there is no evidence for such underhand dealing. Nonetheless, Guilio Ricordi had indeed secured the composer who was to be, as we now know, the successor to Verdi, and Ricordi published all of Puccini's subsequent operas except one.[23]

Ricordi then suggested that Puccini and Fontana lengthen the opera into a two-act version, since opera houses would prefer a longer work. Given the bipartite structure of the original, this was fairly easy: the second act starts with "*L'Abbandono,*" the symphonic intermezzo thus acting as the prelude to that second act. The new version was presented—again, with great success— at Turin's Teatro Regio in December 1884. For the La Scala production in January 1885, Roberto's *romanza* "*Torna ai felici dì*" ("Return to the happy days") was added and other passages extended. In 1886 minor alterations (and a major cut in Roberto's *scena*) led to a third printed edition, the one in use ever since (Budden, *Puccini* 48). It was soon heard outside Italy: in Buenos Aires, then one of the great opera centres, in 1886, in England in 1897, and in New York in 1908. Gustav Mahler conducted the first German performance in Hamburg in 1892.

The reaction of La Scala audiences was less enthusiastic than elsewhere, perhaps because they were more conventional. The singer Teresa Stolz wrote to Verdi, reflecting the conservative view that "This piece made no effect, either—all descriptive music in which the singer appears to do little more than mime" (qtd. in Carner 45). Indeed, the inherent flaws in the work are now fairly obvious. Dramatic conflict is almost completely absent because of the concentration on two incidents that are essentially tableaux: Roberto's departure and his encounter with the Wilis. Consequently, there is little psychological conflict—only moments of psychological states. In Act I, Anna's declaration of love (and her fears for when Roberto is away) may provide an opportunity for Puccini to write an aria, but it is conventional in its content. In Act II, Roberto has little of the psychological angst of Faust in a similar situation: the concentration is on the inevitability of the Wilis' physical destruction of the hero. Elements of the original story that might have provided exactly the kind of conflict that opera thrives on, such as Conrad's confrontation and duel with Roberto, are cut completely, and others, such as Anna's death, are not seen. Nor are there psychological confrontations in what remains. The dramatic potential inherent in the meeting of Roberto and Anna as a Wili is reduced to a *fait accompli*, while Fontana's one main addition—the expansion of the curse of Guglielmo, Anna's father, into a full *preludio* and *scena* for him alone—misses the obvious possibility of the father actually meeting Roberto at this point.

One of Puccini's biographers, Vincent Seligman, describes *Le Villi* as "about as bad as a libretto could be" (qtd. in "Work" 3), and most commentators have similarly dismissed it. However, that is to look at Fontana's libretto in conventional operatic terms, and so miss the point. There are conventional elements to the opera: it is divided into numbers (complete with the standard opening chorus after the prelude), but it is also attempting some quite startling innovations that anticipate twentieth-century operatic ideas. That Fontana's ideas do not fully succeed suggests that his concepts were more advanced than his ability to translate them successfully to the operatic stage. Nonetheless, like Puccini's music, the libretto bestrides the old and the new and deserves more consideration than it has generally been given.

The whole construction is in the shape of an arch, with the orchestral intermezzi at the apex—something that must have been more obvious in the one-act version. The rising part of the arch is spring, with its flowers, whereas in the falling part it is winter, with the score specifying snow; the first part is in daylight, the second in darkness. The strong dramatic effect of both the change of season and of lighting on stage is something that is all too easy to overlook based on the score or a recording. At the base of the arch the opening dance of the villagers (No. 2 in the score) is matched by the closing dance of the Wilis (No. 10) and by their dance at the apex: the tryst of love matched by the tryst of death. Anna's *scena "Se come voi piccina"* ("If I were tiny like you," No. 3) is matched by Roberto's Act II *"Ecco la casa"* ("Here is the house," No. 9): the theme of Anna's "Do not forget me" flower song—an echo of Giselle's flower song, at exactly the same dramatic moment, in Loder's *Night Dancers*[24]—contrasts with Roberto's anguish and thoughts when, with the flowers of May, love blossomed for him. The lover's duet (No. 4) is matched by Guglielmo's *scena* (No. 8): the former has the reiterated, *"Ah! Dubita di Dio, / Ma no, dell'amor mio non dubitar!"* ("Doubt your God, but no, never doubt my love!"), and in the latter the father asks God to forgive him for calling on the Wilis to take revenge on the faithless lover. In Number 5, the traditional *preghiera* to close an act, Guglielmo blesses the couple and Roberto leaves; its counterpart is the Wilis' "Witches' Sabbath Dance" (No. 7). The central No. 6 is the intermezzo showing Anna's funeral cortege.[25]

Such a structure has considerable symbolic potential, with Anna as the centre of that symbolism: love and life, death and revenge, light and shadow, spring and winter. It also reinforces the not inconsiderable anti-clericism inherent in the libretto, part and parcel of deconstructing both the social norm and Italian operatic tradition. The idea of doubting God before doubting love was hardly a message of which the Catholic Church would approve. Guglielmo's call for revenge—let alone revenge by the forces of darkness—is also not exactly a Christian sentiment, as he himself recognizes.

Nor does Roberto have any choice in his fate. The Wilis say he is damned before he actually sees them, and there is no suggestion that he thinks he can repent. When he wonders whether Anna is still alive, he decides to knock on Guglielmo's door, but he cannot lift his hand to do so—the suggestion is that there are supernatural forces at work, and in his demise he is closer to Marlowe's Faustus than Goethe's Faust. The final ironic "Hosanna" from the Wilis not only reminds one of the ending of Boito's *Mephistopheles*, but also mocks religious values, and clearly involves a pun on the heroine's name (especially as Roberto has sung that name three words earlier).

One can, perhaps, then understand why Fontana essentially created a series of tableaux that conveniently (and rather conventionally) coincide with the divisions of a "numbers" opera. The libretto, at least, is less concerned with the physiological profiles of the characters—hence there is no real necessity for dramatic conflict—than with the forces behind those characters, be they love, revenge, or, especially, fate.

Perhaps, too, in his rather muddled way, Fontana recognized that an orchestra could provide that psychological layer, a layer of comment, in a way that Italian opera had not really attempted. Certainly he wrote the libretto later that he had agreed to do, in part because he had heard Puccini's *Capriccio sinfonico* (Budden, *Puccini* 42), and Puccini clearly responded to Fontana's work, writing to his mother that there was "ample scope" in the libretto "for the descriptive, symphonic kind of music, which attracts me because I think I ought to succeed in it" (42).

What Fontana did give Puccini in the libretto were the opportunities for strong arias for the soprano and tenor, conventional operatic elements, such as the choruses and the prayer scene at the end of Act I, and more than ample opportunities for the dance: in the opening dance with the villagers, in the "Witches' Sabbath," and in the Wilis' dance at the end. What he did not give Puccini is what we now know, with hindsight, was Puccini's strength: the exploration of the relationships between men and women, usually in more extreme psychological circumstances. Nor was Puccini the kind of composer to respond to the type of symbolism that Fontana was hinting at, at least not until the very end of his career, with *Turandot*, and by then he had the examples of Strauss and von Hofmannsthal before him. Puccini, for all his innovations, essentially evolved Italian opera, rather than throwing the traces over: that had to wait until the middle of the twentieth century, in the operas of Dallapiccola and Nono.

Of course, all this was ahead for Puccini. The fascination is with what he actually did do with this flawed libretto at this very early stage of his career. As one might expect, he looked both backwards and forwards. The very opening *preludio* (No. 1) indicates some of those influences: one hears Tchaikovsky in the woodwinds answering the strings and then a Wagnerian moment complete with Wagnerian brass,[26] before Tchaikovsky returns again. The influence of the French also permeates the score, from Massenet and

Gounod: in the first part of the opening chorus, for example (*Le Villi* 1:111), or in the passage that starts with Guglielmo's prayer in Act 1 (*Le Villi* 1:123, at rehearsal figure 24), where Gounod meets Wagner. It is most obvious in the dance of the second part of the opening chorus, which is so indebted to Bizet that it is almost a pastiche, even if it draws on material from Puccini's own Scherzo in A minor for string quartet, written in 1881 (Budden, *Puccini* 50).[27] Indeed, Puccini had sneaked into La Scala without paying to hear *Carmen* in March 1883, so it was fresh in his mind (*Puccini* 41). Some have considered the "Witches' Sabbath" to be similarly influenced by Bizet, but its origins go back further, through Wagner to Weber, and with a nod, too, to Boito.

Catalani himself believed that *Le Villi* was derived from his operas *Elda*, premiered in 1880, and *Dejanice* (1883), which we know Puccini admired (Burton 107–08). Certainly, *Le Villi*'s characteristic open fifths are found in *Dejanice*, and Roberto's *romanza* in Act II (No. 9) has been seen as drawing on Admeto's "*Mio bianco amor*" from the same opera (Carner 338–39). More audible, perhaps, is the influence of Verdi, as one might expect. It is clear in the layout and some of the phrasing of the choruses in Act I (in the "*Coro d'introduzione*," No. 2, complete with trumpet interjections) and in the cello accompaniment in Guglielmo's *scena* (the least inspired writing in the opera, matching the lack of inspiration in the libretto). Less obvious, but equally strong, is the influence of the sea music of *Simon Boccanegra*, leading here to one of the few occasions when Verdi himself did tone-painting. The influence can be heard in the orchestral accompaniment of the opening of Anna's aria ("*Se come voi piccina*") and in Guglielmo's *scena* in the passage that follows "*S'io po*" (*Le Villi* 2:77), especially in the violins' falling phrases. Verdi's opera in its revised form had been premiered at La Scala two years earlier, and, in a letter written just before writing *Le Villi*, Puccini mentions the 1883 La Scala revival (*Puccini* 41)—the implication is that he attended that revival, though he does not state so specifically.

These, then, are the understandable influences of a young composer starting out and writing in a hurry. But, while they may now be obvious to us, to contemporary Italian audiences much of Puccini's music in *Le Villi* was equally and understandably startling. Although other young Italian composers were absorbing similar influences, the music of Massenet, Wagner, and Bizet was still new in Italy, and to integrate their styles into an opera that was clearly also in an Italian tradition was even newer. Whatever the deficiencies of the libretto, one can understand why the original audiences were so enthusiastic, and why many thought the great new Italian opera composer might have been discovered.

Then there are the unmistakable glimpses of the mature Puccini personal style. The opening two orchestral bars that start Anna's aria, "*Se come voi piccina*," could have walked out of the pages of, say, *Tosca*. The orchestral passage in *L'Abbandono* that starts at rehearsal figure 31, and which has been heralded at rehearsal figure 30, is unmistakably pure Puccini, with its melody starting high and falling away, its orchestral colours, its slight air of melancholy (it is in D minor), and its unfolding of the melodic phrase, which only lasts some seven bars before becoming more conventional (*Le Villi* 2:15–16). Anna's Act I aria, "*Se come voi piccina*" (No. 3), sometimes heard on its own in recital, and Roberto's *romanza* (No. 9) both suggest the melodic Puccini that was to come, though the melodic lines are not as long-breathed.

What is palpable, however, is the "descriptive, symphonic kind of music" Puccini felt so attracted to, which permeates the score. Contemporary audiences immediately recognized that the importance of the orchestral contribution was something new in Italian opera, and either heralded it as a welcome influence from beyond the Alps, as they had done with Catalani's Wagner-influenced operas, or as a pernicious import that obscured the purity of the traditional Italian opera vocal line. The orchestra in *Le Villi* is much more than accompaniment to that vocal line, and it is more than additional overall colour. It regularly adds commentary, amplifying the emotions of the situations on stage.

A good example is Roberto's "*scena drammatica—romanza*" (No. 9). This is quite a complex series of emotions, with a dramatic orchestral introduction, the Vilis regularly calling out, Roberto seeing the cottage, reacting to the Vilis, recalling in the main aria the days of old, being unable to knock on the door, finding he is unable to pray, and cursing the "*cortigiana vil*" ("vile whore") who enticed him in Mainz, all in the space of about thirteen minutes. The musico-dramatic flow of this section is compelling, entirely through-composed, and it is the orchestra that carries that flow. The actual vocal writing is fairly conventional, if effective, but the orchestral writing, in Italian terms, is not. Reminiscences of earlier music is heard in the orchestra, tying in the emotions both with the happy days and the Vilis, and the orchestral textures are much thicker than was then customary. Especially effective is the sudden emergence in the orchestra of a funeral march, with great tympani strokes; it has been quietly heralded a little earlier in the orchestra, without the timpani (*andante mesto*, sad and somewhat slow, eight measures after rehearsal fig. 47), but here (*andante mesto*, somewhat slow, eight measures after rehearsal figure 48), it breaks out in full.[28] At the end of this there is an extraordinary orchestral comment. Roberto sings *"Forse ella vive!"* ("Perhaps she lives!") and goes to knock on the cottage door. The oboe reminds us of the lover's tune in the first half, but then a dark solo cello takes over and sinks down into a solo double bass. In a moment that should be full of anticipation and the hope of joy, we are given Roberto's actual subconscious state, and that cello and double bass tell us in no uncertain terms that there is no hope whatsoever. The whole scene is an indication of the dramatic mastery that Puccini was to develop so vividly.

Then, of course, there are the two central orchestral interludes. The first, the representation of Anna's funeral, is the kind of affecting and powerful orchestral statement of the emotional and dramatic situation that was shortly to become so important to new Italian opera, in which the orchestra, for a brief period, becomes the main protagonist—the orchestral interlude. The second, the "Witches' Sabbath Dance" of the Wilis, might have been startling to contemporary Italian audiences (and is in itself quite bombastically exciting, as well as providing material for the second half), but would have not been so to non-Italian audiences, for it is indebted to German and French models in a style Puccini never returned to. Essentially it is a ballet section, rather than an orchestral interlude. But having a ballet in opera was not in the Italian tradition, being left to the French. The importance of the orchestra is actually diminished here, since it is the dancing and the Vilis that dominate, though its centrality is quite restored as it goes immediately into the opening of Roberto's *scena*.

The other remarkable element of the score is the extent to which the second half (Act II in the revised version) is built on, or recalls, material already heard in the first half. That might, of course, be seen simply as a composer in a hurry needing material to finish a score; however, it does serve to give unity to the whole work and to recall the emotions of the events of the first half in the different circumstances of the second. Furthermore, there seems to be a more complex intent. If one accepts that Fontana's libretto is deliberately designed to have two mirror halves, then Puccini's reliance in the second on the material of the first becomes a much more central and deliberate concept.

The immediate importance of the music to the development of Italian opera was not, however, what it heralded in Puccini's own music, but the influence it had on Mascagni. Puccini and Mascagni were friends and indeed shared an apartment, and most commentators claim that Mascagni played the double bass at the premiere of *Le Villi*—at which time Mascagni was working on *Guglielmo Ratcliff*, an opera directly based on Heine. Mascagni scholar Alan Mallach states that Mascagni actually watched from the wings alongside Puccini (Mallach, *Pietro Mascagni* 28), and Mascagni subsequently wrote, revealingly: "Here I was watching my dearest friend reach the goal that I myself have dreamed of for so long, and I was burning with desire to imitate him, and yet I could not see any possibility of doing so…Oh, art! My beautiful art! Would I never, then, be able to reach the glory that I longed for, which I dreamed about even wide awake?" (qtd. in Mallach, *Pietro Mascagni* 29).

Mascagni was to achieve that glory in his winning entry for the next Sonzogno competition in 1890. In *Cavalleria rusticana* Mascagni has clearly learned from Puccini—not the least in avoiding some of the weaknesses of Fontana's libretto. Most obvious is the concept of the orchestral intermezzo, perhaps the most celebrated moment of the opera, which was immediately emulated by other Italian composers, notably Leoncavallo in *Pagliacci* (1892). Equally obvious is the importance of the orchestral contribution and commentary, but less noted is the dramatic example of Puccini's opera. The libretto of *Le Villi* may be dramatically naive, but the music certainly is not: it is taut, concise, and dramatically flowing; a good performance seems shorter than its actual length of just one hour. Mascagni clearly learned the importance of such a musico-dramatic concision (though not immediately— *Guglielmo Ratcliff* is considerably more diffuse, but it does contain three orchestral intermezzi), and in doing so created the *verismo* movement.

The *verismo* subject of *Cavalleria rusticana*, with its story of the heightened emotions of ordinary Sicilian peasants, reflects the literary vogue for such realistic stories exemplified by the works of Giovanni Verga, on whose story the opera is based.[29] Puccini's opera is, of course, from a very different literary tradition, but there are some features in *Le Villi* that do anticipate *verismo*, especially in the ending of the opera. In Adam's ballet—and indeed in the Moncrieff play and in Loder's opera—Giselle is essentially a victim, and in all three versions one gets the sense that she would much prefer to have her lover restored to her, so she could be the good little wife. In Fontana's libretto, and in Puccini's music, there is no such implication; quite the contrary: she wants revenge, and she gets it. Roberto, too, seems compelled towards a psycho-sexual apotheosis (also reflected in the music). In the final action, again not obvious from a recording, Anna is simply standing there as *"Roberto va verso Anna come spinto da una forza"* ("Roberto moves towards Anna as if propelled by an invisible force"), and the Vilis close in behind him, supported by the male chorus singing offstage as *"spiriti intern"* ("unseen spirits"). He attempts to escape to Guglielmo's cottage, but he is chased by Vilis into Anna's waiting arms and consumed. Anna here anticipates a Salome or an Electra, rather than a nineteenth-century Italian opera heroine, and the whole sequence is closer to the heightened psychological realism of the *verismo* operas. The music at the very end, too, anticipates the kind of cruel brashness *verismo* revelled in.

It is Mascagni's opera, however, not Puccini's, that has been credited with the start of *verismo*. If there is an irony in that, there is also an irony in the fact that, if Mascagni was undoubtedly the more famous opera composer for the next decade, Puccini, eschewing *verismo* until the late one-act opera *Il tabarro* (1918), eventually eclipsed him nationally and internationally.

Puccini's next opera was also to a Fontana libretto, but *Edgar* (1889), without all the virtues of concision of *Le Villi*, was not a success. Indeed, Puccini wrote, "In setting the libretto of *Edgar* I have, with all respect to the memory of my friend Fontana, made a blunder. It was more my fault than his" (qtd. in Carner 57). It was not until *Manon Lescaut* (1893) that Puccini really found his mature voice, as well as two librettists, Luigi Illica and Giuseppe Giacosa, who were not only more sympathetic to his aims but whom he could also control.

Puccini's later success and opera-goers' familiarity with his later style have eclipsed *Le Villi*, rather in the same way that familiarity with Gilbert and Sullivan has been detrimental to audience appreciation of such British Romantic operas as Loder's *The Night Dancers*. Paradoxically, if Puccini had written nothing more (and Mascagni and Leoncavallo had carried the mantle of Italian opera), *Le Villi* would probably be much better known and its anticipation of later developments in Italian opera more obvious. For, if one temporarily suspends knowledge of Puccini's later work, it has much to recommend it: a fast-paced, tuneful, punchy one-act work with interesting psychological features, good choruses, a supernatural element, and two powerful arias. Its dramatic shortcomings are not nearly so obvious if one realizes Fontana's scheme (which indeed opens the kind of production possibilities not normally associated with a Puccini opera), and it needs to be given without any break to emphasize that scheme. If *Edgar* deserves its current obscurity, *Le Villi* certainly does not.

The dawn of the twentieth century saw the end of that Gothic Romantic thread that had wound right through the arts of the previous century, and which was so based on Germanic, Scandinavian, and Slavic oral traditions. That thread had partly been interwoven with the literary discoveries of such oral traditions, which had started early in the nineteenth century and continued throughout it. By the early twentieth century it was the turn of musical, rather than literary, folklorists (most famously Bartók and Kodaly) to rediscover the musical equivalents of that oral tradition, and that changed the nature of the music that would be written for such folk-inspired subjects.

Attitudes to women, so clear in Adam's ballet, Moncrieff's play, and Loder's opera, were also moving beyond the nineteenth century into a Freudian age, exemplified by Strauss's *Salome* (1905) and *Elektra* (1909), a movement perhaps hinted at in Puccini's—or rather Fontana's—*Le Villi*.

(Freud was to publish *Studies in Hysteria* two years after the opera's premiere.) In France, the French symbolism movement (a very different treatment of myth subjects) led to Debussy's opera *Pelléas et Mélisande* (1902). Britain turned to its own folklore heritage, especially the musical legacy, and where such folk subjects were attempted operatically, as in Broughton's *The Immortal Hour* (1914), they reflected Celtic origins. In Italy, *verismo* briefly ruled, with local subjects created in poster-paint colours, before Italian opera largely returned to historical or exotic foundations—exemplified respectively by Francetti's *Cristoforo Colombo*, 1892, and by Puccini's own *Madama Butterfly*, 1904. Puccini himself turned to subjects that were actually closer to the long Verdi tradition of the concentration on the relationships between the sexes, set in such heightened circumstances that were readily equitable with reality, be they those of Tosca or of the artists in *La Bohème*.

Adam's seminal ballet, Moncrieff's melodramatic play, Loder's British Romantic opera, and Puccini's first attempt at *verismo*, then, all belong to a particularly nineteenth-century fascination with the supernatural (and a rather Gothic supernatural at that) that was part and parcel of the century's fascination with—and rediscovery of—the kind of folk and fairy tale that had produced the concept of the Wilis in the first place, notably in the 1841 ballet *Giselle*. All four works belong firmly to the sensibilities of the nineteenth century, despite that embryonic awareness of the psychological underpinnings of such a fascination in the Puccini, and together form a fascinating quartet of reactions to one particular folk tradition.

By the twentieth century, however, the forest glade had become deserted, the Witches' Sabbath (and, indeed, witches themselves) had become things remembered from a mist-filled, superstitious past, and the Wilis had faded back forever into their lotus-flowers. Adam's ballet, of course, lives on, in part because classical ballet delights in, and retains over generations, traditional choreography. Otherwise, apart from the occasional reference here or there, the Wilis survive only in a pair of obscure operas and an unknown play, to evoke epochs with very different sensibilities, and to make us think twice before jilting our lovers.

Notes

1. The playbill states "presented for the first time," but someone has inserted "here" by hand, and it is quite clear from this, the second, playbill that the work had been performed before moving to the Royal Pavilion.

2. The review is in a press cutting pasted to the playbill, verso. The newspaper source has been lost.

3. They also have voices like woodpeckers. Indeed, in the versions that Keightley recounts, from Serbia and Dalmatia, the Vilas seem quite benign, though they have some supernatural powers.

4. He was actually a sub-king who owed allegiance to the King of the West Saxons.

5. St. Walpurga has a town in Saskatchewan, Canada, named after her. She wrote accounts of her brothers, both of whom were saints themselves, but the *Catholic Encyclopedia* makes no mention of her supposed reputation for chastity (Cassanova).

6. The amaranth has a long association with beauty that does not fade: Keats, Shelley, and Coleridge all refer to it. The plant also had religious associations in classical Greece, China, and Mesoamerica.

7. They also included some colourful characters. Balfe was discovered as a young man by Rossini and had parallel careers as an opera singer in France, Italy, and England. Wallace, a friend of Berlioz, emigrated with his wife and family to Australia, where he founded the first music school and the first music festival in the country, and then disappeared (without his family) to the Far East and South and North America for a few obscure years, before returning to England (White, *History* 263–89). His sister Elizabeth was a successful opera singer.

8. The original was in English. It is now usually heard in the German version, translated by Theodor Hell.

9. And he was as wayward as some of his fellow composers: as "Ernest Loder von Löwe," he married Louisa Forster in 1849, bigamously, as he was still married to, though separated from, the singer Elizabeth Watson (Temperley, "Edward James Loder").

10. Fortunately there was no injury, as the fire was soon put out. Madame Albertazzi was rising out of the stage trap when her dress brushed against one of the lights ("Occasional Notes").

11. Soane's only other opera libretto was written much earlier, in 1826, for Bishop's "fairy opera" *Alladin*, produced at Drury Lane (White, *Register* 69). He was later to collaborate with Loder on the 1848 operetta *The Andalusian* and on the 1852 masque *The Island of Calypso*.

12. Temperley simply states that it was based on a French version of the German folktale—one presumes he means Adam's ballet ("Raymond and Agnes" 307).

13. This game is well known in Britain, but Sloane feels he has to explain it in a footnote in the libretto, saying it is common in Germany. It is indeed referenced in Goethe's *Faust*.

14. The fine overture has been recorded on CD by the Victorian Opera Orchestra, conducted by Richard Bonynge: *British Opera Overtures*, SOMM Recordings SOMMCD0123.

15. Scribe wrote the libretto for Verdi's *Les vêpres siciliennes* in 1855, and (with A. de Leuven) that for Balfe's *Le Puits d'amour* in 1843.

16. In 1886 Verdi wisely advised Riccordi to buy Casa Lucca. The sale was completed in 1888.

17. Opera composition was an exclusively male preserve in nineteenth-century Italy. The only Italian woman opera composer of note has been Francesca Caccini (1587–1641), who was one of the pioneers of the art form.

18. These included one for Ponchielli which the composer never set. Strangely, almost every writer on *Le Villi* seems to have ignored Fontana's already considerable experience as a librettist. He was to write another twenty operas after *Le Villi*.

19. It could still have been seen in St. Petersburg, however.

20. Heine's *Über Deutschland* is referred to as *De L'Allemagne*, the title of its French translation, elsewhere in this collection.

21. Interestingly, the *Musical Times* notice of the revival at the Teatro dal Verme in 1885 specifically states that a *chorus* for female voices "relates Robert's betrayal of his bride at Mayence, her sufferings, and her death"—presumably an error, unless the theatre was using a now-lost version (C.P.S.).

22. Based on a novel by Edward Bulwer-Lytton, whose works had been adapted by Verdi (*Aroldo*) and Wagner (*Rienzi*).

23. Sonzogno had his revenge. Ricordi turned down Mascagni's *Cavalleria rusticana*; after it won the next Sonzogno competition in 1880, it went on to be the most successful Italian opera of the end of the nineteenth century.

24. The two flower songs are placed where they are for the same dramatic reasons—Fontana would not have known about Loder's opera.

25. Mallach claims that Anna's aria was added for the revision—in which case it was matched by the addition of Roberto's "*Torna ai felici dì*" into No. 9 (Mallach, *Autumn* 68). But that seems to be contradicted by a record of Puccini's playing Anna's *romanza* to Ricordi in August 1883; the source is a letter to Fontana dated August 30, 1883 (Ashbrook 9).

26. *Le Villi* 1.2, at rehearsal figure 1. In the printed score the measures are not numbered. All score references are to the undated Edwin F. Kalmus edition, which is a reprint of the original Riccordi 1884 edition.

27. Camera, reviewing the premiere in *Corriere della Sera*, wrote that "from time to time it seems one is hearing not a young student, but a Massenet or a Bizet" (qtd. in Mallach, *Autumn* 67).

28. The closest musical parallel of the effect is perhaps Britten's powerful orchestration of the Scottish ballad "The Bonnie Earl of Moray."

29. Stanislao Gastaldon actually submitted an opera, *Mala Pasqua!*, based on the same story for the same Songonzo competition, but withdrew it as he already had a professional performance scheduled, which took place a month before the Mascagni premiere (Mallach, *Autumn* 34). Domenico Monleone then submitted his own version of *Cavalleria rusticana*, even more compressed, to the 1907 Sonzogno competition. It was premiered in Amsterdam coupled with Mascagni's version, and the double-bill successfully toured Europe. Sonzogno sued (on the grounds that Verga has assigned sole operatic rights to Casa Sogonzo) successfully, and the opera had to be rewritten to a new libretto (Baxter).

Works Cited

Ashbrook, William. *The Operas of Puccini*. Ithaca, NY: Cornell UP, 1992.

Baxter, Robert. "Cavalleria rusticana." *Opera Quarterly* 19.2 (2003): 304–06. Project Muse. muse.jhu.edu/journal/148.

Biddlecombe, George. *English Opera from 1834 to 1864 with Particular Reference to the Works of Michael Balfe*. New York: Garland Publishers, 1994.

Bowring, John. *Poetry of the Magyars*. London, 1830.

Budden, Julian. *Puccini*. Oxford: Oxford UP, 2002.

———. "The Genesis and Literary Source of Puccini's First Opera." *Cambridge Opera Journal* 1.1 (1989): 79–85. openmusiclibrary.org/journal/cambridge-opera-journal/.

Burton, Deboarah. *Essays on Puccini's Operas*. Hillsdale, NY: Pendragon Press, 2012.

C.P.S. "Giacomo Puccini's Opera 'Le Villi.'" *Musical Times* Dec. 1, 1889. openmusiclibrary.org/journal/the-musical-times/.

Carner, Mosco. *Puccini: A Critical Biography*. London: Duckworth, 1992.

Casanova, Gertrude. "St. Walburga." *Catholic Encyclopedia*. Vol. 15. New York: Robert Appleton, 1912.

Cox, John Edmund. *Musical Recollections of the Last Half-Century*. Vol. 1. London: Tinsley Bros., 1872. 2 vols.

Karr, Alphonse. "Les Willis." *Contes et nouvelles.* Paris: Hachette, 1856. n.p. *La Bibliothèque Électronique de Lisieux.* www.bmlisieux.com.

Keightley, Thomas. *The Fairy Mythology.* London: G. Bell, 1878.

Loder, Edward James. *The Night Dancers: A Grand Romantic Opera (in Three Parts), Partly Founded on the Story of Giselle.* C. Jefferys, 1846.

Mallach, Allan. *Pietro Mascagni and His Operas.* Boston: Northeastern UP, 2002.

———. *The Autumn of Italian Opera.* Boston: Northeastern UP, 2007.

McCarren, Felicia M. *Dance Pathologies: Performance, Poetics, Medicine.* Stanford: Stanford UP, 1998.

Moncrieff, W.T. *Giselle; or, The Phantom Night Dancers: A Domestic, Melo-dramatic, Choreographic, Fantastique, Traditionary Tale of Superstition in Two Acts.* London: J. Limbard, 1842.

"Music." Review of *The Night Dancers. Fine Arts Journal,* Nov. 14, 1846: 27–28.

"Occasional Notes." *Musical Times* Apr. 1, 1906: 243.

Pavilion Theatre. *Giselle, or, The Night Dancers.* Mixed playbill with press cutting attached verso. Oct. 18, 1841. *East London Theatre Archive.* 2009. University of East London. www.elta-project.org/browse.html?recordId=1345.

Puccini, Giacomo. *Le Villi.* Boca Raton, FL: Edwin F. Kalmus. Publication No. A4604.

———. *Letters of Puccini.* Ed. Guiseppe Adami. Trans. Ena Makin. London: Harrap, 1974.

Rotter, Andrew J. "Gender Relations, Foreign Relations: The United States and South Asia, 1947–1964." *Journal of American History* 81.2 (1994): 518–42. jah.oah.org/.

St. John, Percy. "Drury Lane, October 3." *Our Tatler. Mirror of Literature, Amusement, and Instruction,* monthly edition 2 (1846): 254–55. books.google.com.

Stephens, John Russell. "Moncrieff, William Gibbs Thomas." 2004. *Oxford Dictionary of National Biography.* www.oxforddnb.com/.

Temperley, Nicholas. "Edward James Loder." 2015. *Grove Music Online.* www.oxfordmusiconline.com/grovemusic/.

———. "The English Romantic Opera." *Victorian Studies* 9.3 (1966): 293–301.

———. "Raymond and Agnes." *Musical Times* 107.1478 (1966): 306–07. openmusiclibrary.org/journal/the-musical-times/.

Thoms, William J. *Lays and Legends of Various Nations.* George Cowie. London, 1834.

White, Eric Walter. *A History of English Opera.* London: Faber and Faber, 1983.

———. *A Register of First Performances of English Operas.* London: Society for Theatre Research, 1983.

"Work." *Opera Quarterly* Autumn 1984: 1–4. Project Muse. muse.jhu.edu/journal/148.

4

(Re)creating *Giselle*

Narrative and the Ballerina

NARRATIVE is the stuff of stories. In the worlds of ballet and video games, there is a recent move to tell better stories. According to Marcia B. Siegel, "story ballets have a stranglehold on the audience right now." Narrative is not new to ballet, but the postmodernist focus on form over content did witness a devolution of the plot-driven ballet once so popular among librettists. However, today the most attended and applauded performances among ballet-goers are those of *Giselle*, *Sleeping Beauty*, and *Swan Lake* (see, for instance, Balanchine and Mason 193–208; Alfort 40–41)—all plot-driven Romantic ballets from a bygone era. Why are productions of traditional, classical performances still the standard of the ballet world? Perhaps the key lies within the narrative. Similarly, the video game industry is witnessing a significant rise in popularity of narrative-focused games in which the player determines the plot line of a story. Although the indie gaming world is no stranger to interactive narrative experiences, AAA games such as BioWare's successful role-playing game *Jade Empire* and their *Mass Effect* series are prime examples of the continuingly increasing demand in the commercial world for quality narrative experiences as opposed to mere gameplay-driven events. However, both realms are limited in their portrayals of dance, specifically ballet. In the research and creation of our interdisciplinary interactive ballet video game *iGiselle*, our research team has identified video games as an important medium for reshaping the cultural and social narratives of dance. Not only is *iGiselle* a contemporary political and aesthetic reworking of the original Romantic ballet (1841), but—because of the narrative choices in the scripting—this interactive quest game also allows players to assert agency in the otherwise gaze-motivated genres of dance and dance video games, specifically.[1]

I would like to note that I am working here from the assumption that both games and dance *can* be read as narratives and studied through literary narratology practices. Graeme Kirkpatrick argues that dance and game "are caught up in a paradoxical refusal of textual or discursive meaning" and that, in both cases, "there is an inherent ephemerality about this vanishing content and...its very transience is somehow essential" (120). While I acknowledge the premise of Kirkpatrick's argument within a formalist analysis of the aesthetics of both the gaming and dancing genres, I suggest that while the genres may attempt to refuse discursive meaning, dance and game nevertheless do contain a discursive meaning that is translated from the aesthetic and circulated among various publics. In the case of *Giselle*, I suggest that it is primarily the ballet's narrative and discursive tropes[2] that are recognizable and translatable across different media and have been reproduced throughout time and across the social imagination.[3] Similarly, while I recognize the ongoing debate on the usefulness of applying narrative discourse to gaming, my goal is not to defend the validity of one side versus the other.[4] *iGiselle* arose from a desire to explore the possibilities of retelling the traditional balletic story of *Giselle*, and, as the game genre was elected as our narrative medium, my chapter starts from the position that narrative discourse holds potential for both the cultural and political interventions of game and dance.

Giselle is the ballet that contemporary critics—or at least the majority of critics since the wake of western first-wave feminism—love to hate. While the quintessential Romantic veneration of the feminine ideal has become the standard for classical ballet, audiences have come to understand Giselle's love-driven descent into madness, subsequent death, and final act of forgiveness as a retrogressive portrayal of gender dynamics and romantic melodrama.[5] Sally Banes outlines two standard readings of Giselle, suggesting that, "depending on how the role of the hero is played, the first act of the ballet may be read as the story either of a peasant girl's seduction and betrayal by a nobleman or of a tragically futile love affair that violates class boundaries" (23); on either reading, however, this warring between class and gender is reconciled in the second act by the transcendental nature of enduring love. This seemingly simplistic libretto charting a boy-meets girl, boy-betrays-girl, girl-forgives-boy storyline has generally fallen into two camps of analysis: one stresses the victimization in women's roles, the other celebrates their historical representation, but both centre around the acts of madness and forgiveness. Is Giselle's madness (which is consequentially linked to the debate surrounding her death as a natural death or as suicide) a liberatory response to societal constraints placed upon women in the nineteenth century? Or is it merely a hysterical feminine reaction to unrequited love? Is her final act of forgiveness of Albrecht an assertion of bourgeois individuality and female community? Or is it merely a reaffirmation of the system of patriarchy? Regardless of the cultural and social meaning we attribute to Giselle's actions, what unites all of these analyses is the way in which we interpret Giselle's expression of herself through embodied acts. Giselle's physical manifestation of madness as a peasant girl in the first act and the manifestation of her altered female identity and sexuality as a Wili in the second act are interpreted according to the ways in which she expresses herself through dance. As Cyril W. Beaumont articulates, "the theme of Giselle is unique and ideal because its mainspring is *the dance*" (23). Dance is the medium for both Giselle's body and spirit.

The interconnection between women, dance, madness, and the supernatural or spiritual achieved a particularly notable rise to prominence in nineteenth-century literature, in both Gothic *and* realist fiction. Marion Smith traces the inspiration of Théophile Gautier's libretto to two sources:

the first, Victor Hugo's 1829 poem "Fantômes," in which a young Spanish girl's love for dancing leads to her demise; the second, Heinrich Heine's *De l'Allemagne*, begun in 1833, which recounts a folktale about ghostly brides who rise from their graves at midnight to dance in the moonlight and seduce young men to their death (Smith 170–71). Molly Engelhardt notes other literary echoes in *Giselle* as well. "The Dance of Death," a short story published in *Blackwood's Edinburgh Magazine* in 1832, portrays a pretty, but poor, foreign young woman who is passionately fond of dancing and who marries a wealthy gentleman. In a dream she "imagines dancing with a young attractive man who through the course of the dance slowly transforms into Death" (Engelhardt 126). "First Love," a story by Catherine Gore written in 1842, portrays an act of wild dancing that leads to a young woman's cardiac arrest. Emily Brontë's 1847 novel *Wuthering Heights* features a dramatic death scene in which Catherine and Heathcliff engage in a metaphoric pas de deux, reminiscent of the dance-to-death scene in *Giselle*, where "the dance figures as the catalyst and context of cardiac arrest" (Engelhardt 134). In Henrik Ibsen's 1879 play *A Doll's House*, Nora Helmer, a conflicted housewife, tells her husband Torvald, "I would play the fairy and dance for you in the moonlight" (Act II), and then proceeds to engage in a tarantella, a wild and frantic dance reminiscent of Giselle's mad scene and the "Dancing Mania" discussed by Engelhardt. However, these are not the only literary appearances of a Giselle-like figure.

As Nora Foster Stovel's chapter in this collection reveals, the iterations of *Giselle* in nineteenth-century literature appeared far and wide. Engelhardt argues that one of the primary factors contributing to the rising interest and connection between women and dance in Victorian literature was female dancers' "ambivalent position in society and in the social imagination" (86). The female dancer's ability to navigate both the public and private worlds, both as an agential labouring body and as a figure of an eroticized gaze, challenged the boundaries of Victorian ideologies and encapsulated both the anxieties and hopes of social modernization (93). While literary narratives in the nineteenth century feature the trope of the dance and the dancing body—in these instances, the dancing female body—to negotiate ideals concerning gender identity and sexuality, they also deal with a particular type of female body: that of the white, European, heterosexual woman. Nevertheless, despite the risk of writing a master or homogeneous narrative of representations of female dancing bodies in this era, it is clear that, generally speaking, the literary associations between women and dance fail to critique dominant cultural notions of female corporeality.

But what does all of this have to do with video games? In 2003 John Carmack, the founder of ID Software and creator of the series of first-person shooter games *Doom* and *Quake*, said that "story in a game is like story in a porn movie: it's expected to be there, but it's not that important" (qtd. in Howitt 2014). Carmack's comment highlights the way in which narrative has traditionally fit into the genre of gaming, at least in regard to AAA games. It is a model in which "gameplay forms the meat of the experience as players test their physical and mental skills, and narrative is often delivered in cut-scenes that nestle between the action sequences" (Howitt 2014). The prioritization of gameplay can often lead to a discrepancy between plot (or narrative) and skill-based events. This disconnect in the relationship between "discourse and the act that produces it" is known as ludonarrative dissonance (Genette 27). In short, narrative, traditionally, has taken a backseat to gameplay in the history of video gaming.

A similar disconnect can be found in the world of ballet. Smith argues, for instance, that there is a distance between the original production of *Giselle* that appeared on stage in 1841 and the *Giselle* that is performed today. According to Smith, the original choreography of the libretto of *Giselle* read much more like an opera. It featured significant mime scenes: emotional dialogues and soliloquies whose gestures functioned to enrich the storyline of *Giselle*, ultimately working "moment-to-moment in getting the story across" (167). Today, however, "nearly all of these ballet-pantomimes, and their elaborate, detailed stories, have utterly vanished from the stage, to be replaced by ballets in newer styles which usually tell their stories in more abstract ways or tell none at all" (Smith 167–68). We could say that, in the performance history of *Giselle*, narrative has taken a backseat to dance. This is the moment where video games and ballet meet.

There has been a recent push in the gaming industry to reprioritize, or at least better integrate, the role of narrative into the medium of video games. According to Jonathan Ostenson, "the games of today have come to rely more and more on the elements of fiction in their design, and they represent unexplored territory in studying the nature and impact of narrative" (71). The indie gaming world has been particularly interested in producing games focused on compelling storytelling, and often this means challenging the social relations, gender dynamics, and political conventions that dominate AAA games. For example, in 2013 the Fullbright Company came out with *Gone Home*, a first-person adventure exploration video game that deals with issues of family, gender, sexuality, and coming-of-age. According to Matt Connolly, "In an industry full of big budget shooters, *Gone Home*'s eschewal of violence to focus on exploration and storytelling has brought near-universal critical acclaim." In an interview, one of the cofounders of Fullbright, Steve Gaynor, explained the centrality of elements of narrative, such as conflict, character, setting, and sequencing, to the creation of the game:

> *Coming off of* BioShock [Infinite] *stuff,[6] the part that really inspired us about those games was the sense of exploration—going around a first-person environment, finding the story in the environment, and putting together the story of the place as you go...We can make this story about just a normal family, a group of people that live in this house in contemporary America, and there doesn't also have to be zombies coming out the walls.* (qtd. in Connolly)[7]

Other examples of indie games invested in expanding the realm of interactive fictional gameplay include Nina Freeman's vignette game *Freshman Year* (2015), which explores issues of sexual abuse, and Zoë Quinn's *Depression Quest* (2013), an interactive fiction game that tells the story of an individual living with depression. The indie gaming community is pushing back against the dominant trends in commercial and mainstream gaming and working towards developing games based on inclusivity, complexity, and diversity.

Ballet, similarly, provides ample terrain for narrative possibilities, particularly the reworking of gender, class, and race politics. Beginning in the twentieth century, there have been several attempts to rework *Giselle* within the ballet genre. Two notable cases I would like to further examine here are Fergus Early and Jacky Lansley's 1980 production of *I, Giselle* and Dance Theatre of Harlem's 1984 production of *Créole Giselle*.[8] According to Vida L. Midgelow, *I, Giselle* "embodies the agendas of the 1970s feminist movement, representing a critique of *Giselle* and the ballet genre while at the same time maintaining a respect for the ballet" (15). True to the postmodern deconstructionist trend towards reflexivity of form, Early and Lansley's reinvention of the Romantic ballet begins by challenging the conventions of historical dancing bodies and using multiple female bodies to dance the role of Giselle—one for Act I and another for Act II, while slide projections of other famous ballerinas who have performed the role of Giselle are cast onto the backdrop of the stage (Midgelow 15). This pluralism serves not only to allow for visual reminders of the types of bodies that have historically symbolized the role, but also to further contrast the transformation of Giselle from Act I to Act II. Inverting the original narrative of the ballet, Early and Lansley have an hysterical Albrecht die in the first scene of Act I, ultimately repositioning the role of Giselle as one of triumphant agency over passive victimhood (Brown 46). The ballet is no longer centred on the figure of Albrecht and the ways in which his actions affect Giselle's; instead, when Giselle enters the realm of the Wilis, she makes a deliberate choice to enter a sisterhood. The choice to join the Wilis and their realm unpenetrated by men, as opposed to the coercion of the original libretto, infuses the ballet with "feminist celebrations of womanhood and community" (Midgelow 16). *I, Giselle* maintains the major plot points of the original ballet but allows for contemporary ideas of female agency to reconceptualize the gendered dynamic of the narrative.

Créole Giselle challenges a different aspect of historically visual dancing bodies: whiteness.[9] In Frederic Franklin and Arthur Mitchell's reinterpretation of *Giselle*, the story is "relocated...from its feudal German Rhineland setting to the farms and plantations of 1841 Louisiana's free people of color" (Gaiser 269). The transposing of the archetypal Romantic ballet from an idealistic pastoral Europe to a politically, socially, and economically charged world of American slavery contests the idyllic aestheticization of whiteness that has become a fundamental component of ballet's history. While the rest of the narrative remains relatively unaltered, primarily centred on the conflict of class identity, and the choreography danced by black bodies is "the same choreography that other dancers in (white) ballet companies performed," according to Gaiser, this "choreography read as new when performed by black bodies" (270). The fact that critics interpreted the classical choreography of *Créole Gisele* as "new" when performed by black bodies, despite being criticized by some as an appropriated means of legitimation for black dancers, highlights the exclusionary history of *le ballet blanc* and gives a whole new meaning to the term. *Créole Giselle* attempts to remove the ballet from its historical material conditions—the racially essentializing conditions of the Romantic ballet in particular.

There have been numerous other notable reproductions and recreations of *Giselle*, such as Mats Ek's twentieth-century contextualized *Giselle* (1982)[10] and Michael Keegan-Dolan's Irish retelling of the original story (2003).[11] First performed by the Ballet Cullberg, Ek's[12] *Giselle* is set in an isolated rural community where its protagonist essentially functions as the naive village misfit. Eventually betrayed by the aristocratic Albrecht, who finds himself falling for the "richness of her imagination and her sweetness," Giselle is led to an insane asylum in Act II by her fiancé Hilarion (Boccadoro 2004). Ek emphasizes the social norms surrounding female sexuality in the ballet, transforming Myrtha into the austere sister of the ward. As Boccadoro explains, "the nurse serves as a defense against sexual attraction in this self-contained world where the inmates are condemned to frustration." The Wilis-turned-psychiatric-inmates are, Ek hints, "being held here as a result of challenging the structure and rules in their own social class" (Piquero). Met with both resounding approval and reproachful scorn, Ek's retelling of the classical ballet remains one of his most enduring pieces to date.

Continuing to push the line of radicalism, Keegan-Dolan's production plays with both form and content. Combining speech, song, text, and action, Keegan-Dolan's *Giselle* appears as a blending of opera, theatre, and dance. Michael Crabb's brief synopsis of the ballet, set in the Irish Midlands, is enough to glean the ways in which this is no longer the world of Gautier:

"In Keegan-Dolan's telling, the ballet-mad mother of Giselle McCreedy has committed suicide. Her father has retreated to the top of a hydro pole, leaving his now dumbstruck and asthmatic daughter to the less than tender, loving care of her psychotically cruel, incestuously inclined brother, Hilarion." In this story, Albrecht is a bisexual line-dance instructor who seduces Giselle while also harbouring lust for the local butcher's son—a revelation Hilarion forces his sister to witness, which ultimately leads to her death.[13] While there is no intermission between acts, the second half of the ballet features gender-bending Wilis—here, men dressed as women—in a dystopian scene of aerial choreography and gruesome violence. Keegan-Dolan captures the essence of the original ballet, while pushing its conflicting themes to their darkest edges.

Despite these divergent rewritings, the traditional narrative of the ballet still remains the most widely circulated to date. Why do audiences continue to fill seats to sold-out shows to be told the same story over and over again; a story we like to think of as outside of *our* time? In her recent review of the National Ballet of Canada's version of *Giselle* (2016), Martha Schabas asks, "Can 2016 audiences stomach a work of art that paints women as victims-turned-predators, eternally mourning the betrayal of disloyal men?" The answer seems to be that they can. Perhaps this has something to do with the way in which the story is told to us. What would happen if audiences could choose the path Giselle takes in her narrative, if audiences could even choose their own Giselle? What would happen if we made ballet an interactive experience? If we accepted Ostenson's premise that "video games represent some of the most important storytelling in the 21st century" (71) and Banes's notion that the dancing body is a medium that is "shaped by—and in part shape[s]—society's continuing debates about sexuality" and identity (1), then we could use ballet narrative as a prime location for the intersection of divergent work. *iGiselle*, as an interactive, interdisciplinary narrative game, could attempt to employ dance as a tool to express embodied identity through the construction of alternative narratives.

This is where our University of Alberta research team enters the scene. A project initiated by Stovel, who did indeed dare to ask the question of what would happen if we could change the narrative of *Giselle*, became a means not only of participating in the rewriting of the history of Romantic ballets but also of reworking the history of video game narratives. An interdisciplinary project emerged, bringing together worlds that are, in general, exclusionary: Computing Science, Physical Education, English and Film Studies, Music, and Art and Design. Armed with paper and pen, computer and programming language, and dancers and choreography, the potential for narrative re-creation was infinite in our hands. Where should we begin? Questions quickly emerged: what would be the parameters for narrative development? Who and what should be our characters, setting, audience, conflict, and climax? What should be our narrative goals? To reconsider ballet stories through feminist lenses? To overturn the authority and canonicity of Romantic ballets? To introduce the layperson to ballet culture? The kind of narrative options we created would ultimately tell a story in and of themselves. Narrative trees quickly branched into endless possibilities. Part of our challenge would also be to integrate the interactive artificial intelligence component, using player modelling to sustain an emotional trajectory. How, then, did we unify the divergent interests and backgrounds of our research team at the level of narrative, and how much change was too much?

Realizing our *Giselle* storyline could be everything and anything, we regrouped. Dance and gaming, like any art forms, are reflections of social moments; and ballet and the video game are as much about the dancers and the players as they are about the dancing and the game playing. If we were to take the title of *Giselle* and use it as a signifier for our game, then we had to somehow deliver on the promise of a game that is reminiscent of the original *Giselle*. How, then, did we stay true to the original ballet while also adapting it for our time? Marie-Laure Ryan suggests that virtual reality is a form of storytelling concerned with immersion and interactivity (2–3). How could we create an interactive experience that immerses our players enough to provoke an emotional form of engagement? At its core, the ballet *Giselle* engages with the intertwining themes of vulnerability, risk, love, sexuality, betrayal, redemption, and forgiveness. What are the cultural conditions that would make our *Giselle* an expression and exploration of these original themes, and our player satisfied with and convinced by the updated choices?

Ultimately, the final constraints of our narrative choices stemmed from a more practical, as opposed to an ideological, set of parameters. Temporal, financial, and physical conditions decidedly shaped the nature of our narrative. As dance is one of the driving forces of this game, we had to make sure that our visual representation of dance was adequate. Additionally, focusing on reworking the narrative, as opposed to reworking the dance form, became our primary motive; therefore, we chose to stick with classical ballet choreography—pointe shoes and all. Given the method we selected to compose the graphics for our game—photography and subsequent Photoshop editing—this required working with *real* bodies skilled in the art of classical ballet. Realistically, this meant pooling our physical resources from the local dance community in Edmonton, requesting time and labour on a volunteer basis. The aesthetics of our game, particularly with regard to the appearance of characters, is therefore based on a representative sample of our volunteer population, as opposed to a representative sample of a much broader population (with variable physical characteristics in terms of size, racial background, [dis]ability, etc.), according to our ideological goals. The audition process required participants to be skilled in both ballet technique and acting ability. As a result, most of our dancers are university students with ballet training, with a few exceptions on both ends of the dance experience spectrum. Our dancing bodies are perhaps more typical of the traditional ballet world than ideally intended, but there is some diversity within the group's makeup.

With time and limited financial resources pressing down upon us—such can be the nature of scholarly work—we also had to make feasible choices with regard to the number of aspects of the narrative we could play with in our game. Surveying the many adaptations and iterations of *Giselle* in both literature and dance, we opted to work with the themes we found at the core of the majority of these works: primarily, love, madness, and revenge. The goal of *iGiselle* was to create an interactive narrative—meaning that the player needed to feel sufficiently immersed in the world of *iGiselle* to make decisions with dramatic or significant effects on events. We felt that the most consequential decisions in the world of the original *Giselle* regarded moral decisions concerning the interpersonal relationships that affected multiple parties and the outcome of the narrative.

What unfolded in the next few stages was a condensed and intense period of brainstorming, white-board charting, drafting, and editing. To offer a brief synopsis, then: *iGiselle* follows the narrative of a young dancer, Giselle Woods, who is in the process of joining a new company led by a promising new artistic director, Albert Albertson, who plans to debut a modern production of the ballet, *Giselle*. The points of conflict *iGiselle*'s protagonist, Giselle, must face include weathering professional pressures from her overbearing mother; negotiating a confusing relationship with her director, Albert; and staving off the animosity of other dancers within the company while confronting her own fears and desires in the process. Although some of these conflicts may seem stereotypical in their nature, they do illuminate some of the real pressures that have faced female dancers throughout the history of ballet and, in so doing, offer players a chance to participate in, observe, and rewrite that world. The metanarrative element (the ballet within the ballet) also puts these problems into dialogue with one another. The game reaches a climactic point when Giselle injures herself while preparing for her principal role, which may or may not be the result of malice on the part of one of the other characters in the game, and falls into a coma, where she encounters Myrtha and her Wilis, who compel Giselle to make a decision between enacting revenge or choosing forgiveness.

In re-centring the climactic conflicts of the original ballet, *iGiselle* deprioritizes the problematic romantic love aspect of the original narrative that has come to characterize not only the world of *Giselle* but also the worlds of countless balletic stories, whether on the stage, in film, or in literature. While the ballet is entitled *Giselle*, the story of the original libretto belongs more to Albrecht than to the titular character. George Balanchine and Francis Mason offer an illuminating reflection on Albrecht: "Giselle's death brings a sincerity to Albrecht's life he otherwise might not have known. His awareness of guilt makes him mature" (208). Balanchine and Mason's comment suggests that *Giselle* is Albrecht's coming-of-age story, a lesson in responsibility, and it is he who lives, while Giselle is resigned to death, peacefully, in the end. While Giselle's expression of noble spiritual love may be the very thing that saves Albrecht, it is an act that is very much historically situated with regard to the position of women in society. As Sally Banes argues, "*Giselle* represents its heroine as a female nurturer firmly ensconced in the new, private bourgeois domain, turning her back on female community and terrorist female activism" (24). Giselle's expressions of agency and individuality are therefore inseparable from the socio-political climate of post-Revolutionary France, of which the Wilis are particularly reminiscent.

According to Joellen Meglin, the Romantic ballet conveyed a "horror of congregations of women...Women acting in concert were characterized as vindictive, wrathful, and remorseless; they were the fearsome oppressed who would vent their fury in judgment of the oppressors. The corps de ballet was a kind of irrational mob taking justice into its own hands" (qtd. in Banes 30–31). I would argue that the same holds true for heteronormative women portrayed in AAA games. Anita Sarkeesian identifies certain tropes regarding women in video games, including the following: exotic fantasies, sinister seductresses, women-as-rewards, background decorations, and damsels in distress. While all these women may be in precarious situations, their danger stems more from their association with sexuality than anything else. These fearsome female automatons not only are victims of their desire for heterosexual love, often jilted and scorned by their former male lovers, but they also now use their allure and appeal to bring men to their death. The famous dance-to-death scene involving Hilarion and the Wilis only serves to highlight the treachery of mad, dancing women. As Engelhardt suggests, this public "exhibition of female mobility and corporeality" problematized the role of women at the time of composition (86). However, like *La Sylphide*, which is also a story of "marriage, of socially licensed sexuality, and of what is possible and impossible, sanctioned and forbidden, with respect to courtship" (Engelhardt 86), *Giselle* seeks to restore order to the gender hierarchy. While Wilis may be alluring and appealing, they also are clearly designated as evil. This dichotomization of good and evil follows a prescriptive gendered agenda that wreaks havoc in a contemporary setting.

How could *iGiselle* rewrite the Wilis to represent both an empowered community of female agency *and* a space of danger and moral dilemma, without rendering them stereotypical, hostile, and dangerous sexualized temptresses? In *iGiselle*, the end goal of the Wilis depends on the path the player chooses, but their scorn stems less from romantic wrongdoings than from the larger inner obstacles Giselle encounters. Each Wili represents a thematic struggle Giselle has faced in the game thus far. She must decide if a professional dance career is what she ultimately wants for herself; if her actions thus far have been the result of her active choices or simply have been reactionary (passive) responses to others; if love is something that matters to her or not; and if she wants to leave this community of women or stay, thereby enacting revenge or forgiveness in the process.

Ultimately, the most difficult part of deciding the types of narrative paths to create for an interactive story was deciding how to interpret particular choices. As we developed the script, questions of a moral nature needed to be asked and answered: should we moralize revenge as bad and forgiveness as good, following the original ballet? Would Giselle's expression of romantic love lead her to a happy ending? Is death an adequate or even warranted outcome of the narrative? Where our game falls short is in the player's ability to enact the exact plot he or she may wish to see unfold in the game. True agency is not a possibility in this particular interactive narrative; therefore, our game remains more limited in its possibility for agency than is commensurate with our original goals.

Eventually, the game leads players to three types of endings with minor variations between them. First, the game can end with Giselle enacting revenge and remaining in the realm of the Wilis, either as one of Myrtha's community or by seizing the power and becoming the new leader. Second, Giselle can enact revenge on one of multiple parties (Albert/Albrecht, Betty/Berthe, or Beatrice/Bathilde) and wake up to play out the consequences of her decisions. Or, finally, Giselle can choose forgiveness and either remain with the Wilis, free them, or wake up to a new life where she can decide her own terms. Regardless of these decisions, her continued romance with Albert is not a possibility in any ending. The goal of the game was to allow Giselle to assert her own agency without the conflicting interest of romantic entanglements, which we saw as a key problem area within the original ballet. While this is problematic in the agential limitations of the player, it is an effect of our decision to diminish the place of the heterosexual and stereotypical romance aspect of Romantic ballets.

Our primary narrative is not, in the end, drastically different from the original libretto; nevertheless, it allows the player to rewrite the narrative at the level of romance (although to a limited extent), betrayal, and forgiveness, if he or she chooses. Allowing the protagonist-player a choice is the primary way in which we have enabled a higher degree of agency than that which Giselle finds within the original ballet. We have also restructured the mid-way point of the ballet itself. Rather than accept the original Giselle's death as the primary event required for character development and rising action, we have taken the spectral forest of Act II—a space in which we see the precarious blurring between the real, unreal, and hyper-real—and turned it into a dream state. Here, Giselle's own suppressed unconsciousness functions as her primary obstacle or opponent, as opposed to external and less controllable nemeses. Both Myrtha and the Wilis, then, are Giselle's fears, anxieties, and moral dilemmas materialized, forcing her to confront her weaknesses and obstacles and choose whether or not to assert active control over her life. The choice of revenge or forgiveness in this way becomes an action solely of Giselle's own choosing, leaving less room for her victimization.

So how does our Giselle measure up to the original titular character? Balanchine and Mason say of *Giselle* that "the heroine is given a basis in real life, to make her real and unreal at the same time" (195). While our Giselle may not be the 1841 ideal of womanhood, *iGiselle* presents a Giselle who is a more realistic portrait of a heterosexual, white woman facing similar life circumstances today. In the process of writing *iGiselle*, we have created what Midgelow defines as a "reworking" of an "authentic" text: "reworkings...are engaged in a dialogue with tradition, often challenging established premises" (11). Our reworking of the Romantic ballet relies on familiarity with the traditional tropes, themes, and motifs of the original *Giselle* in order to "deconstruct the past, engaging with it only to enter into an interpretive discourse" (11). Taking the original *Giselle* as our primary text, we have opted to reconceptualize the "aesthetic and political terrain" established in the original telling in order to uncover the historical contextualization and contemporize the narrative for a twenty-first-century audience (Midgelow 14).

In practice, our game functions a little like a choose-your-own-adventure; the player's gameplay also impacts the narrative branch she or he will pursue. As we could not conceive of all alternative possibilities within our narrative, given the basic constraints of our project, our game does have some focalized branching and a degree of linearity, but there is the potential for a reader-player's experience to be different from another reader-player's, depending on the interactive choices she or he makes. As the game came together and we were able to put our narrative into action, we found that our Giselle still has the potential to have more ties to the original 1841 character of Giselle than we might originally have intended. In this discovery, we came to the realization that it was not as difficult as we had first thought to conceive of a contemporary context in which the original *Giselle* still rang relatively true. Maybe the Romantic ballet is not as retrogressive as we had come to assume; perhaps that is why it is has remained so popular in the ballet world today. Rather, we just need to find the cultural conditions that give this social narrative form.

Notes

1. Unlike traditional console video games, games designed for gesture consoles necessarily reduce the number of options offered to a player due to issues regarding human motion tracking. As a result, the complexity of game play is reduced, and the scope of player agency is narrowed. We found this to be a problem in our own use of Kinect for *iGiselle*. The sensor did not always recognize the gestures and motions we attempted to convey; therefore, our choice of ballet postures was limited by the mechanism of the device.

2. This statement is not intended to dismiss the aesthetic value of the ballet's dance, music, scenery, and costumes; however, their construction and production affect the discursive meaning of the ballet within public imaginations.

3. For example, in *Reworking the Ballet: Counter Narratives and Alternative Bodies* (2007) and *Reading Dance: Bodies and Subjects in Contemporary American Dance* (1986), Vida L. Midgelow and Susan Leigh Foster, respectively, discuss the circulation of dance and

representations of dance—Foster pays special attention to literary representations of dance—among various audiences, readers, and publics.

4. For more on this debate, see Murray ch. 1–3; Juul; Aarseth; and Gee ch. 1–2.

5. This statement is not intended to homogenize or generalize all audience responses to the classic version of *Giselle*, but a cursory look at ballet performance reviews (e.g., Anderson; Schabas) and scholarly studies (e.g., Smith, "What Killed Giselle?"; Bruner) reveal these dominant narratives.

6. *BioShock Infinite* (2013) is a first-person shooter game with elements of role-playing, developed by Irrational Games. Gaynor worked on the second instalment of the *BioShock* series.

7. I would like to thank Pascale Thériault at the University of Montreal for his suggestions on behalf of the Groupe Féministe Vidéolodique.

8. First performed by Dance Theatre of Harlem at the London Coliseum in New York City on July 18, 1984.

9. Issues of racial homogenizing and stereotyping also proliferate within the gaming industry. For example, according to Sandy Ong, black characters are often stereotyped as comedic or enforcer-type sidekicks, and narrowly typecast as athletes, gangsters, rappers, and impoverished children of broken homes. Similar typecasting occurs for Asian, Latino/Latina, and other minority populations in AAA games. 2K Games' recent release of *Mafia III* (2016) is one of few commercial games to feature a black (male) protagonist, Lincoln Clay. Informal communities and organizations, such as Blacks in Gaming (BIG) and I Need Diverse Games, recently have emerged in response to the need to diversify the gaming industry.

10. Mats Ek's *Giselle* premiered in Sweden, performed by the Cullberg Ballet (1982).

11. Keegan-Dolan's *Giselle* was first performed by Fabulous Beast Dance Theatre at Samuel Beckett Theatre in Dublin, Ireland, in September 2003.

12. Ek is known for his reinterpretations of ballet classics, including *Swan Lake* (1987), *Sleeping Beauty* (1996), *Carmen* (1992), and *Romeo and Juliet* (2013), as well as *Giselle*.

13. Similarly, in his 2013 production of *Giselle*, José Navas, Director of Compagnie Flak in Montreal, portrays Albrecht and Hilarion as lovers. The world premiere was on April 25, 2013, at the Queen Elizabeth Theatre in Vancouver, British Columbia.

Works Cited

Aarseth, Espen. "Genre Trouble: Narrativism and the Art of Simulation." *First Person: New Media as Story, Performance, and Game.* Ed. Noah Wardrip-Fruin and Pat Harrigan. Cambridge, MA: MIT Press, 2004. 45–55.

Alfort, Bérengère. "Qu'est-ce qui fait couris Giselle?" *Les Saisons de la Danse* Dec. 2000: 40–41.

Anderson, Zoë. "Tale of Betrayed Love, Death and Forgiveness Is Lucidly Told." Rev. of *Giselle*, performed by the Royal Ballet. *The Independent*. Feb. 29, 2016. www.independent.co.uk.

Balanchine, George, and Francis Mason. *101 Stories of the Great Ballets: The Scene-by-Scene Stories of the Most Popular Ballets, Old and New*. New York: Anchor, 1975.

Banes, Sally. *Dancing Women: Female Bodies on Stage*. London and New York: Routledge, 1998.

Beaumont, Cyril W. *The Ballet Called Giselle*. 2nd ed. New York: Dance Horizons, 1969.

BioWare. *Jade Empire*. Microsoft Game Studios, 2005.

———. *Mass Effect*. Microsoft Game Studios, 2007.

———. *Mass Effect 2*. Electronic Arts, 2010.

———. *Mass Effect 3*. Electronic Arts, 2012.

Boccadoro, Patricia. Rev. of *Giselle*, choreography by Mats Ek. *Culturekiosque* July 13, 2004. www.culturekiosque.com/dance.

Brown, Carol. "Inscribing the Body: Feminist Choreographic Practices." Diss. University of Surrey, 1994.

Bruner, Jody. "Redeeming *Giselle*: Making a Case for the Ballet We Love to Hate." *Studies in Dance History* (1997): 107–20.

Connolly, Matt. "Why This Indie Game Studio Chose a Feminist Drama over Guns and Zombies." *Mother Jones* Sept. 20, 2013. www.motherjones.com/media/2013/09.

Crabb, Michael. "*Giselle*: Radically, Ribaldly Revised." *Toronto Star* May 5, 2010. www.thestar.com.

Engelhardt, Molly. *Dancing Out of Line: Ballrooms, Ballets, and Mobility in Victorian Fiction and Culture*. Athens, OH: Ohio UP, 2009.

Freeman, Nina. *Freshman Year*, 2015. ninasays.so/freshmanyear.

Fullbright Company. *Gone Home*. Fullbright Company, 2013.

Gaiser, Carrie. "Caught Dancing: Hybridity, Stability, and Subversion in Dance Theatre of Harlem's Creole *Giselle*." *Theatre Journal* 58.2 (2006): 269–89.

Gee, James Paul. *What Video Games Have to Teach Us About Learning and Literacy*. 2nd ed. New York: Palgrave Macmillan, 2007.

Genette, Gérard. *Narrative Discourse: An Essay in Method*. Ithaca, NY: Cornell UP, 1983.

Howitt, Grant. "Writing Video Games: Can Narrative Be as Important as Gameplay?" *The Guardian* Feb. 21, 2014. www.theguardian.com.

Ibsen, Henrik. *A Doll's House*. [1879]. Project Gutenberg, 2008. www.gutenberg.org.

Juul, Jesper. "Games Telling Stories?—A Brief Note on Games and Narratives." *Game Studies* 1.1 (2001).

Kirkpatrick, Graeme. *Aesthetic Theory and the Video Game*. Manchester: Manchester UP, 2011.

Midgelow, Vida L. *Reworking the Ballet: Counter Narratives and Alternative Bodies*. London and New York: Routledge, 2007.

Murray, Janet Horowitz. *Hamlet on the Holodeck: The Future of Narrative in Cyberspace*. Cambridge, MA: MIT Press, 1997.

Ong, Sandy. "The Video Game Industry's Problem with Racial Diversity." *Newsweek* Oct. 13, 2016. www.newsweek.com.

Ostenson, Jonathan. "Exploring the Boundaries of Narrative: Video Games in the English Classroom." *English Journal* 102.6 (2013): 71–78.

Piquero, Lu. "Mats Ek: Expression & Fluidity." *Ballet Bag* July 13, 2012. www.theballetbag.com.

Quinn, Zoë. *Depression Quest*. Quinnspiracy, 2013.

Ryan, Marie-Laure. *Narrative as Virtual Reality 2: Revising Immersion and Interactivity in Literature and Electronic Media*. Baltimore: John Hopkins UP, 2015.

Sarkeesian, Anita. *Feminist Frequency*. feministfrequency.com. 2009.

Schabas, Martha. "*Giselle*: A Riveting Classic from the National Ballet—Just Ignore the Outmoded Gender Commentary." Rev. of *Giselle*, by the National Ballet of Canada. *The Globe and Mail* June 17, 2016. www.theglobeandmail.com/arts.

Siegel, Marcia B. "A Newly Old *Giselle*." *Hudson Review* (2011). hudsonreview.com/issue/autumn-2011.

Smith, Marion. *Ballet and Opera in the Age of Giselle*. Princeton and Oxford: Princeton UP, 2000.

———. "What Killed Giselle?" *Dance Chronicle* 13.1 (1990): 68–81.

II

Creating *iGiselle*

SERGIO POO HERNANDEZ
& VADIM BULITKO

5

Artificial Intelligence for Managing
the Interactive Ballet Video Game, *iGiselle*

Introduction

Storytelling is an important art form. Stories are used not only to entertain
but also to convey ideas, experiences and historical events, usually with the
intention of eliciting emotion from the audience. The emotional response
of the audience is a significant factor in audience engagement and thus has
implications for education, training and public policy decision-making. People
expect an emotional connection from modern games to the point that one
review of *Titanfall* (Respawn Entertainment, 2014) criticized the expressly multi-
player game for lack of story-driven emotional engagement (Brown, 2014).

The crucial matter to consider is the emotional response a particular
person will have to a section of narrative. Writers of traditional narratives
employ several mechanisms, such as description, dialogue, and—of course—
plot, to invite reader engagement and elicit emotion. Filmmakers can also
call upon background music, camera angles and colours to cue emotion in
their viewers (Tan, 2011; Smith, 2003). Yet contemporary narrative-rich video
games bring in the added complexity of interactivity and, hence, emergent

non-linear narratives. How can video game developers hope to elicit certain emotions—or any emotion at all—from an unknown player who is shaping the story dynamically by controlling his or her in-game avatar?

Video game developers have tackled this challenge in a variety of ways. One possibility is to make the narrative primarily emergent. Games such as Bethesda Softworks' *Fallout* series (developed by Obsidian Entertainment), first released in 2012, fill the game world with a great number of mini-narratives or side quests and characters for the player to interact with in the hope that there will be something for everyone in the game world. The disadvantage of this approach is that the main story takes a back seat to the minor details, and the resulting player experience usually lacks tension. For instance, in BioWare's *Mass Effect 2* (2010), players are told that the galaxy is on the brink of destruction, yet they can choose to solve domestic conflicts, unify broken families, or enjoy dancing in a nightclub. An opposite approach is to write a linear story and hope that the topic is universal enough to elicit emotional engagement in a broad range of players. A classic example is Valve's 2004 release, *Half-Life 2*, where human beings are oppressed by technologically advanced aliens. However, combining a narrative arc that sustains tension (through suspense, for instance) with open-world exploration is an enormous challenge (Petit, 2014).

Artificial Intelligence for Player-Experience Management in a Narrative-Based Ballet Video Game

Typically, researchers in artificial intelligence (AI) have addressed these challenges by attempting to manage the player's experience on a per-player basis. Such AI experience managers approximate a human game master— a person who, in the world of traditional pen-and-paper role-playing games, assesses players' emotions and shapes the story to elicit certain emotional responses from them (Laws, 2002). If the story universe is encoded in a computer-readable form, then stories that are consistent with both the player's actions and authorial goals can be automatically generated via AI planners (Riedl et al., 2008). The disadvantage of this approach is that it becomes more difficult for the game developers to anticipate and direct the player's emotional response. To this end, AI researchers have attempted to model the player's state explicitly and shape the narrative specifically to influence it. For instance, one recently developed AI experience manager attempts to infer the player's inclinations towards different play-styles and then selects the next section of narrative to maximize the player's perception of fun and agency (Thue et al., 2007; 2011).

In this chapter, we approach the problem of automatically shaping the narrative on a per-player basis from a different angle. Answering the call for explicit emotion modelling in AI-driven storytelling (Poo Hernandez & Bulitko, 2013), we let the authors explicitly specify a trajectory in a space of emotions that they would like their players to experience. So, instead of providing concrete narrative goals (for example, "Grandmother is eaten by the wolf" in an interactive version of "The Little Red Riding Hood" story [Riedl et al., 2008]) and hoping that accomplishing these goals will somehow elicit the needed emotional response from the player, we let the author specify emotional "key frames" at certain narrative points. For instance, the author can specify that at a certain point in the game the player should be hopeful, but also somewhat fearful. Our AI system will then pick concrete narrative events that it expects will put the particular player in a particular emotional state at the specified time.

We approach this goal by extending and combining several existing AI approaches to the interactive narrative experience management. Specifically, we encode the narrative world in a planning language and represent the stories themselves as plans in the spirit of the Automated Story Director (ASD) (Riedl et al. 2008). We infer the player's inclinations towards different play-styles, using a player model inspired by Player-Specific Stories via Automatically Generated Events (PASSAGE) (Thue et al. 2007). We use an appraisal model of emotions to predict the player's emotional response to a candidate narrative (Ortony, Clore, & Collins, 1990; Marsella & Gratch, 2003; Lazarus, 1991). Our first contribution is thus a novel combination of several existing AI approaches and the introduction of a new computational model connecting play-style modelling to goal inference to emotion prediction to narrative selection. Our second contribution is the specific implementation of the narrative planning module within our system. The resulting approach is called Player Appraisal Controlling Emotions (PACE) and is presented in this chapter.

We have been able to evaluate this approach in a unique test bed: possibly the first interactive narrative-oriented ballet video game. In addition to providing a rich test bed for PACE, the video game touches on such cross-disciplinary issues as exercise games (Lanningham-Foster et al., 2009) and gender representation and inclusion in video games (Norris, 2004; Consalvo, 2012). In the rest of this chapter, we formulate the problem more precisely; review relevant existing work and its applicability to the problem at hand; present our approach in the case of *iGiselle*; discuss the implementation within the interactive ballet video, the planned empirical evaluation and the hypotheses it will test; and conclude with suggestions for future work.

Problem Formulation

The problem we set out to tackle in our research was two-fold. First, we wanted to give players a sense of narrative agency by allowing them to shape the story in meaningful ways and feel that, ultimately, their choices matter. Second, we wanted the player to follow an author-specified emotional trajectory. We attempted to solve both problems by developing an AI-managed interactive narrative in which, as the game unfolds, narrative events are produced by an AI experience manager (the ASD) and are influenced by the player's choices; the player's choices are expressed by his or her avatar's actions, whereas the author's desires are expressed in the form of a target emotional trajectory for the player.

To use the terminology of the Procedural Game Adaptation (PGA) framework (Thue & Bulitko, 2012), we structured the video game narrative as a Markov Decision Process (MDP), with the player being the decision agent. The MDP states are narrative events, and the MDP actions are the narrative choices the player makes. The MDP structure can be defined to ensure plot consistency: for example, if the player kills the wolf early in the game, Little Red cannot be eaten by the wolf later. Unbeknownst to the player, his or her actions are monitored by the ASD, which uses this information to adjust the MDP's transition function while the game is running. This mapping from the player's actions to the MDP adjustment is implemented via several AI techniques, which are algorithmically detailed in the discussion that follows.

Related Work

Our approach to the problem we identified built on work done in two fields of research: AI experience management in the context of interactive narrative in video-game-like systems, and the use of goal-appraisal models to compute and infer a player's emotional state.

The ASD represents the narrative as a plan and uses an AI planner to build a narrative from a formal description of the story world and *a priori* given authorial goals (Riedl et al., 2008). However, not all plans, or sequences of events, result in interesting and emotionally rich narratives. The ASD lacks any model of the player's emotions or play-style preferences. Instead, it forces the author to build an exemplar narrative manually. During the game, the player is monitored for rupturing the exemplar narrative by taking in-game action. Such ruptures are then repaired by invoking the automated planner Longbow (Young, 1994). While a narrative rupture can be repaired in many different ways, the planner selects the repair most similar to the handcrafted exemplar narrative, thereby pulling the player back towards the original story. The lack of explicit player-specific emotion modelling prevents the ASD from solving our problem by itself. We, however, incorporate parts of the ASD in our approach.

Explicit play-style modelling in interactive storytelling was implemented in PASSAGE (Thue et al., 2007; 2011) where the player's actions were mapped to inclinations towards five distinct play-styles borrowed from pen-and-paper game mastering (Laws, 2002). The inclinations were used to select from a handcrafted library of narrative segments in an attempt to maximize the player's feelings of enjoyment and agency. PASSAGE neither allowed the game designer to specify an arbitrary emotional trajectory on which to keep the player nor explicitly modelled the player's emotional state. While PASSAGE cannot solve our problem by itself, we use a PASSAGE-inspired play-style model in our approach.

Player-Specific Automated Storytelling (PAST) (Ramirez & Bulitko, 2015) combined the AI planner of ASD and the play-style model of PASSAGE in an attempt to repair player-induced ruptures in the exemplar narrative in a player-specific way. Longbow within PAST combined proximity to the exemplar narrative with predictions of the player's enjoyment to select the best repair for a rupture. To predict the amount of fun the player would have along a candidate repair, PAST used a PASSAGE-style model of play-style inclinations, automatically updating it from the player's actions. This prediction of fun experienced along a possible narrative can be viewed as rudimentary emotion modelling. However, it is insufficient to solve our problem, as PAST did not allow the author to specify an arbitrarily shaped emotion curve even in the case of fun, but rather always attempted to maximize it. Furthermore, PAST could not be easily extended to support other emotions.

The other field of existing work focuses on inferring the player's emotional state (Lin, Spraragen, & Zyda, 2012). For narrative-rich games the models based on goal-appraisal appeared a natural fit. Such models compute the player's emotional state as a result of the interaction between the player's goals and the likelihood of his or her achieving them. For example, the possibility of a failure elicits fear, whereas a definitive failure elicits despair. A well-known appraisal model is OCC (Ortony, Clore, & Collins, 1990). OCC is capable of modelling twenty-two different emotions and has been used in several systems such as EM (Reilly, 1996), Émile (Gratch, 2000), and FearNot! (Aylett et al., 2005; 2007). Émile computes the probability of an agent's success based on its current intentions and the plan the agent has developed to achieve those intentions, and it uses this probability to determine the agent's emotional state. EMotion and Adaptation (EMA) (Marsella & Gratch, 2003) complements an appraisal-based emotion modelling with a coping mechanism and thus can be used to control an NPC's appearance (Kenny et al., 2007), as well as actions within a game. While insufficient to solve our problem by itself, we incorporate an appraisal-style model into our approach.

A few projects attempted to shape narrative by explicitly representing the player's emotions. *Moe* (Weyhrauch, 1997) used a target intensity curve and annotations on narrative events supplied by the author to guide the narrative. A similar approach was implemented in Façade (Mateas & Stern, 2003), where each plot point was manually annotated with a tension value by the authors. Then an AI drama manager would choose the plot point whose tension value was estimated to be closest to the target tension curve. Our approach is similar, but it allows us to model a broader range of emotions and explicitly recognizes that the same plot point may elicit radically different emotional responses from different players. A different approach is used in Distributed Drama Management (DDM), where the non-playable characters model the player's current and future emotions and use them to choose an action to perform (Weallans, Louchart, & Aylett, 2012). Our approach is similar, but it is not character-centric.

With advances in biometric readers, researchers have attempted to explicitly read the player's emotional state and use it to shape the game. For instance, skin conductance, heart rate and facial electromyography (EMG) can be used to infer the player's level of tension and thus dynamically adjust the layout of a game level and enemies encountered by the player (Nogueira et al., 2013). A similar but sensorless approach was implemented in the commercial game *Left 4 Dead* where the tension level of the player, inferred from such observable variables as the avatar's health level and shooting accuracy, was used to modulate the influx of enemies the player combats (Booth, 2009). While the latter approach allowed, in principle, the game designer to specify an arbitrary target tension curve, the changes to the game were limited to elements of the gameplay with no AI-managed narrative. An additional problem with biometrics-driven approaches is that only the player's current state can be read, whereas generating future narrative requires a prediction of the player's future emotional response.

In summary, none of the related work reviewed in this section could solve our problem directly. However, most contain elements, such as play-style modelling and narrative generation with AI planning, that could be incorporated into our approach.

Our Approach

As we described in the introduction, our method, PACE, combines elements from existing AI experience managers in a novel approach. We will first illustrate the ideas with an example and then follow up with details.

Intuition

Consider an interactive story based on the classic Romantic ballet *Giselle* (Gautier et al., 1841) where the player controls the titular heroine. At the end of a ballet class, the player decides to leave the studio (fig. 5.1) and head out to a party. It is now up to the AI experience manager to select the next section of narrative for the player to experience. Upon arrival at the party, using the automated planning approach from the ASD, PACE computes two possible narratives with different scenarios: one, the player socializes with her friends; two, the player confronts a rival dancer. Which one should be presented to the player?

As our goal is to elicit a specific emotional response from the player, the answer depends on the player's reaction to each of the two narrative candidates. To make the selection we predict the player's emotions, using an appraisal model. Suppose the author specified a target curve for the evolution of the player's hope. Then PACE predicts the emotional intensity of hope elicited in the player by socializing with friends, as well as by confronting her rival, and chooses the narrative most likely to keep the player closer to the target curve. This process is done in four steps, as follows:

1. PACE maintains a model of the player's inclinations towards different play-styles (Thue et al., 2007). For this example, suppose there are three archetypical play-styles: storytelling, showing off, or being modest. Using author-supplied annotations on the player's past actions, PACE has computed the player's inclinations towards these three play-styles.

2. Given the play-style model of the player, PACE can now infer how desirable certain narrative goals are to him or her. Suppose the author has previously identified two possible goals that a player may be pursuing at this point in the story: *maintaining a successful career* and *leading a fulfilling*

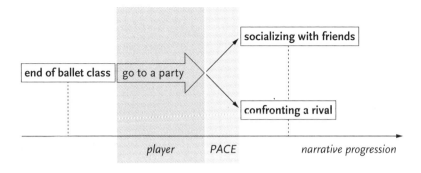

Figure 5.1: The player goes to a party. What happens next?

personal life. The author has also provided a mapping between play-style inclinations and goal desirability. Using the mapping and the player's inclination modelled in step one above, PACE computes the desirability of a successful career and the desirability of a fulfilling personal life to the player.

3. PACE uses the goal desirabilities and author-supplied probabilities of reaching these goals from each of the candidate narratives to predict the player's emotional response. If the socialize-with-friends narrative is chosen, then the probability of the player's having a successful career will be lower than the probability of having a fulfilling personal life. Using the appraisal model of emotions (Marsella & Gratch, 2003), PACE estimates the intensity of the emotion of hope, should this narrative be presented to the player. On the other hand, the confronting-a-rival narrative places the player's chances of having a successful career substantially higher than the chances of having a fulfilling personal life. Appraising the two goals ranks the intensity of hope lower for this narrative than it would under the socialize-with-friends narrative, because this player's preferred goal is *leading a fulfilling personal life.*

4. PACE compares the predicted values of hope elicited by the two candidate narratives with the target value of hope that the author wanted the player to experience at this point in the narrative. If socializing with friends brings the player's hope closer to the target curve (fig. 5.2), then

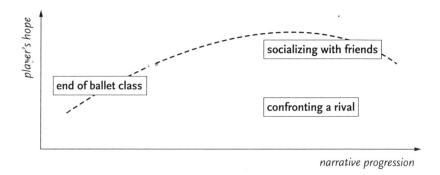

Figure 5.2: PACE *selects the "socializing with friends" narrative section, keeping the player along a target curve for the emotion of hope.*

that section of the narrative will be presented to the player when he or she arrives at the party. This process is applied to each scenario in the narrative.[1]

Implementational Details

While reusing elements from PAST, we replaced its narrative-oriented automated planner, Longbow, with a domain-independent planner. Switching to the de facto standard planning domain description language (PDDL) allowed us to take advantage of recent advances in automated planning research.

We currently use FastDownward planner (Helmert, 2006), running the LAMA implementation (Richter & Westphal, 2010). This planner was chosen because of its versatility and performance, as it won the Sequential Optimization track and was the runner-up in the Sequential Satisficing track in the Seventh International Planning Competition (Coles et al., 2012).

The planner is guided by a heuristic function which PACE sets as the deviation of the emotions to be elicited by a candidate narrative from the target emotions specified by the authors. Thus, PACE is able to compute the best narrative without explicitly computing all alternatives.

Figure 5.3: iGiselle *game interface.*

iGiselle

We evaluated PACE in a novel test bed called *iGiselle*: an interactive version of the classic Romantic ballet *Giselle* (Gautier et al., 1841) created in a video game. An interactive ballet provides narratives with the potential to elicit a variety of emotions, along with an opportunity to investigate gender issues in video games.[2]

In *iGiselle* the player takes control of Giselle and experiences the narrative via a combination of still images, music and voiceovers. To further immerse the player in the game we forgo a traditional game controller and have the players indicate their narrative choices by assuming dance positions (fig. 5.3) which are recognized with the Microsoft Kinect sensor. The game makes use of four poses: fifth *en haut*, first arabesque, *retiré devant* and fourth lunge. Unlike other systems that interpret the meaning of gestures, such as Viewpoints AI (Jacob et al., 2013), we utilize these poses because they do not occlude the player's limbs, which makes them easier for the sensor to recognize.

Figure 5.4: Photographing against a green screen (left). The resulting composite image (right).

The development of the multimedia content was done in two phases. First, working with writers, we developed a non-linear narrative graph that allowed the player to explore various narratives by controlling the heroine. The narrative graph was then encoded as states and actions in PDDL. Then, to capture the multimedia content for the narrative graph, we worked with ballet dancers, voice actors, choreographers and scriptwriters. Eleven actors were photographed against a green screen (fig. 4), and their images were later composited onto separately captured background images. This process afforded us a greater freedom in scheduling our time with the actors as well as in the choice of locations for the background images. Finally, a cell-shading-style process was applied to the composite images to achieve the desired aesthetic effect (fig. 5.4).

For the audio component of the game, we recruited a cast of ten voice actors who were recorded in a studio reading their lines from the script. The audio was later processed and imported into the game. Finally, an original soundtrack was composed for the game, by Wayne DeFehr, with various tracks setting the sound stage for the different parts of the story (see Chapter 7 in this volume).

To evaluate the effectiveness of PACE we conducted a user study in which human subjects either experienced *iGiselle* managed by PACE, using emotional modelling of the player (the experimental condition), or *iGiselle* managed by a baseline AI manager (the control condition). The subjects then filled out a post-experience questionnaire on their enjoyment of the story, the emotions they experienced, etc. The results of the evaluation are discussed in our previous publication (Poo Hernandez, Bulitko, & Spetch, 2015).

Future Work

In addition to evaluating PACE with *iGiselle*, as described above, we plan to explore applications of PACE to simulations used for education and training. In particular, we are considering applications of emotion modelling to shaping training scenarios for neonatal emergency care. As with most emergency response training, opportunities for live exercise are limited, and mistakes can have catastrophic consequences (Bulitko & Wilkins 1999). As a result, medical instructors have shown interest in intelligent training systems that are similar to video games (de Ribaupierre et al., 2014, Bulitko et al., 2015). With PACE, an instructor will be able to specify the target emotional trajectory for the trainee, which PACE will then attempt to implement by dynamically shaping the training scenario in response to the trainee's actions.

Another interesting avenue for future work is the development of narrative-rich exercise games. While a number of exercise-oriented video games have been developed (Morelli et al., 2014), few of them immerse the player in a rich narrative. Using *iGiselle*, we are planning to compare the level of story engagement the player would experience by controlling Giselle via our interface, as opposed to a gamepad.

Yet another area of further research involves improving how to calculate the goal desirability and goal likelihood values. Current implementation uses hand-coded values for the goal desirability and goal likelihood. Alternatively, these values could also be obtained by interviewing test players and then relating their goal preferences to their play-style inclinations. Another method would be to set up test scenarios in which the players' choices will be data-mined for goal desirabilities. The evaluation of such methods would include their cost-effectiveness.

Conclusions

PACE is an AI experience manager that provides the player with a sense of narrative agency, while attempting to keep him or her on an author-specified emotional trajectory. In this chapter we have shown how PACE is implemented in terms of the MDP-based framework PGA in order to accomplish these tasks. We have also demonstrated its application to an innovative story-based video game related to the Romantic ballet *Giselle*.

Authors' Note

The *iGiselle* project was funded by the Natural Sciences and Engineering Research Council of Canada (NSERC), Kule Institute for Advanced Study (KIAS), and the WISEST, HIP, and Science-without-Borders programs at the University of Alberta. This essay is an updated version of our previous publication (Poo Hernandez, Bulitko, & St. Hilaire, 2014). The republication is by permission from the Association for Advancement of Artificial Intelligence (AAAI), which holds the copyright for our original publication.

Notes

1. The algorithmic details of the PACE operation can be found in our previous publication (Poo Hernandez et al., 2014).

2. The development of *iGiselle*, the video game, was directed by Vadim Bulitko. The artificial intelligence part (PACE) was designed by Vadim Bulitko (lead) and Sergio Poo Hernandez. The software development team consisted of Sergio Poo Hernandez (lead), Igor Pereira Machado, Renato Ribeiro, Sarah Beck, and Trevon Romanuik. Scriptwriting was done by Emilie St. Hilaire (lead), Laura Sydora, Sarah Beck, Nicole Papadopolous, Sergio Poo Hernandez, and Nora Foster Stovel. Character photography was done primarily by Vadim Bulitko, while Emilie St. Hilaire captured the background images. Compositing and editing were carried out by Emilie St. Hilaire, Sergio Poo Hernandez, Allyson Shewchuk, Luke Slevinsky, and Jesse Underwood. Dance choreography was created by Nicole Papadopolous and Laura Sydora. The soundtrack was composed by Wayne DeFehr. The voiceover recording and editing team consisted of Nicole Papadopolous, Kevin Hoskin, Emilie St. Hilaire,

Laura Sydora, Sergio Poo Hernandez, Allyson Shewchuk, Luke Slevinsky, and Jesse Underwood. The visual cast consisted of Aphra Sutherland, Andrea Ginter, Kandise Salerno, Nathan Lacombe, Charles Nokes, Kiera Keglowitsch, Tara Gaucher, Rachel Ginter, Karly Polkosnik, Sierra Lacombe and Justin Kautz. Voice actors included Dawn Harvey, Jessica Watson, Jeanine Bonot, Grant Eidem, Yvonne Desjardins, Dale MacDonald, Sarah Beck, Leah Beaudry, Nicole Papadopolous, and Larissa Thompson. Pirkko Markula, Emilie St. Hilaire, Sarah Beck, Susan Howard, Sunrose Ko, Geoffrey Rockwell, Oliver Rossier, Mark Riedl, Alejandro Ramirez, David Thue, and Christina Gier all supported the project in various roles. Special gratitude goes to Nora Foster Stovel and Pirkko Markula.

References

Aylett, R.S., Louchart, S., Dias, J., Paiva, A., & Vala, M. (2005). FearNot!—An experiment in emergent narrative. In T. Panayiotopoulos, J. Gratch, R. Aylett, D. Ballin, P. Olivier, & T. Rist (Eds.), *Intelligent virtual agents: 5th International Working Conference, IVA 2005: Proceedings* (305–16). Berlin: Springer-Verlag.

Aylett, R., Vala, M., Sequeira, P., & Paiva, A. (2007). FearNot!—An emergent narrative approach to virtual dramas for anti-bullying education. In M. Cavazza & S. Donikian (Eds.), *Virtual storytelling. Using virtual reality technologies for storytelling: 4th International Conference, ICVS 2007: Proceedings* (202–05). Berlin: Springer-Verlag.

BioWare. (2010). *Mass Effect 2* [video game]. Redwood City, CA: Electronic Arts.

BioWare. (2014). *Dragon Age: Inquisition* [video game]. Redwood City, CA: Electronic Arts.

Booth, M. (2009). The AI systems of *Left 4 Dead* [Keynote address]. In C.J. Darken & G.M. Youngblood (Eds.), *Proceedings of the Fifth Artificial Intelligence and Interactive Digital Entertainment Conference*. Cambridge, MA: AAAI Press.

Brown, P. (2014, May 7). *Titanfall* review—through the eyes of a lapsed combatant. *Gamespot*. www.gamespot.com/reviews/.

Bulitko, V., Hong, J., Kumaran, K., Swedberg, I., Thoang, W., von Hauff, P., & Schmolzer, G. (2015, July 3). RETAIN: A neonatal resuscitation trainer built in an undergraduate video-game class (preprint). *arXiv*. arxiv.org/pdf/1507.00956.pdf.

Bulitko, V., Solomon, S., Gratch, J., & van Lent, M. (2008). Modeling culturally and emotionally affected behavior. In M. Mateas. & C. Darken (Eds.), *Proceedings of the Fourth Artificial Intelligence and Interactive Digital Entertainment Conference* (10–15). Cambridge, MA: AAAI Press.

Bulitko, V., & Wilkins, D.C. (1999). Automated instructor assistant for ship damage control. In R. Uthurusamy & B. Hayes-Roth (Eds.), *Proceedings of the Eleventh Conference on Innovative Applications of Artificial Intelligence* (778–85). Cambridge, MA: AAAI Press.

Coles, A., Olaya, A.G., Jimenez, S., Lopez, C.L., Sanner, S., & Yoon, S. (2012). A survey of the Seventh International Planning Competition. AI Magazine, 33(1), 83–88.

Consalvo, M. (2012). Confronting toxic gamer culture: A challenge for feminist game studies scholars. Ada: A Journal of Gender, New Media, and Technology, (1). adanewmedia org/2012/11/issue1-consalvo.

de Ribaupierre, S., Kapralos, B., Haji, F., Stroulia, E., Dubrowski, A., & Eagleson, R. (2014). Healthcare training enhancement through virtual reality and serious games. In M. Ma, L.C. Jain, & P. Anderson (Eds.), Virtual, augmented reality and serious games for healthcare 1 (9–27). New York: Springer.

Gautier, T., Coralli, J., Perrot, J., & Adam, A. (1841). Giselle [ballet]. Perf. Bolshoi Ballet. Bel Air Classiques, 2012. DVD.

Gratch, J. (2000). Émile: Marshalling passions in training and education. In C. Sierra, M. Gini, & J.S. Rosenschein (Eds.), Proceedings of the 4th International Conference on Autonomous Agents (325–32). New York: Association for Computing Machinery. doi:10.1145/336595.337518.

Helmert, M. (2006). The Fast Downward Planning System. Journal of Artificial Intelligence Research, 26, 191–246.

Jacob, M., Coisne, G., Gupta, A., Sysoev, I., Gav Verma, G., & Magerko, B. (2013). Viewpoints AI. In G. Sukthankar & I. Horswill (Eds.), Proceedings of the Ninth Artificial Intelligence and Interactive Digital Entertainment Conference (16–22). Cambridge, MA: AAAI Press.

Kenny, P., Hartholt, A., Gratch, J., Swartout, W., Traum, D., Marsella, S., & Piepol, D. (2007). Building interactive virtual humans for training environments. In Maintaining the Edge...Transfoming the Force: Proceedings of the Interservice/Industry Training, Simulation & Education Conference (Vol. 2007). www.iitsecdocs.com/volumes/2007.

Lanningham-Foster, L., Foster, R.C., McCrady, S.K., Jensen, T.B., Mitre, N., & Levine, J.A. (2009). Activity-promoting video games and increased energy expenditure. The Journal of Pediatrics, 154(6), 819–23.

Laws, R.D. (2002). Robin's Laws of good game mastering. Austin, TX: Steve Jackson Games.

Lazarus, R.S. (1991). Emotion and adaptation. New York: Oxford University Press.

Lin, J., Spraragen, M., & Zyda, M. (2012). Computational models of emotion and cognition. Advances in Cognitive Systems, 2, 59–76.

Marsella, S., & Gratch, J. (2003). Modeling coping behavior in virtual humans: Don't worry, be happy. In J.S. Rosenschein, M. Wooldridge, T. Sandholm, & M. Yokoo (Eds.), Proceedings of the Second International Joint Conference on Autonomous Agents and Multiagent Systems (313–20). New York: Association for Computing Machinery. doi:10.1145/860575.860626.

Mateas, M. & Stern, A. (2003, March). Façade: An experiment in building a fully-realized interactive drama. In *Proceedings of Game Developers Conference, Game Design track* (Vol. 2, 82–106). www.cc.gatech.edu//~isbell/classes/reading/syllabus.html.

Morelli, T., Liebermann, L., Foley, J., & Folmer, E. (2014). An Exergame to improve balance in children who are blind. In T. Barnes & I. Bogost (Eds.), *Proceedings of the 9th International Conference on the Foundations of Digital Games*. Society for the Advancement of the Science of Digital Games. www.fdg2014.org/papers/fdg2014_wip_13.pdf.

Nogueira, P.A., Rodrigues, R., Oliveira, E., & Nacke, L.E. (2013). Guided emotional state regulation: Understanding and shaping players' affective experiences in digital games. In G. Sukthankar & I. Horswill (Eds.), *Proceedings of the Ninth Artificial Intelligence and Interactive Digital Entertainment Conference* (51–57). Cambridge, MA: AAAI Press.

Norris, K.O. (2004). Gender stereotypes, aggression, and computer games: an online survey of women. *Cyberpsychology & Behavior, 7*(6):714–27.

Obsidian Entertainment. (2012). *Fallout: New Vegas* [video game]. Rockville, MD: Bethesda Softworks.

Ortony, A.; Clore, G.L.; & Collins, A. (1990). *The cognitive structure of emotions*. Cambridge: Cambridge University Press.

Petit, C. (2014, April 22). Balancing freedom and story in *Dragon Age: Inquisition. Gamespot*. www.gamespot.com/articles.

Poo Hernandez, S. & Bulitko, V. (2013). A call for emotion modeling in interactive storytelling. In G. Sukthankar & I. Horswill (Eds.), *Proceedings of the Ninth Artificial Intelligence and Interactive Digital Entertainment Conference*, 89–92. Cambridge, MA: AAAI Press.

Poo Hernandez, S., Bulitko, V., & St. Hilaire, E. (2014). Emotion-based interactive storytelling with Artificial Intelligence. In I. Horswill & A. Jhala (Eds.), *Proceedings of the Tenth Artificial Intelligence and Interactive Digital Entertainment Conference* (146–52). Cambridge, MA: AAAI Press.

Poo Hernandez, S., Bulitko, V., & Spetch, M. (2015). Keeping the player on an emotional trajectory in interactive storytelling. In A. Jhala & N. Sturtevant (Eds.), *Proceedings of the Eleventh Artificial Intelligence and Interactive Digital Entertainment Conference*, 65–71. Cambridge, MA: AAAI Press. www.semanticscholar.org.

Ramirez, A. & Bulitko, V. (2015). Automated planning and player modelling for interactive storytelling. In *IEEE Transactions on Computational Intelligence and AI in Games, 7*(4), 375–86.

Reilly, W.S. (1996). *Believable social and emotional agents* (Report No. CMU-CS-96-138). Carnegie Mellon University, School of Computer Science.

Respawn Entertainment. (2014). *Titanfall* [video game]. Redwood City, CA: Electronic Arts.

Richter, S., & Westphal, M. (2010). The LAMA planner: Guiding cost-based anytime planning with landmarks. *Journal of Artificial Intelligence Research, 39*(1), 127–77.

Riedl, M.O., Stern, A., Dini, D., & Alderman, J. (2008). Dynamic experience management in virtual worlds for entertainment, education, and training. *International Transactions on Systems Science and Applications* [Special Issue on Agent Based Systems for Human Learning], *4*(2), 23–42.

Smith, G.M. (2003). *Film structure and the emotion system.* Cambridge: Cambridge University Press.

Tan, E.S. (2011). *Emotion and the structure of narrative film: Film as an emotion machine.* London: Routledge.

Thue, D. & Bulitko, V. (2012). Procedural game adaptation: Framing experience management as changing an MDP. In M. Riedl & G. Sukthankar (Eds.), *Proceedings of the Eighth Artificial Intelligence and Interactive Digital Entertainment Conference* (44–50). Cambridge, MA: AAAI Press.

Thue, D., Bulitko, V., Spetch, M., & Wasylishen, E. (2007). Interactive storytelling: A player modelling approach. In J. Schaeffer & M. Mateas (Eds.), *Proceedings of the Third Artificial Intelligence and Interactive Digital Entertainment Conference* (43–48). Cambridge, MA: AAAI Press.

Thue, D., Bulitko, V., Spetch, M., & Romanuik, T. (2011). A computational model of perceived agency in video games. In V. Bulitko & M. Riedl (Eds.), *Proceedings of the Seventh Artificial Intelligence and Interactive Digital Entertainment Conference* (91–96). Cambridge, MA: AAAI Press.

Valve. (2004). *Half-Life 2* [video game]. Bellevue, WA: Valve.

Weallans, A., Louchart, S., & Aylett, R. (2012). Distributed drama management: Beyond double appraisal in emergent narrative. In D. Oyarzun, F. Peinado, R.M. Young, A. Elizalde, & G. Méndez (Eds.), *Interactive Storytelling: Fifth International Conference, ICIDS 2012* (132–43). New York: Springer, 2012.

Weyhrauch, P. (1997). *Guiding interactive drama.* Carnegie Mellon University, School of Computer Science.

Young, M.R. (1994). *A developer's guide to the Longbow discourse planning system* (Tech. Rep. 94-4). University of Pittsburgh, Intelligent Systems Program.

6

Re-playing *iGiselle*

Dance, Technology, and Interdisciplinary Creation

Introduction

iGiselle is a ballet-based video game that re-imagines the 1841 Romantic ballet *Giselle*. Our interdisciplinary team included researchers from the departments of English and Film Studies, Computing Science, Music, and Art and Design, and from the Faculty of Kinesiology, Sport and Recreation, at the University of Alberta. We used simple audio and visual components to create an interactive game exploring alternative narrative options for a contemporary retelling of *Giselle*. We implemented emotion-modelling techniques to map player styles within the game and used a Microsoft Kinect as a gameplay controller, thereby requiring players to interact with the narrative via ballet-inspired, full-body poses.

There are several aspects of the *iGiselle* project worthy of analysis: I will focus on the steps undertaken in the creation of the game and the creative re-imagining of *Giselle* that took place. After situating *iGiselle* within the discourse of computer interaction design I will propose ways of seeing beyond the default movements and viewpoints often assumed by designers, thus thinking past *iGiselle* towards potential future projects that would go further in exploring some of the valuable questions raised by the *iGiselle* project. Drawing on Donna Haraway's concept of feminist objectivity, I propose a situated, embodied approach to research and creative practice that can help research teams work through disciplinary boundaries as well as explore technological engagements that extend beyond regimented movements and typical user interfaces. In the following chapter, I will dance my way through several ideas, united within the *iGiselle* project, beginning with a framing of the body in technology and the body in dance. There is much to be explored in this territory, and thus my introductory approach will resist favouring a single aspect of the *iGiselle* project or a single lens through which to reflect upon it.

The Development of *iGiselle*

I was invited to work as a research assistant on the *iGiselle* project because of my interest in interactive art installation and bodily engagement with digital technologies. I worked with the *iGiselle* team during the final year of my Master of Fine Arts degree. Early in the development of *iGiselle*, we explored several game platforms that would allow us to re-imagine *Giselle*. Our choices were informed by our capacities as a small team, and the first major component we developed was the narrative for our game. Having watched five ballets from the Golden Age of Romantic and Classical ballet—*La Sylphide, Giselle, La Bayadère, Swan Lake,* and *Sleeping Beauty*—we found that the story of *Giselle* resonated with us most strongly, and so we used it as the basis for our game narrative. The experience of having Nora Foster Stovel guide us through the historical and artistic significance of each performance provided us with a useful introduction to the form, and we discussed ballet at length in a casual setting as we got to know one another.[1] Within our video game we wanted to be attentive to contemporary issues related to dance and ballet, such as representations of the female body, gender roles, and the physically demanding nature of ballet, while still maintaining some structural resemblance to the original story of *Giselle*. We reflected on how bodily representations and gender politics are being addressed increasingly within gaming culture. Critical discussions about sexualized representations of female bodies in games, as well as the male-dominated culture evident within gaming communities, are pushing the industry towards a more diverse and egalitarian culture. These issues were not overtly included in our game narrative, but they were present in our minds as we created *iGiselle*. A common critique of the representations of women in video games and especially women of colour is that these characters overwhelmingly represent stereotypes and often die or are killed within the game. As interdisciplinary scholar David J. Leonard points out, "more than 90% of African-American women function [in video games] as props, bystanders, or victims" (2). A parallel can be drawn between Giselle's lack of agency (and that of women in Romantic and Classical ballet more generally) and the roles of women in games. To illustrate these parallels, I offer the following brief outline of our *iGiselle* narrative.

Giselle is an aspiring young dancer who lives with her mother and has just been accepted as a new company member at Valiance Dance. On Giselle's first day with the company she meets the promising young artistic director, Albert, who immediately takes a liking to her. Giselle also encounters Henry, a childhood friend, and Beatrice, who quickly becomes Giselle's romantic and professional rival.[2] Giselle is given the lead role in the company's production of *Giselle*, to the great pleasure of her mother, Betty, and to the dismay of Beatrice. The role proves to be very demanding for the young dancer, who should be mindful of her heart condition, but Albert and Betty push Giselle hard in preparation for opening night. Albert spends a lot of time alone with Giselle, and they develop a strong attraction to one another. Giselle's mother throws a party in honour of her daughter's success, and Albert takes the opportunity to publicly announce that he believes he and Giselle should get married. (Here, the player must decide whether to accept or refuse Albert's proposal.)

The first act of *iGiselle* ends with an accident, and in Act II Giselle finds herself in a dark forest surrounded by the Wilis (ethereal ghostly women who were jilted before their wedding day) led by the vengeful Myrtha. Giselle is swept up by the Wilis and forced to dance tirelessly under the power of Myrtha, Queen of the Wilis. Myrtha then informs Giselle that her accident was in fact an attack planned by someone close to her. Myrtha and two other Wilis bring Giselle on a haunting tour of recent events in an effort to convince her that Albert, her mother, and her rival Beatrice have all been conspiring against her. Myrtha then asks Giselle whether she will take revenge upon the guilty person, and the player must decide who is guilty as well as whether or not to take revenge. There are several possible endings for the game, depending on what choices the player has made: Giselle leaves the dance world to pursue her academic interests; Giselle helps her mother set up a dance academy; Albert is exposed for his incompetence and neglect, and his career is ruined; Beatrice has an accident and never dances again; or, in the most dire scenario, Giselle never wakes up from her coma and must remain a Wili forever.[3]

Given the diverse backgrounds of our team members, our approaches to narrative were varied, and we had lively discussions about the creative direction and details of the story. Our plan for paralleling the original 1841 *Giselle* libretto worked well, given the objectives of our colleagues in computing science who wanted to design an artificially intelligent system that would repair narrative breaks while keeping the player on an author-specified emotional arc. It might have felt counter-intuitive to ground the story on a predetermined emotional arc, had we been creating a narrative from scratch. This example demonstrates the different approaches of members of our interdisciplinary team; the resulting creative work is a hybrid of our ideas, respective areas of expertise, and aesthetic sensibilities. By working together, taking a curiosity-driven approach, we shared expertise and exchanged ideas, converging around the central research question of what would happen if Giselle did not die, and we examined options for providing a player with alternatives to explore within this classic tale.

After developing our story into a script, our next step was to acquire the visual components for the game. We considered the popular game design platform Unity but decided after a few trials that this tool would require resources well beyond our capabilities, and we found limitations in it as well. For example, the stock characters readily available all had the slim physiques typically found in games, and the clothing had to be tight because the physics within the game platform could not handle the processing required to emulate looser fabric. We concluded that by using photography as a medium we would have more flexibility and would be able to achieve a distinctive aesthetic for *iGiselle*.

We held auditions for local dancers interested in working with us, and then photographed each character against a studio green screen in numerous ballet poses and still-shots with various facial expressions. The background imagery was added, subsequently, in post-production. We also held auditions for voice actors to narrate our story. This simple combination of auditory and visual storytelling allowed us to create an engaging interface with minimal programming and computer-processing power.

The Kinect is a motion-capture device used for gestural gaming developed by Microsoft, first introduced in 2010. The Kinect was meant to appeal to novice players, who might be less comfortable with a traditional game controller that can include a dozen buttons and joysticks (Pham). Whereas our use of the Kinect relied on the player striking a single pose emulating the ballet position shown on-screen, the most advanced gestural interfaces track a player's movements in real time throughout a game. This advanced tracking was not necessary for our game, since we used the Kinect as a game controller to allow the player to experience ballet poses first-hand. We had to simplify the dance positions, however, for technical reasons related to body occlusion and limb-tracking problems that we encountered. We also chose simple poses in order to maintain accessibility among players with different levels of physical ability. Although relatively simple, the ballet poses may present bodily positioning that is foreign to some players, thus making them more aware of their bodies. For dancers, the positions might be reminiscent of early training experiences. When a narrative rupture occurs, the players have on-screen options to choose from and must assume the physical pose associated with their choice. Once the dancer is in position, the Kinect registers the player's matching posture, and the game continues. The physical engagement required by the players emphasizes the degree of skill required to perform classical ballet and helps the players to feel engaged in the story by investing more fully in their narrative options.

The potentialities of this type of physical, embodied engagement with digital media are explored in the following sections through the work of select philosophers and cultural theorists. While the *iGiselle* project demonstrated much of the generative potential discussed in the following sections, the full possibilities for *haptic creativity*, as defined by Myers and Dumit below—which propose rendering data sensible, thus prompting embodied engagements—extend beyond what we were able to implement in *iGiselle*, but they point towards exciting new avenues in this emerging hybrid genre of research.

Historical and Theoretical Framework

Human-computer interaction (HCI) is a major field of research that seeks to develop technological innovation in the gaming and entertainment industry, as well as in everyday applications. Traditionally, the approach within computing science and commercial enterprise has taken for granted a disembodied perspective on technological interactions, due in part to the Shannon-Weaver model of information that has dominated discourse in the information age ever since its development in the mid-twentieth century (Hansen xvi). This influential model of communication is more concerned with the probability of data being accessed than with the information contained within the communication signal itself (Hansen xvi). As digital technologies have become ubiquitous, however, user interface (UI) and user experience (UX) design have become key areas of development. UX and UI designers consider how the human body and the senses engage with technological objects. Similarly, full-body immersion that engages all the senses has been a goal within the creative arts since at least the nineteenth century when, most notably, composer and theatre director Richard Wagner revolutionized opera by seeking to synthesize the visual, musical, poetic and dramatic arts. More recently, virtual reality (VR), in development since the late twentieth century, has been striving to create convincing computer-generated environments that transcend the constraints of physics and allow the user to float freely through virtual environments. Impressive developments have been made in this area, including increasingly mainstream VR headsets. These headsets are equipped with two small screens that subsume a viewer's field of vision, giving the illusion of a three-dimensional space that shifts in relation to directional head movements. The limitations of this sort of immersion quickly become apparent, however, as the users have no body within the virtual world and thus cannot see their own hands (or, at best, may see a crude polygon-based rendering of a body), thus adding to the disembodied nature of the immersive VR experience. Sound is usually added to VR through headphones that can block out ambient noise, but these add weight to the apparatus and can be distracting or uncomfortable.

Through the following discussion of the body in technology and the body in dance, I will demonstrate some of the ways that dance offers insight into how embodied haptic experience with technology can bring greater immersion and engagement with digital media and virtual environments, ideally offering a more immersive and enjoyable experience for the viewer. What is at stake for users is the possibility of a more sustainable relationship with digital technology, wherein an embodied perspective on the technological form and media content encourages critical reflection on forms of engagement. Furthermore, these same methods of thinking through the body require the kind of comfortable discomfort and risk-taking that can help researchers working interdisciplinarily to open their practices to alternative ways of working and embracing partial knowledge.[4]

The Body in Technology

Persuasive challenges to the disembodied nature of interactions with digital technology have emerged in recent decades in the fields of philosophy, science and technology studies, and feminist cultural theory. Mark Hansen draws on the work of Donald Mackay to shift the focus from the well-established Shannon-Weaver model of information, with its focus on what information is, to a model that takes into account what information *does*. As Hansen points out, "The central notion of information in Shannon and Weaver's work is that the information carried by a message or symbol depends on its probability of being selected" (xvi). Hansen lays out the framework for a new phenomenology, in which the body is central to understanding digital media; according to Hansen, the body provides the material link between digital data and perception. The framing function of the physical body is required to make sense of information that is fundamentally meaningless without the actions taken by a user to decode it with the appropriate tools and knowledge. Drawing on Henri Bergson's understanding of embodiment, Hansen suggests that "media convergence under digitality actually increases the centrality of the body as framer of information: as media lose their material specificity, the body takes on a more prominent function as selective processor in the creation of images" (xvi). Hansen's description of the digital image places importance on the means through which a digital image becomes accessible and highlights the selective nature of perception. He emphasizes how information is filtered and chosen, based on what is most relevant to the perceiver (83). If we view digitality through the lens of Hansen's model, then, we may appreciate that physically repositioning a user of technology is one means of exploring alternative modes of bodily engagement that can shape perceptual experience. More specifically, a player assuming a ballet-inspired pose in iGiselle can be seen as enacting Hansen's description of the framing function of the body in perceiving digital images—the main difference being that a player is more actively engaged in embodied perception when the physical-digital connection is made explicit through a specific physical posture. "Rather than having an existence independent of the potential action of the perceiver, the image exists only in and through the actions of the perceiving body" (58).

N. Katherine Hayles presents embodiment as a non-dualistic concept that is crucial to understanding the relations at play in technological interactions.[5] Hayles's term "mindbody," borrowed from Mark Hansen, signifies an emergent unity among complex, interactive and holistic entities ("Flesh and Metal" 299). The thrust of Hayles's argument is a call to consider the interactions that emerge between entities, rather than accepting their "precoded" and "prevalued" status ("Flesh and Metal" 298). That is, she proposes to "focus on the idea of relation and posit it as the dynamic flux from which both the body and embodiment emerge," rather than thinking dualistically about the mind and body ("Flesh and Metal" 298). Hayles highlights the rich and complex relations of the mindbody as these relations extend into and constitute perception, sensation, and proprioception (one's sense of one's own body in space). Hayles's argument supports placing importance on the body and embodiment when designing compelling interactions with technology. Following from Hayles's proposition that the mindbody is constituted by the unity between action and perception, what new relations might emerge through embodied interactions between humans and machines?

I reference the work of Hansen and Hayles because these two well-known figures highlight the importance of the body in perception and particularly in technological interactions. With emphasis on the importance of a holistic approach to new media forms that value the full spectrum of aesthetic experience and perceptual sensory processes, there is less risk of falling into a troublesome and limiting disembodied aesthetic experience. This approach can help maintain a connection to embodied perceptual experience and push innovative thinking to go beyond the habitual in design, research, and creative processes, allowing greater generative risk-taking to come into play. To present the socially constructed nature of bodily movements, particularly in classical ballet, I turn now to Marcel Mauss's concept of *habitus* and then to Natasha Myers and Joe Dumit's work on *haptic creativity*.

In an influential 1935 essay, Mauss examines how members of cultures and societies use their bodies in particular ways. He looks at physical habits that serve more than biological necessity in order to address the social nature of various gestures and techniques. Mauss uses the Latin term *habitus* to highlight the acquired nature of habit beyond incidental customs, as would be implied by the French term *habitude*. Mauss is fascinated by the causes of shifts in habitus that occur over time and across cultural differences. These adaptations are equivalent to such learned techniques as those acquired to play instruments or use specialized equipment; consequently, Mauss refers to the body as the human's "first and most natural instrument" (75). While there is a risk of returning to dualistic thinking in conceiving of the body as an object or instrument, Mauss describes the social, psychological and biological elements that constitute the habitus as being "indissolubly mixed together" (74). Mauss's terminology is useful when we come to consider the body as a form of technology, which is then further extended by prosthetic technological devices that are employed, often with proprioceptive capacity. The study of classical ballet is an ideal example of applying learned techniques to the body as an instrument. The techniques practised by dancers alter their physical way of being in the world (and their physique)—much as the use of instruments becomes natural and affords enhanced movement and ability. As dancers learn techniques for movement, their new abilities for bodily expression lead to a new understanding of space and their positioning within it, enabling greater aptitude for learning further techniques.

On a similar note, Hayles describes "the force of habits to shape embodied responses—especially proprioception, the internal sense that gives us the feeling that we occupy our bodies rather than merely possess them" ("Flesh and Metal" 299). As Hayles reports, video game players insist that to be successful at a game they must project themselves proprioceptively into the simulated game space ("Flesh and Metal" 300). She points out that humans have one of the longest periods of neotony, which is characterized by the capacity to develop and change the nervous system, allowing for adaptations to new techniques and new technological instruments ("Flesh and Metal" 300).

An exciting example of this model of technologically enhanced proprioception and its effects on perception, understanding, and ways of being is presented by Myers and Dumit, who characterize the physical bodies of scientific researchers as "excitable tissues," in work that offers unique entryways to reconsidering perception, affect and action in laboratory experimentation (239). Myers and Dumit also draw upon the work of Bergson, a philosopher who argued that perception and movement combine to produce, in the body's nervous tissue, a "kind of motor tendency in a sensory nerve" that produces affect and responsive actions (qtd. in Myers and Dumit 239). Myers and Dumit's model of haptic creativity is part of a wider reorientation towards alternative modes of understanding scientific processes and different scales of life. There is increasingly a recognition of the limitations of scientific models that omit partial knowledges in favour of claiming absolute truths. In light of this recognition, Myers and Dumit explore alternative ways of engaging with their objects of study, through a model that highlights the positionality of the researcher by critically engaging bodily positions and movements. By studying a biologist who uses time-lapse media to visualize living cells and a geologist working with interactive 3D visualizations, for instance, the authors find that both scientists "engage their technologies to become entangled *kinesthetically* and *affectively* with their data" (240, emphasis original), resulting in personal and individualized engagements with responsive media and thus maximizing what Myers and Dumit call haptic creativity. In their view, such research practice alters the spatial and temporal scales of visual media and interactive models to render data sensible, often in a playful manner. Furthermore, haptic creativity is an experimental approach that can lead researchers into new territories, lead them to question what might be possible to know, and allow leaps into previously inconceivable discovery. Moreover, this practice results in shared excitement when the researchers convey their experience and understanding to others. On this point, the authors invoke Bruno Latour's provocation—"Is not being moved, or rather, put into motion by the informants exactly what we should mean by an enquiry?" (qtd. in Myers and Dumit 241).

In Myers and Dumit's work, the term *mid-embodiments* describes the partial and tentative nature of a body that is in the process of studying, experiencing, and understanding data through haptic inquiry. In their terms, this process creates a relationship between researcher and subject matter that resembles the relationship between "partners in a contact improvisational dance" (249). This comparison challenges us to take seriously the possibility that dance itself may be a type of physical exploration that can yield knowledge not available for discovery by other means. Related work from the world of dance supports an embodied exploratory process.

The Body in Dance
"The Dancer's Body" is José Gil's contribution to the collection of essays edited by Brian Massumi, entitled *A Shock to Thought*, which explores the expressive philosophy of Giles Deleuze and Felix Guattari within the context of cultural studies, philosophy, and art theory. Gil discusses the work of Merce Cunningham at length. As a choreographer, Cunningham became

well known for introducing elements of randomness and for deconstructing or re-composing customary sequences of organic movement. This approach led to new kinds of unusual dance movements, such as shifting the body's gravitational centre to explore motions that seem counter-intuitive and thus illuminate alternative bodily movements. Cunningham's work was considered revolutionary because of the way it deconstructed the language of dance. When asked how he did it, Cunningham would say, "'How do you do it?' By doing it" (125). Cunningham's words echo Zen philosophy, which guided his methodology and practice. Gil describes Cunningham's technique of "emptying out movement" (121), which is reminiscent of the well-known Zen aphorism of needing to empty one's cup before filling it up again; to Gil this aphorism applies to the mental state of a practitioner of meditation, or, in this case, a dancer. If the dancer begins as a sort of blank slate, open to spontaneous action, her movements will have to create their own logic and meaning through the process of being created and sequenced iteratively and responsively. This could be considered a break from her habitus. As difficult as this may be to imagine, it must be even more challenging to perform. With repeated effort, however, the result can be compelling and always new. A list of other artistic forms that employ this improvisational principle includes abstract expressionism in visual art, improvisational performance art, and a number of musical styles including jazz, compositions by John Cage, or performative noise music. It is not as common in theoretical or academic work, due to the importance of structural and institutional norms, but the idea of emptying one's disciplinary cup before engaging in cross-disciplinary collaboration is a promising one that could help guide those hoping to follow research questions into unexplored territory through creative cross-disciplinary journeys. This could result in a non-objective positioning that is open to alternative and responsive ways of thinking and being.

The potential of this sort of exploration is vividly described by Zeynep Gündüz, who explores the relationship between bodies and interactive technologies in order to understand how the boundaries of the body are redefined by technology, particularly in dance. Gündüz reflects on her first-hand experience in a contemporary dance class with the Belgian dancer and choreographer Peter Jasko, who instructs dancers to experiment with improvisation that alters habitual movement patterns. As a result of this exercise, Gündüz states, "the body teaches itself innovative ways of moving because the discovered new sensations not only expand the body's movement vocabulary but affect the body's experience of being-in-movement" (312). A shift in perspective can open up research opportunities as well. To emphasize why this move is critical, I now turn to Haraway's definition of feminist objectivity.

Embodying Situated Objectivity

In her oft-referenced publication "Situated Knowledge: The Science Question in Feminism and the Privilege of Partial Perspective," Haraway addresses the power dynamics at work in scientific fields of inquiry and examines how claims of objectivity have constructed and perpetuated colonial, patriarchal and relativistic authority at the expense of genuine inquiry. She refers to this rhetoric and teleological power structure as a "God trick" that works to validate all-knowing claims that are unquestioningly posited from the point of view of nowhere ("Situated Knowledges" 584). Instead, she calls for a feminist objectivity that includes partial perspective and situated knowledges; such an approach, Haraway argues, can prompt greater responsibility in scientific pursuits by requiring scientists to be attentive to forms of knowledge that may challenge institutional traditions. The following passage is particularly relevant to interdisciplinary research:

> The science question in feminism is about objectivity as positioned rationality. Its images are not the products of escape and transcendence of limits (the view from above) but the joining of partial views and halting voices into a collective subject position that promises a vision of the means of ongoing finite embodiment, of living within limits and contradictions—of views from somewhere. ("Situated" 590)

Haraway's critique of the all-seeing, all-knowing perspective in scientific inquiry relates to her later writing on cyborgs (*Simians*). Cyborg imagery encompasses the contradictory, complex, animalistic and technological characteristics of the posthuman. The Romantic Giselle of 1841 was conceived of as an ethereal creature born to dance, love, and then die. As re-imagined in *iGiselle*, this heroine belongs to many worlds and has complex relationships contingent on those around her and dependent on the choices she makes. Giselle has agency that is transferred to and reliant upon the game player. She may still not survive the game, but we envisioned our Giselle as a cyborg, and we hoped that players would conclude that, to borrow an appropriate line from Haraway, "I would rather be a cyborg than a Goddess" (*Simians* 181).

Contradictory views can (and hopefully do) arise in cross-disciplinary work. Accepting these frictions, learning to see, move and maybe even dance through them, holds promise for innovative research. Similarly, research that drives technological development could benefit from a shift in perspective in how we conceive of the roles of the senses, the body, and of our technological tools. Here, too, emptying one's cup of once-cherished notions about what technology does and for whom seems critical to progressive and sustainable development.

Conclusion

I have offered here an analysis and theoretical framing of the body in technology and the body in dance in relation to what I believe are some of the most interesting aspects of the *iGiselle* project. My reflections on interdisciplinary research have been informed by my experience on this project, considered alongside contemporary feminist theory. This experience has clarified for me the importance of interdisciplinary and transdisciplinary[6] collaboration. Recent literature on interdisciplinarity places value on the exploration of practices that extend beyond disciplinary affinities in favour of methods that are responsive to the needs and creative potential present within a research project. For example, Natalie Loveless refers to such methods as involving "situated accountability," and she calls for "responsive and 'response-able' dialogue between sources, inspirations, discourses, and stakes" (98). This discourse on interdisciplinarity goes beyond the scope of this chapter, but it represents an exciting field of inquiry born out of the acknowledgement that interdisciplinary research represents some of the most innovative work currently being undertaken in—and beyond—the academy. This acknowledgement is crucial to the support of ground-breaking knowledge production. Loveless is interested in the potential for truly interdisciplinary work that could emerge from research-creation methodologies; indeed, the difficulties inherent in the disciplinary model common to educational institutions have long been criticized. This issue was well articulated in 1976 by Samuel Bowles and Herbert Gintis:

> With the specialization of jobs in the economy has come a fragmentation of studies and research. Increasingly, students and researchers are discouraged from dealing with a whole problem, just as the worker is forbidden to produce a whole product. The artificial compartmentalization of intellectual pursuits allows the development of advanced technique within each area and simultaneously militates against the application of comprehensive moral standards or the consideration of the larger social consequences of one's work. (209)

By bringing together dance and HCI design, as well as video games and Romantic ballet, the *iGiselle* project succeeded in reconsidering each of these entities individually—and together. There is no question that cross-disciplinary approaches can result in research that benefits every domain considered, re-combined, and re-imagined. I have pushed this research further into the theoretical domains explored in this chapter as an extended analysis of this unique project, of which I feel fortunate to have been a part.

Notes

1. We also received an introduction to the world of video games with the guidance of our colleagues in the Department of Computing Science.

2. Similar characteristics and narrative threads are shared by characters in *iGiselle* and in the original 1841 *Giselle*, namely, Albert and Albrecht, Henry and Hilarion, Beatrice and Bathilde.

3. In the original *Giselle*, Prince Albrecht is forgiven by Giselle and spared by the Wilis, but we did not want to rely on a narrow conclusion that would have the players "win or lose" the game depending on whether or not they chose forgiveness.

4. I am referring here to Haraway's concept of partial knowledge, which I explain further in the concluding section of this text.

5. Hayles introduces this position at the end of her well-known publication *How We Became Posthuman* (1999) and further explores it in "Flesh and Metal: Reconfiguring the Mindbody in Virtual Environments" (2002).

6. A concise description of the differences between interdisciplinarity and transdisciplinarity is offered by Henry Daniel (drawing on the work of Basarab Nicolescu): "Interdisciplinarity and transdisciplinary are thus two very different concepts that serve two very different intentions. The former goes between and tries to mediate, while the latter goes across and tries to create new frameworks and solutions to address a wider set of concerns" (462).

Works Cited

Bergson, Henri. *Matter and Memory*. New York: Zone Books, 1991.

Bowles, Samuel, and Herbert Gintis. *Schooling in Capitalist America: Educational Reform and the Contradictions of Economic Life*. New York: Basic, 1976.

Daniel, Henry. "Writing Dance in the Age of Technology: Towards Transdisciplinary Discourse." *Forum for Modern Language Studies* 46.4 (2010): 460–73.

Gil, José. "The Dancer's Body." In *A Shock to Thought: Expression After Deleuze and Guattari*. Ed. Brian Massumi. London: Routledge, 2002. 117–27.

Gündüz. Zeynep. "Digital Dance: Encounters Between Media Technologies and the Dancing Body." *At the Interface / Probing the Boundaries* 85.1 (2012): 309–33.

Hansen, Mark. *New Philosophy for New Media*. Cambridge, MA: MIT Press, 2004.

Hayles, N. Katherine. "Flesh and Metal: Reconfiguring the Mindbody in Virtual Environments." *Configurations* 10.2 (2002): 297–320.

———. *How We Became Posthuman*. Chicago: U of Chicago P, 1999.

Haraway, Donna. "Situated Knowledges: The Science Question in Feminism and the Privilege of Partial Perspective." *Feminist Studies* 14.3 (1988): 575–99.

———. *Simians, Cyborgs and Women: The Reinvention of Nature*. New York: Routledge, 1991.

Henry, Daniel. "Writing Dance in the Age of Technology: Towards Transdisciplinary Discourse." *Forum for Modern Language Studies* 46.4 (2010): 460–73.

Leonard, David. "'Live in Your World, Play in Ours': Race, Video Games, and Consuming the Other." *Studies in Media & Information Literacy Education* 3.4 (2003): 1–9.

Loveless, Natalie. "Practice in the Flesh of Theory: Art, Research, and the Fine Arts PHD."
    Canadian Journal of Communication 37.1 (2012): 93–108.

Mauss, Marcel. "Techniques of the Body." *Economy and Society* 2.1 (1973): 70–88.

Myers, Natasha, and Joe Dumit. "Haptic Creativity and the Mid-embodiments of
    Experimental Life." In *A Companion to the Anthropology of the Body and Embodiment.* Ed.
    F. Mascia-Lees. Oxford: Wiley-Blackwell, 2011. 239–61.

Pham, Alex. "E3: Microsoft Shows Off Gesture Control Technology for Xbox 360." *Los Angeles
    Times.* Technology. June 1, 2009. latimesblogs.latimes.com/technology.

7

Renewing Adolphe Adam's Score

Creating the Music for iGiselle

CREATING THE MUSICAL SCORE for Nora Foster Stovel and Vadim Bulitko's innovative ballet-themed video game *iGiselle* involved the customary creative process: one per cent inspiration and ninety-nine per cent perspiration. After the initial fun of researching musical concepts and listening to music by nineteenth-century composers, including Adolphe Adam's 1841 score for *Giselle*, and formulating my ideas for this project, the composition of *iGiselle* involved many revisions and reiterations.

While preparing to compose the music for *iGiselle* I researched the roles played by music in Adam's *Giselle*, beginning with *Grove Music Online*. In the early to mid-nineteenth century, ideas concerning the meaning of music were undergoing radical changes, and these new ideas, such as the concept of "tone poems" (also known as "symphonic poems"), influenced my approach to composing the music for *iGiselle*. Franz Liszt called his compositions of 1848–1858 *symphonische Dichtung* (symphonic poems), reflecting the concept of music gaining currency at the time: classical works should represent narratives, poems, or scenes; and, by referencing texts and scenes outside itself, music could create a heightened emotional effect. German composer Carl Loewe described one of his 1828 pieces as a *Tondichtung* (tone poem), suggesting that this conception of music had already become influential. As English musicologist Hugh Macdonald argues, "the symphonic poem met three nineteenth-century aesthetic goals: it related music to outside sources; it often combined or compressed multiple movements into a single principle section; and it elevated instrumental program music to an aesthetic level that could be regarded as equivalent to, or higher than opera." Roger Scruton explains Liszt's contribution to this concept through his idea of "programme music":

> He considered the idea of exalting the narrative associations of music into a principle of composition to be incompatible with the continuance of traditional symphonic forms. In this break with the western musical tradition, his term "programme music," then, came to be applied not only to music with a story, but also to music designed to represent a character (Strauss's Don Juan *and* Don Quixote) *or to describe a scene or phenomenon (Debussy's* La mer).

Thus, musical scores supported the narrative arc of operas and ballets and expressed characters' emotions and relationships.

A similar musical-narrative connection was what I aimed for in my score for *iGiselle*, a score that consisted of six musical pieces, or themes, designed to be inserted throughout the game as appropriate. The opening 16 bars of the first piece present a musical theme in the melody that introduces the emotional content of Giselle's initial dance practices at Valiance Dance. The music at this point is simple and light, with a melody carried in the solo strings that expresses Giselle's hopefulness. The brief parting dialogue between Giselle and her mother, Betty, underscores the importance of this moment, as Giselle leaves the support of her mother for the challenges of dancing in this new studio. The everyday quality of the words contrasts with their importance as a turning point for Giselle when she says, "See you after class, Mom!" and her mother replies, "Good luck, Giselle. Make me proud. Don't overdo it, Dear, remember your heart condition." Betty's voice "trails off" as Giselle turns to enter the ballet studio, and she reflects on having to let her daughter go, while Giselle crosses the threshold into a world that is out of her maternal control (Act I, Scene 1). Supporting Betty's feelings, the solo strings in the music are joined by lines that harmonize with the alto voice; these are intended to represent Betty's good wishes for her daughter as they part.

Adam's score for *Giselle* can be understood in terms of the musical concepts of the nineteenth-century symphonic poem through its motifs, or brief musical phrases, that are associated with specific characters in the ballet. Thus, the music conveys the characters' relationships as the plot unfolds, involving the love triangle of Albrecht, Giselle, and Hilarion. Clearly the music in *Giselle* is intended to play a vital part in telling the story, as Christina Gier explains in Chapter 2 of this volume.

Throughout the process of creating the musical score for *iGiselle*, I was influenced by the storytelling possibilities of music itself and by music's potential to express characters' emotions. For example, the second musical theme begins with a swelling two-note pattern from the string section. Then the soft attack of the clarinet that takes the melody, with the string section responding in an 8-bar motif that is conversational in tone, supports the connection that Albert and Giselle are starting to feel for each other. At the end of the clarinet's second statement, the second-last note goes a half-step too low before settling on the tonic, or home note, that provides the conclusion to the phrase. Movements like this just outside the scale suggest the emotional tension of the events of the narrative. As the narrator indicates at the beginning of the third scene, Albert and Giselle "begin to develop feelings for one another" as they work out the choreography for the Valiance Dance premiere of *Giselle* (Act I, Scene 3). The emotions Giselle experiences in *iGiselle* are now becoming intense. Together with having suddenly been cast as the lead in *Giselle*, the first ballet production of a new dance company, Giselle also feels pressure from her mother, who is proud of her daughter but afraid that she will fail and cause her embarrassment.

The emotional palette of the music also helps support the drama that is building in the scene that follows. Betty organizes a party for all the dancers to celebrate Giselle's breakout role, but, as the video game's narrator explains, "Betty enjoys the party with pride, but she keeps a close eye on Giselle, constantly watching to make sure Giselle doesn't embarrass her." The underlying emotional tension that Giselle feels from her doting, yet critical, mother is reflected in the music's repeated strings that sound gentle and well-meaning at first, but eventually become repetitive and irritating. Adding to the push and pull of feelings in this scene, Beatrice, Giselle's rival for the title role in the ballet and for the attentions of Albert, the director of Valiance Dance, is "brooding in the corner of the room," feeling jealous of Giselle's sudden success in Albert's new dance company (Act I, Scene 3). The crowning moment of this scene, however, which heightens the emotional intensity, is Albert's announcement: "Everyone, I'd like to have your attention. Giselle, I've decided we should get married!" This dramatic announcement is the culmination of the romance that has developed during their private rehearsals. Musically, the woodwinds carrying the melody throughout the first half of the sound piece emphasize the ambivalence of the position into which Giselle is now thrust: suddenly successful and the centre of attention, she is also vulnerable and isolated, as even her good friend Henry, based on the character of Hilarion, begins to distance himself from her.

Marriott's historical overview of Adam's score for *Giselle* emphasizes the importance of Adam's use of woodwinds to convey the emotional content of the music. Adam's use of the oboe, which Marriott calls the "expressive solo writing" that Adam draws on to paint the sonorous canvas that conveys emotional shadings "with economy of means," influenced my use of the clarinet to support the emotional shifts that Giselle experiences. Marriott explains Adam's method, which influenced my compositions for *iGiselle*: "Throughout the ballet, colourful orchestration makes much of the typical orchestral resources of the time. Contrast of individual instrumental sounds was particularly a feature of the developing French orchestral tradition...and Adam was especially skilled in writing French theatre music." In a similar vein, the music for the third piece I composed for *iGiselle* builds to include brass instruments, representing the involvement of the partygoers in the announcement and the excitement it inspires. At the end of this musical section the woodwinds return from the start of the piece, bringing the focus back to the personal level of the individual relationships.

This narrowing of the emotional scope to a personal level was an important feature of Adam's score as well—an approach that contrasted with the music of "heroic grandeur" that most French composers created for the nineteenth-century theatre: "Processions, ceremonies, and rituals, tableaux, and spectacular stage effects were strong features of such long, grandiose productions" (Marriott). These spectacles were characteristic of the ideals of the Romantic Movement, which encouraged the expression of emotion, in contrast to the rational formalism of the preceding era. These ideals are defined, for example, in E.T.A. Hoffman's celebratory 1810 review of Ludwig van Beethoven's *Fifth Symphony*. As music critic Jim Samson explains, "it was Hoffmann's fusion of ideas already associated with the term 'Romantic,' used in opposition to the restraint and formality of Classical models, that elevated music, and especially instrumental music, to a position of pre-eminence in Romanticism as the art most suited to the expression of emotions" (qtd. in "Romantic Music"). Orchestral music's potential to express emotions can be heard throughout Adam's score for *Giselle*, which interweaves motifs, rhythmic patterns, and orchestral textures to emphasize the emotions in the intensified theatre of personal relationships.

Similarly, the crescendo of emotions following Albert's announcement in Act I, Scene 3, that he wants to marry Giselle is supported by the music for *iGiselle*. Here the narrative presents three options for the game player, each with an expected emotional response from Giselle. The first response is anger, as Giselle is upset by an announcement that does not respect her privacy and autonomy: "How can he think I would want to get married right now?" The second option emphasizes her ambivalence, suggesting that she might have entertained the idea herself, as she turns to her mother for advice: "What do you think I should do, Mom? He caught me off guard." The third option conveys Giselle's excitement at the possibility of marrying the director of the dance studio she has just joined: "Can you believe he proposed tonight? I'll be Mrs. Albertson!" Each scenario turns on Giselle's response to Albert's accelerating their romantic relationship, while emphasizing the element that Romantic writers, artists and musicians considered paramount—the inner world of emotion.

The music accompanying the moment following Albert's announcement conveys strong emotion, reflecting the intimate world of Giselle and Albert's deepening relationship. The woodwinds begin by carrying the melody once again, tossing the motif back and forth with the flutter of the grace notes, as if an animated conversation were taking place between two people. In the middle of the piece the emotional intensity swells as the string sections take over the motif. The woodwinds also join in, buoyed by the sense of possibility in the pleasant harmonies of the intervals of the thirds and sixths throughout these passages. Then this wave of emotion begins to quiet, emphasized by the grounding effects of the lower brass and woodwinds that play only the first notes of the 1–2–3 waltz rhythm pattern. Although cymbals are often used to create grand dramatic effects, in this clip the cymbal sounds are quiet, drawing the listener closer, just as Giselle and Albert's relationship is becoming more intimate.

Because my score was intended to accompany a ballet video game and relate to the physical movements of the dancers, the music vocabulary is also in conversation with the dance vocabulary to tell the story of *iGiselle*. Adam employed programmatic orchestration to help tell the story of *Giselle*, as well as motifs to represent the characters. Similarly, in *iGiselle* the waltz time signature is used at the beginning to indicate Giselle's excitement as a new member of Albert's dance studio. The waltz rhythm returns again in the fifth theme, where Albert has just finished pushing the dancers to exhaustion as they rehearse for their upcoming performance of *Giselle*, culminating in the light fixture falling onto the stage, narrowly missing Giselle, and contributing to plunging her into a coma. The fast pace of the dance is echoed in the *vivace* tempo of the music, but, in contrast with the first waltz, this second one contains more harsh, shrill tones in the melody and the harmonizing lines, to emphasize the tension that the dancers, especially Giselle, feel in preparing for their premiere performance. In the waltz can be read the features of this popular nineteenth-century dance form, but the brass instruments' repeating phrases, which continue to rise near the top of their registers, highlight the dancers' stress. This tense music underscores Giselle's mother's lack of sympathy for Giselle's accident—instead blaming her for the near-tragedy. Her mother's cold response, frightening in its lack of emotion, contributes to Giselle's portentous nightmare of being "trapped in a dark forest dancing forever with no hope of escape" (Act I, Scene 6).

Together with referencing nineteenth-century concepts of story and emotion in orchestral music evoked by Adam's *Giselle* score, the music for *iGiselle* is inflected by concepts of sound from the world of video games. For example, several theorists argue that the purpose of video game soundscapes, especially in the big blockbuster titles—ranging from *Call of Duty: Black Ops* to *Skyrim* and *Halo*—is to lift the players out of their seats and transport them to this imagined world, where the players can gain powers and a kind of immortality based on their achievements in the game. This argument is expressed by composer Walter Murch, who explains the power of sound to create imaginary worlds:

> This metaphoric use of sound is one of the most flexible and productive means of opening up a conceptual gap into which the fertile imagination of the audience will reflexively rush, eager to complete circles that are only suggested, to answer questions that are only half posed...Sound is as much an aesthetic choice as it is a reproduction of the imagined space. (qtd. in Collins 135)

The high-resolution sound effects, intense musical scores, and fast-paced dialogue present an unfamiliar, but more challenging, more rewarding world for the gamer. The player, wearing quality headphones or surrounded by a professional sound system, is transported to virtual worlds that the sound plays an integral role in creating. Game sound expert Karen Collins explains how many blockbuster games not only create an emotional effect through the soundscape, but also have a physical effect on the gamer through the sheer volume of the sound (137). A similar perspective is shared by K.J. Donnelly, William Gibbons, and Neil Lerner, researchers of the increasingly powerful effects of video game music, who state, "In a matter of only a few decades, game music has developed from extremely modest beginnings (the primitive bleeps and throbbings of early video games) into a medium of great complexity, affective expressivity, and increasing interactivity" (viii). Music professionals working in the gaming industry echo these opinions about the integral role that sound design plays in creating dynamic experiences for games. For example, in a recent interview, the music supervisor with Ubisoft Montréal, Bénédicte Ouimet, argues that "music is a huge element in a game. It helps create a link between the game developers' intentions and the players' experiences; all the while defining the fantasy and the mood. The atmosphere plays a large part in the game appreciation; even if we don't necessarily notice the music, we feel it."

The music for *iGiselle*, although subdued in many places, has a similar purpose in helping to construct the world of the game through stimulating sound. In *iGiselle* the music is created by using an ensemble of software-based orchestral instruments, including woodwind, brass, and string sections calculated to help players travel back in time to the mid-nineteenth-century setting of the original *Giselle* ballet. This score, composed of orchestral instruments, uses fewer decibels than the big video games with their range of high-intensity effects and electronic sounds, but the *iGiselle* score emphasizes the intimate scale of the relationships—as opposed to the setting of some video games, which are epic in scale, often allowing players to use advanced weapon systems to eliminate a mutant army and free a distant planet.

The intimate scale of the music in *iGiselle* underscores the personal world that the gamer pursues, even when it enters the dream sequences of Act II, where the setting moves from the everyday world of the dance studio to the fantastical world of the imagination. The main purpose of this part of the game, which breaks from the narrative of the original *Giselle*, is to allow Giselle to see the motivations affecting the behaviour of the people around her. When Giselle awakens in a dark forest in Act II, Scene 1, the figure of Myrtha appears and murmurs: "I'm afraid you've had an accident, Dear. You are here while your body rests and recovers. But don't worry. I'll take care of you and help you discover who has done this to you…Giselle, things are not always what they seem. You are a victim of jealousy and betrayal." The Wilis, ghostly figures drawn from the original ballet, reveal to Giselle the main insights she needs to understand what is going on in this world of the game: Albert's financial difficulties with Valiance Dance, Beatrice's jealousy of her success, and her mother's selfishness. The sixth theme that plays throughout this scene serves a vital role in transporting the player back to the atmosphere of the Romantic era. Here the instruments are drawn not from a full orchestra, but from a smaller ensemble of orchestral instruments to emphasize the personal dynamics evolving in the narrative. The higher-pitched quick, sharp phrases repeated throughout, plus the added timpani, dramatize the upsetting nature of the information the Wilis are imparting to Giselle.

The distinction between sounds that both players and characters in the game can hear (known as *diegetic sound*) and the sounds that only the players can hear (known as *non-diegetic sound*) allows the player to become further immersed in *iGiselle* as the music advances the concluding moments' narrative and conveys the characters' emotions (Collins 132). At the end of the game the sixth theme appears again, this time to introduce the concluding resolution of the musical motif, ending ultimately on the tonic of the D major chord—a sound the characters do not hear, as it plays only in the gamer's world. The resolution of the animated patterns and higher pitches that occur earlier in the piece helps to support the gamer's satisfaction at having given Giselle the agency to act autonomously, instead of following the advice of others.

The final consideration when composing the score for *iGiselle* involved the choice of software, since few composers use live orchestras to create musical support for games. Instead, composers often use composing software, or digital audio workstation (DAW), such as Avid ProTools, Motu Digital Performer, Steinberg Cubase, or Apple Logic Pro, with several banks of orchestral samples. A popular Virtual Studio Technology (VST) instrument that is used on many DAWs was developed by Native Instruments in Germany in 2002. Their samples, which include the Vienna Symphonic Instruments orchestral library, can be downloaded from their website and used in their computer program called Kontakt. Such compositional software allows the player to enter the world of Adam's nineteenth-century ballet score because of the emotional impact these orchestral sounds create. Dave

Stewart details the technical innovations for sound reproduction that the Vienna Symphonic team developed, including their "Symphonic Booth" and "Silent Stage," to reproduce the sound of an orchestra playing in a venue of any size—from a rehearsal studio, such as the Valiance Dance studio in *iGiselle*, to a huge concert hall. Such high-resolution instrument sampling allows composers to create highly accurate and refined nuances in the musical score, which was my goal as I composed music to accompany the world of *iGiselle*. For example, the third musical theme (heard in Act I, Scene 3) progresses from the trio lines of the flute, oboe, and violin and builds to a crescendo when the string section enters in the middle of the passage, helping to evoke the emotional complexity of Giselle's world. The pristine quality of the samples becomes important at the end of the sound cue, which suddenly quiets, suggesting Giselle's isolation, concluding with the gentle sound of a lightly tapped cymbal.

Each level of the musical score for *iGiselle*, with its storytelling power, its emotional expression, its entwined relation to the physical discipline of ballet, and its potential to immerse the player in the game, has an impact that contributes to the overall effect of this interactive gaming experience by drawing on both musical concepts influential during the mid-nineteenth century when Adam composed his score for *Giselle* and on principles employed in twenty-first-century video game musical scores.

Works Cited

Collins, Karen. *Game Sound: An Introduction to the History, Theory, and Practice of Video Game Music and Sound Design*. Boston: MIT Press, 2008.

Donnelly, K.J., et al. Preface. *Music in Video Games: Studying Play*. Ed. Donnelly et al. New York: Routledge, 2014, viii–xv.

Forbes, Elizabeth. "Adam, Adolphe (Charles)." *Grove Music Online*. Oxford UP. www.oxfordmusiconline.com/grovemusic.

Høholt, Henning. "Giselle—La Scala Milan in Paris." *Kulturkompasset* Feb. 6, 2015. www.kulturkompasset.com.

Marriott, Bruce. "The Musical World of Giselle." *ballet.magazine* March 2005.

"The Most Comprehensive Solo String Collection Ever Created." Overview
   of Vienna Symphonic Library—Solo Strings I Upgrade to Full
   Library. *ADK Pro Audio.* ADK Media Group. www.adkproaudio.com/
   vienna-symphonic-library-solo-strings-i-extended-library-2.

Nebel, Cecile. "Théophile Gautier and the Wilis." *Dalhousie French Studies* 39/40 (Summer/
   Fall 1997): 89–99. www.jstor.org/stable/40837168.

Ouimet, Bénédicte. "Music in Video Games." *Alice Studio de Performance.* Ubisoft
   Entertainment. Feb. 1, 2016. montreal.ubisoft.com/en/music-in-video-games/.

"Romantic Music." *Wikipedia.* en.wikipedia.org/wiki/Romantic_music.

Scruton, Roger. "Programme Music." *Grove Music Online.* Oxford UP.
   www.oxfordmusiconline.com/grovemusic.

Stewart, Dave. "VSL Orchestral Cube & Performance Set Pro Editions." Rev. of Performance
   Set Pro Edition and Orchestral Cube Pro Edition, by the Vienna Symphonic Library.
   Sound On Sound March 2004. www.soundonsound.com.

8

The Ballet Body and Video Games

A Feminist Perspective

In a forest glade, by the mouth of a cave, at the very jaws of hell—these are the settings for aberrant dancing. In these dark, enclosed environs furies wield their vipers, witches concoct their brews, the deranged dwell in agonized introspection, ghostly apparitions flicker in and out of visibility. (Foster, 1996b, p. 242)

AS NEW MEDIA TECHNOLOGIES have become increasingly accessible to general audiences, computer and video games have also become more popular. Although no comparable statistics are presently available for Canadian boys, a recent survey found that 99% of American boys play video games (Irvine, 2018). So do 94% of girls (Irvine, 2018). However, the vast majority of boys do not do ballet, whereas 85% of Canadian dancers are women (Ekos, 2014). Considering such statistics, gaming appears to be a male pastime, whereas ballet is an activity for girls. Yet these two activities, deeply divided by gendered lines and thus an unlikely match, were united in our interdisciplinary project, *iGiselle*, in which we set out to design a computer game based on the narrative structure of a Romantic ballet. Such an alliance is by no means unproblematic, for computer games, as well as ballet, have their critics. Nevertheless, since beginning this project, I, as a non-gaming feminist researcher of dance, have become increasingly fascinated by the possibilities computer games offer for the examination of feminist ethics and the reimagination of dance movement. In this chapter, I highlight some previous feminist assessments of computer games and ballet to examine the potential for marrying these superficially quite different activities.

Scholars generally agree that, because more men than women play video games, the majority of the games are designed to target a male audience (e.g., Dietz, 1998; Ivory, 2006). Although there are several types of video and computer games, including action, adventure, driving and flying, fighting, airborne combat, sports, role-playing, and simulation games, many of them depend on violent action or exploration of space (Jenkins & Cassell, 2008). Often the most violent games sell the most copies (Jenkins & Cassell, 2008). Their popular storylines—the hero overcomes a number of obstacles by either killing, fighting, or destroying them—emphasize stereotypical gender roles. Due to the proliferation of such games, there is a growing body of scholarly literature on the impact of video and computer games on their players. Some of this scholarship presents evidence that young gamers "see video game characters as role models" (Miller & Summers, 2007, p. 733) who, as such, potentially affect the players' body image, self-esteem, gender identity, and behaviour (including sexual). Thus, stereotypical gender representation or excessive violence in these games can shape the ways individuals understand acceptable gender relations or violence in general. Smith, Lachlan, and Tamborinin found that 78% of the 20 most popular video games in 1999 contained acts of violence that "would result in moderate to extreme harm in the real world" (cited in Scharrer, 2004, p. 394), while Dietz (1998) found that 80% of the games she studied (Nintendo and Sega Genesis video games) included violence or aggression as part of the strategy or object of the game. As a result, there has been increasing concern regarding the potential impact of interacting with the virtual world, where such severe violence is commonplace, and several studies have demonstrated an alarming connection between playing violent games and acting aggressively (e.g., Anderson & Bushman, 2001; Anderson & Dill, 2001; Kirsch, 1998; Sherry, 2001).

Despite such critiques of violence and its possible negative impact on player behaviour, some feminist researchers believe that equal numbers of girls and boys should have access to computer games, as a means of increasing women's interest in computer science generally and, more specifically, in the continually growing games industry (e.g., Cassell & Jenkins, 1998). Although the majority of women have played games at some point (Cassell & Jenkins, 1998), and up to 67% identify as game users (Miller & Summers, 2007), they remain, at best, a secondary market for the industry.[1] Others point out, however, that game design has now evolved to include more characteristics that are attractive to women (Dickey, 2006; Taylor, 2003), and, with such a growing market, it is has become increasingly important to cater to female consumers. Because women are the major consumers of ballet, there is not an equivalent need to increase their spectatorship or participation. On the contrary, the majority of feminist critics point to ballet as a potentially harmful or even exploitative and oppressive practice for women. Nevertheless, despite such differences, feminist scholars tend to suggest that the content of both ballet and computer games needs to be changed to better serve girls and women.

Women Characters in Games: Victimized and Sexualized

If it is, indeed, the case that video and computer game characters serve as role models for gamers, it is reasonable to assume that there need to be characters with whom aspiring female gamers can identify. Research to date, however, uniformly demonstrates a general lack of female characters; if present, they appear in stereotypical roles.

Video games include far more male than female characters (e.g., Beasley & Collins Standley, 2002; Dickey, 2006; Ivory, 2006; Miller & Summers, 2007; Scharrer, 2004). In her early study, Dietz (1998) discovered no female characters in 30% of the 33 games she analyzed. Similarly, Beasley and Collins Standley (2002) identified only 14% of all characters in their sample of 48

PlayStation and Nintendo games as female, whereas 72% were male. While five games in Dietz's sample portrayed women as heroes or action characters, women were most often non-playable characters, or NPCs (see also Dickey, 2006; Ivory, 2006). It must be noted that the majority of non-playable characters are also male (Miller & Summers, 2007). Still, the playable male characters are the heroes of the game, with more abilities and weapons than female characters. Male heroes are commonly depicted as very muscular (Scharrer, 2004) and powerful, often garbed in army attire (e.g., Miller & Summers, 2007) and bearing several types of weapons. In fact, Martins, Williams, Ratan, and Harrison (2011) assess the male video game characters they studied as being so much larger than the average American male, with significantly larger heads in particular, that they appeared "block-like" (p. 47) instead of possessing the lean, muscular, mesomorphic V-shaped male ideal found in other media sources. Yet these characters are not simply more muscular than the average male, just larger and blockier, and the researchers conclude that such a body shape is generally attainable for the average male player. Perhaps for this reason, there is little evidence of body dissatisfaction among male gamers.[2] Wack and Tantleff-Dunn (2008) even argue that, "unlike other forms of media, electronic gaming may have a weaker relationship to decreased appearance satisfaction or the formation of unrealistic standards of attractiveness" (p. 365). By contrast, the average female character in video games closely approximates the thin, unattainable feminine body ideal (Martins, Williams, Ratan, & Harrison, 2011).

In a video lecture on computer gaming for her blog *Feminist Frequency*, feminist researcher and game designer Sarkeesian (2013c) estimates that only 4% of all playable characters are female. Whether playable or not, female video game characters, she further argues, tend to fall into the categories of "damsel in distress", "Ms. male character", or highly sexualized background NPCs. Approaching the representation of female characters from a critical feminist perspective, Sarkeesian defines the damsel in distress character as a helpless woman "in a perilous situation," such as being kidnapped (2013a; see also Dickey, 2006; Dietz, 1998). The female character enters this situation passively: it simply happens to her. As a victim, the character then needs to be rescued by a male hero whose love interest or relation the female character commonly is. Princesses figure prominently as damsels in distress who commonly wear stereotypical feminine colours of pink or who are dressed in tight, revealing clothing with bare midriff, high heels, and a noticeable amount of makeup. As Sarkeesian argues, such representation objectifies the woman as a possession that a male character acts upon. Captured women are constructed as weak and incapacitated (by men) for the empowerment of other male characters, their rescuers. Some damsels are brutally murdered to create an incentive for the male character's revenge to initiate the actual game (2013b; see also Dietz, 1988). In their captivity, other damsels turn into evil spirits and actually beg the hero to kill them at the end of the game to be freed from their curses (Sarkeesian, 2013c). In these instances, female suffering is used to initiate male emotionality, but, Sarkeesian argues, the emotion is derived from the male character's failure to fulfill his masculinity, which can then be regained at the end of a successful game.

Some male characters (e.g., Pac-Man) have gained parallel playable female characters (Ms. Pac-Man). This is the second category of female game characters that Sarkeesian identifies. According to Sarkeesian in her fifth *Tropes vs Women* instalment, "Ms. Male Character" (2013d), these characters are defined in connection to the male character as his love interest (or mother) and are often dressed in stereotypically feminine pink clothing. Instead of overcoming objectification and victimization, such a representation reinforces (even if unintentionally) stereotypical gender representation: the male is the powerful active hero, and the female is the weak passive object of the male's actions. As Sarkeesian points out, this ideological construction of gender difference can be harmful, as it justifies women's subordination and, thus, reinforces male dominance. In this scenario, only the subordinate, helpless woman becomes desirable to a man.

In addition to being objectified and victimized, female characters in video and computer games are also sexualized. Several researchers, including Dietz (1998), Beasley and Collins Standley (2002), Ivory (2006), and Scharrer (2004), have observed that female characters wear skimpier and more revealing clothing than the male characters. Beasley and Collins Standley (2002), for instance, report that 86% of female characters in their study were shown with a low neckline that generously exposed their cleavage. Of these characters, 41% were voluptuous, and most of them "unrealistically large breasted" (p. 288). Such clothing accentuates the sexuality of these characters, who are also often engaged in sexualized behaviour. While this applies to most characters, according to Sarkeesian (2014a), the most sexualized are the female NPCs who are also most brutally victimized. These characters, she explains, are non-essential parts of the game plot or its strategy; they are ornamental decorations that the player encounters on the sidelines of his path—often prostitutes, strip-tease dancers, or women of colour—poor, low-life characters who can be instrumentalized as commodities, whose brutal treatment illustrates the male characters' right to kill or mutilate them. The NPCs are also easily interchangeable with other NPCs who exist to be murdered and then disposed of. What makes the treatment of these characters particularly grim is their non-essential position. Because the violence against them is not needed for the game to commence, the player often passively watches such brutality take place on the sidelines. While not initiated actively by the player, such events, as Sarkeesian argues (2014b), normalize overt sexualization and violence against women as a part of the system of patriarchal male dominance. Drawing on Laura Mulvey's gaze theory, Dickey (2006) similarly concludes that game players are constructed "as male subjects with female representations being the object of male gaze" (p. 787).[3] The explanation for this trend that many researchers, including Martins, Williams, Ratan, and Harrison (2011), offer is that, as video and computer games are mostly created by male designers for the male market, their content reflects assumed male preferences regarding femininity. In this, they turn out to be quite similar to Romantic ballets.

Women Characters in (Romantic) Ballet: Willowy Heroines

In contrast to what we find in computer and video games, females typically outnumber males on the ballet stage. The main characters of Romantic ballets are always women, the males playing supporting roles. In addition, ballet productions include a corps de ballet of female dancers who play various levels of supporting roles. Nevertheless, despite such a prominent female presence, several feminist researchers consider ballet a vehicle for patriarchal oppression. The shape of a ballerina's body, particularly, has received attention since the late 1980s from critical and psychoanalytic feminist dance researchers.

Much like Sarkeesian's reading of female characters in computer games, early analyses by Adair (1992) and Sherlock (1993) centre on the ideological construction of the image of the ballet body and how this image was constructed in support of patriarchal hegemony. Like Sarkeesian, these dance writers assert that, when deconstructed, the image of the ballet body reveals underlying ideologies structuring dance and, more broadly, femininity in western society. They conclude that the image of a ballet dancer, although different from the busty, openly sexualized female characters in computer games, emphasizes the characteristics connected with oppressive western femininity. First, these researchers point to the look of the ballet dancer—light, delicate, attractive—and her dance postures—the arch of the foot and the back, the turn-out of the legs, and the upwardness of the chest— that they find associated with western upper-class ideologies of the female aesthetic. Second, ballet characters, like female game characters, are often defined through their relationships to male characters as mothers, lovers, daughters, wives, or fiancées. Finally, although not often targets of equally explicit and brutal male violence as in computer games, ballet characters are divided dualistically into good and evil to reflect the dominant, male-defined ideas of femininity.

In the Romantic ballet *Giselle*, for example, the eponymous character represents the good, innocent, young peasant girl who sacrifices herself to allow her seducer to live, whereas Myrtha, the queen of the supernatural Wilis (ghosts of maidens who died before their wedding day), is a ruthless female who haunts men to distraction and eventually to death to avenge her disappointment. From the critical feminist perspective, such portrayals of women as weak, passive victims dependent on male actions are oppressive to women. Similar to many computer game plots, the ballet *Giselle* depicts its main character as passively waiting for the male hero, Albrecht, to arrive in her village. She eventually perishes because of Albrecht's actions: he is already engaged, but conceals the fact from Giselle, who dies of a broken heart. In Act II, as opposed to what we might find in computer games, Giselle acts to protect Albrecht, but the ending, in which she is awarded peace in death, is similar to the endings of many games. Therefore, although Giselle, unlike many female computer game characters, is the active leading heroine, her actions are clearly defined by the male (or by an evil female) character. Such representation of the ballet body, from a critical feminist perspective, perpetuates the patriarchal hegemony in society.

More recent analyses of the representation of the ballerina's body have employed Mulvey's concept of the male gaze that I introduced earlier in connection to female characters in computer games. Gaze theory has been widely used to analyze the ballet body by feminist dance studies scholars, including Adair (1992), Cooper Albright (1997), Daly (1987), Dempster (1988), Foster (1996b), and Wulff (1998). Much as feminist gaming researchers do, these scholars suggest that ballet, like film in Mulvey's theory, exposes the ballerina as an object for the male audience's desiring gaze. Female computer game characters, as we have seen, often appear in similar skin-tight clothing that exposes their cleavage. The ballerina's clothing emphasizes the dancer's body, and, thus, "the accent is on woman as object rather than subject" (Adair, 1992, p. 41). Her body shape (extreme thinness, a boyish look) is accentuated through her close-fitting leotard, her tutu, which displays the crotch and legs, and her low-cut tops, all of which stress her "to be looked-at-ness" (Adair, 1992, p. 42). Like many female characters in video and computer games, then, both roles and costumes for the ballerina focus on stereotypical portrayals of femininity that correspond to the male fantasy of women and femininity (Adair, 1992). She is, typically, either the virgin or the whore.

To dig deeper into psychoanalysis, some feminist dance researchers draw from Lacan's notion of the phallus. According to Lacanian psychoanalysis, men continually have to deal with their castration anxiety. As a result, they create fetishes that serve as a reassuring substitute for that which the man construes as missing in the woman's body—namely, the phallus. Adair (1992) likens the ballerina's body to the missing phallus and points out that the ballet pas de deux, particularly, emphasizes the ballerina's position as an object of male desire. Foster (1996a) elaborates: "*she* [the ballerina] conveys desire. *She* exists as a demonstration of that which is desired but is not real. *Her* body flames with the charged wantings of so many eyes, yet like flame it has no substance. *She* is, in a word, the phallus, and *he* embodies the forces that pursue, guide, and manipulate it" (p. 3, emphasis original). From a Lacanian point of view, the ballerina lacks a penis, and therefore lacks power, but is symbolically constructed as a phallus to enact male power. According to Foster, the ballerina's legs in particular reveal her phallic identity:

> *She looks like but isn't a penis. Her legs, her whole body become pumped up and hard yet always remain supple...Her sudden changes of direction and shifts of weight, always erect, resemble the penis's happy mind of its own, its inexplicable interest in negligible incidents. Yet, clearly, she is not a penis, she is a woman whose leg movements symbolise those of a penis.* (p. 13)

Therefore, symbolically, a ballerina's body reinforces the patriarchal order in society: "Supporting, underlying, founding, this phallic identity is ballet's perpetual upward thrust" (p. 14).

Read in this way, the ballerina confers phallic power upon male viewers by "enacting their scenarios and appearing as their fantasy projection" (Foster, 1996a, p. 14) and is entirely controlled by male desire. Foster further contends that many female ballet characters, such as Wilis, gypsies, or orientals, are created to attract men's attention, yet they bestow a stoic and potent male identity on the partnering male dancers and the male audience, thus reinforcing sexual difference. From such theoretical perspectives as these, the ballet body does not provide much for feminist projects.

While looking at the female ballet body from a feminist perspective, Banes (1998) rejects the psychoanalytical perspective, particularly the idea of the male gaze, as unsuitable for an analysis of dance. She also refuses a political agenda that labels ballet either as victimizing or celebrating the ballerina figure and, thus, as necessarily oppressive to women. Instead, Banes prefers to locate each ballet character within its historical context and the specific socio-political conditions of the period. Like other feminist researchers of dance, she acknowledges that ballet characters are shaped by debates about sexuality and feminine identity that surround them, but she insists that "they should not be judged as 'progressive' or 'reactionary' according to current postfeminist values" (p. 3). Instead, a careful analysis can illustrate how these images concurrently reinforce and critique "cultural conceptions of corporeality," because, "through dance, men's attitudes toward women and women's attitudes about themselves are literally given body on stage" (p. 1). As her primary tool of analysis, Banes uses the marriage plot that commonly engages the female dance characters in the ballet narrative. This plot, she argues, should not be judged as uniformly aligned with patriarchy, but needs to be analyzed as questioning the values of marriage. In her socio-historical analysis of *Giselle*, for example, Banes ventures beyond the interpretation that sees this ballet as affirming a love that endures beyond life; instead, she offers an illuminating reading of it "as an allegory for the assertion of bourgeois individuality" that reflects issues current during the reign of "citizen-king" Louis Philippe of France (p. 24). According to Banes, Louis Philippe I (reigned 1830–1848), proclaimed king shortly after the French Revolution (and after the defeat of Napoleon), consciously built his socio-political regime around "centrist middle-class principles" in order to disassociate it from the inequalities practised by previous French monarchs. Against this background, Banes defines Giselle's love not as a universal celebration of human emotions but as "a political affirmation of the self and of personal agency" (p. 24). When Giselle falls in love with Albrecht in Act I, Banes argues, she is able to assert agency unusual for the period: to entertain marrying for love instead of through a pre-arranged engagement. At this point, Giselle lacks the social power to act upon her choice, but she is endowed with power in Act II, where she is able to save Albrecht. In both instances, Giselle acts as an individual fulfilling her own purpose.

In addition, Banes sees the ballet as conveying subtle critiques of nobility, as in its depiction of the arrogant, unfeeling nobleman at liberty to seduce innocent maidens in the countryside: a critique that aligned with the political climate of post-revolutionary France. To Banes, Act II of *Giselle* is an allegory of an aristocratic space where fighting and unfairness reign. In this act, on her reading, several meanings materialize in the Wilis. They could be read as a group of spiteful terrorist women who resembled the activist women of the French Revolution—a threat that now needs to be tamed for post-revolution peace and calm. They could represent the anti-nun sentiment of the time, fed by rumours of shady sexual practices in cloisters. Finally, they could be an allegory for the increasingly large number of single, lower-class women trapped in their social positions with few choices regarding marriage or work. On Banes's reading, Giselle transcends the circumstances of these single women by actually being able to marry Albrecht, albeit only for one night and only symbolically, and then escaping an existence as a Wili by descending to her grave to rest in peace. In many ways, then, Giselle as Banes sees her "upholds the right to individual choice, so crucial to the bourgeois ethos, in the face of hierarchical, autocratic laws regarding both marriage and revenge" (p. 34).

Banes (1998) complicates the narratives of Romantic ballets by reading their treatments of the marriage plot against the social and political conditions of the ballets' inception. Even if the audience remains unaware of these conditions, Banes's work adds new layers to our understanding of the role of the female characters in ballet. Furthermore, Banes's work points the way to interpreting the narratives of some computer games in which women are the active playable characters, following similar logic. Indeed, several female action heroes do exist in computer games.

Popular Action Heroines

Among the most famous video or computer game action heroines is Lara Croft, the lead character of the *Tomb Raider* game. Originally created by British Core Design, the first *Tomb Raider* was released in 1996. Since then, Lara has become "one of the most recognizable, globally popular and lucrative media stars working today" (Rehak, 2003, p. 477)—one who, in addition to the game itself, now appears in comic books, men's magazines, music videos, board games, and a motion-picture franchise. The original game was based on a familiar and popular adventure-based narrative format employed, for example, in the *Indiana Jones* movies. In the game, Lara, as an avatar of the player, explores exotic environments to unearth treasures or mystical artifacts from deathtrap-laden tombs (Rehak, 2003), often populated with non-human characters whose role is to protect the tombs' secrets. Feminist researcher Kennedy (2002) attributes the game's success to the "synchronicity between" what were at the time "new techniques" in game design ("navigable three-dimensional game space, a simple but atmospheric soundtrack," and new levels "of cinematic realism" that provided "highly immersive game spaces"), to the game narrative, and to "the controversial (and opportunistic) use of a female lead."

Lara's character was originally created by Toby Gard, an English game designer who wished for a female lead different from the "bimbos" or "dominatrix" types typical of female game characters (cited in "Lara Croft"). He settled for tough South American Laura Cruz, whose name was, however, changed to Lara Croft as more suitable for the English-speaking gaming market. The result was an athletic and fast woman in her late twenties, with long brown hair tied back in a braid or ponytail. Her original costume consisted of a tight, sleeveless, turquoise tank top, tight light-brown shorts, and calf-high boots over long white socks. In the later games Lara's outfit evolved into a crop top and camouflage pants or black shorts. The outfit, in both cases, accentuates Lara's large breasts, small waist, and shapely legs. Her signature accessories include fingerless gloves, a backpack, a utility belt, and two pistols with their holsters tied around her thighs with garters. These features enhance our impression of a muscular, strong, and acrobatic protagonist who is capable of holding her own. Players soon learn that Lara possesses larger-than-life abilities, such as an amazing physical prowess that enables her to back-flip out of buildings, swim underwater, punch tigers, bite foes, ride big vehicles, and master multiple firearms (e.g., Rehak, 2003). With these attributes, Lara Croft was intended as an attractive role model for girls and as an attractive figure for the core gaming market: boys. Gard explained his design concept in an interview for *The Face* magazine: "Lara was designed to be a tough, self-reliant, intelligent woman. She confounds all the sexist clichés apart from the fact that she's got an unbelievable figure. Strong, independent women are the perfect fantasy girls—the untouchable is always the most desirable" (cited in Mikula, 2003, p. 79).

Soon after the launch of the first *Tomb Raider* game, Gard left Core. Since then, instead of a single designer, Core has emphasized collective authorship for the game (Mikula, 2003). Lara's character has become anchored in an officially endorsed background narrative intended to increase her distinction. According to an early version of her biography, Lara was born in Wimbledon (February 14, 1968), the daughter of Lord Croft, a fictional English aristocrat. Lara has been educated in Gordonstoun, an upper-class Scottish boarding school and Prince Charles's alma mater. She is betrothed to the Earl of Farringdon, a fictional nobleman ("Lara Croft"). When she was travelling from her Swiss finishing school with her parents, their airplane crashed in the Himalayas. When both of her parents perished in the accident, Lara was left for two weeks to survive on her own in dire circumstances. This experience inspired her to change her life to seek adventures around the world. As a trained archaeologist and accomplished author, Lara is fluent in several languages. She has also retained a number of signature characteristics that identify her as a member of the British upper class: her refined accent, her polished manners, and her partiality for tea (e.g., Mikula, 2003). According to Rehak (2003), many fan sites pay equal, if not greater, attention to the details of Lara's fictive life than to the game itself.

Despite Gard's efforts to break out of the usual mould for digital female characters, however, some feminist writers find Lara yet "another female 'creation' by a male 'creator' in a long series of patriarchal representations of women" (Mikula, 2003, p. 82). Germaine Greer even describes her as a "sergeant-major with balloons stuffed up his shirt...She's a distorted, sexually ambiguous, male fantasy" (cited in Mikula, 2003, p. 79). Others concur that the popularity of the game is almost all based on Lara's erotic appeal to boy players (Jenkins & Cassell, 2008) instead of her appeal as a role model to girls. Although there are also feminists who welcome an appearance of an active female heroine within the traditionally male genre of gaming, generally the scholarly readings define Lara as a polymorphous figure who reflects postmodern identity in constant flux (Schleiner, 2001).

Rehak (2003), Schleiner (2001), Mikula (2003), and Kennedy (2002) all understand Lara as a non-fixable, continually changing postmodern icon made possible by the new media transcoding—the "endless translation of information between diverse technological frameworks and cultural hierarchies" (Rehak, 2003, p. 479). A consequence of this changeability is, for Rehak, "Croft's *polysemous perversity*, her ability to endlessly resignify," depending on the context and the player (p. 481, emphasis original). Mikula similarly argues that Lara was purposefully created as an "empty sign" to appeal to a very broad global audience to make their own meanings. While an officially endorsed background story was published to somewhat control her sign, Lara is still left open to several contradictory meanings. Mikula emphasizes, however, that some of these seemingly contradictory qualities, while not often assigned to a heroine, represent "the different faces of empowerment in advanced capitalist societies: class, wealth, appearance, physical fitness, strong will, intelligence and independence" (p. 83).

Kennedy (2002) takes a slightly different approach, locating the ambivalences of Lara's character in the continuum ranging from the model of traditional womanhood to a postfeminist bimbo. She compares "stunting bodies" in film—"female figures which, through the performance of extraordinary feats, undermine conventional understandings of the female body"—to Lara's powerful image that acts in traditionally masculinized spaces, using traditionally male tactics. From this perspective, instead of being a victim or a love interest needing to be rescued by a hero, or an icon of capitalist privilege, Lara's "occupation of a traditionally masculine world, her rejection of particular patriarchal values and norms of femininity and the physical spaces that she traverses are all in direct contradiction of the typical location of femininity within the private or domestic space." Schleiner (2001) also sees the possibility of empowerment for female players, proposing that Lara's avatar offers multiple "gender-subject positions," among which the player might oscillate (p. 222). Such often contradictory positions as "Lara as female automaton...Lara as drag queen, Lara as dominatrix, Lara as girl-power role model and Lara as queer babe with shot-gun" provide "possible strategic means for feminists to participate in the formation of new gender configurations" through gaming, in Schleiner's view (p. 225). There is also a notable absence of romantic or sexual intrigue within the game narrative, which gives Lara another kind of independence. Lara can, then, be celebrated as a significant breakthrough in the gaming world, where female lead characters are largely absent. Nevertheless, she can also, as Kennedy points out (see also Cassell & Jenkins, 1998), be seen as a postfeminist icon that emphasizes female participation in traditional male spheres, while retaining their traditional female looks—simultaneously the hero (active) and the heroine (to be looked at).

Despite the multiplicity of possible readings (a multiplicity similar to that found in *Giselle* by such feminist ballet scholars as Adair, 1992; Daly, 1987; Foster, 1996a; and Wulff, 1998), Rehak (2003), Schleiner (2001), Mikula (2003), and Kennedy (2002) all invoke Mulvey's gaze theory to note the voyeuristic appeal of Lara's body. Rehak speculates that male players gaze at her through what Mulvey (1989) defines as twin poles of male gaze: investigation and fetishism. Kennedy reminds us, however, that, according to Mulvey, an active female disrupts such a gaze and, like the ballerina, has to be rendered safe by phallicization of her body. Lara's body, although not equal to the ballerina's body in its resemblance to a phallus, continues to pose a threat, argues Kennedy, even as the threat is "disavowed through the heavy layering of fetishistic signifiers such as her glasses, her guns, the holster/garter belts, her long swinging hair."

Not all researchers, however, characterize the ballerina as a fetish for the male gaze. Although ballerina roles can be seen as representing patriarchal stereotypes, individual ballerinas can turn into iconic celebrities similar to Lara Croft. Fisher (2012), for example, describes ballerina Anna Pavlova as a heroine comparable to female adventure-game protagonists. Pavlova, an early twentieth-century Russian prima ballerina, began her stardom at the famous Royal Imperial Ballet at the Maryinsky Theatre in St. Petersburg. She also established her own ballet company and, after the Russian Revolution, while based in London, rose to international stardom. Pavlova is perhaps best remembered for her solo *The Dying Swan*, choreographed by Michel Fokine to premiere in 1905. While this piece exemplifies the feminine Romantic ballerina stereotype of "a delicate, glossy creature," a dancer in a white tulle skirt, with "the gliding grace and feathery ethereality of ballet," Fisher argues that Pavlova's dancing body and her interpretation of her roles also suggested "strength, expansion, and power" (p. 65). Although often considered "old-fashioned" and "conservative" in comparison to her contemporaries in the Ballets Russes, Pavlova is depicted by Fisher as an innovator, a "post-Romantic" superstar who actively made ballet a serious endeavour that required hard physical training. She was a "demanding, tireless, dedicated, and driven" career woman whose profession required "single-minded devotion" (p. 59). As such, Pavlova, much like the fictional Lara Croft, can be seen as a role model for female admirers wanting to break away from the conventional expectations set for women at the time. With these contributions, Fisher concludes, Pavlova "became a powerful female figure in a world where men dominated all decision-making jobs" (p. 62) and "can be seen today as a precursor of modern feminism" (p. 62).

While not all ballerinas (or action heroines) turn into feminist icons, such scholarship makes clear that a careful and detailed reading of their often subtle tactics within the limitations of the structure of the ballet (or the video and computer game) world is needed before we dismiss them as empowering agents. I have so far focused on the representations and the multiple possible interpretations of these seemingly quite different female heroines in gaming and in ballet. The question that remains is whether the practice of ballet or gaming results in a different relationship with these genres for the practitioner than for the viewer.

Practising Ballet, Practising Gaming

Several researchers distinguish between objectifying and identifying with computer game characters. Kennedy (2002), for example, emphasizes the difference between playing a computer game in which the gamer actively assumes control of a character and viewing movies or ballet performances, where the spectator's role is limited to observation of the events. When the player can actually become the character of Lara Croft, does she continue to be a target of the male gaze?

According to Mikula (2003), identification with the character is a gendered process: female gamers find it important to be able to identify with the character they play much more than male gamers do. Mikula finds that Lara Croft provides opportunity for such identification: "By and large," she claims, "women enjoy 'being' Lara, rather than controlling her" (p. 81), because the character allows for identification with both a strong and capable woman and an excessively feminine character. Somewhat paradoxically, however, "*Tomb Raider* rarely figures among women's preferred games"; Rehak (2003) posits that this is because Lara "remains an emblem of corporate artifice, ideologically laden and therefore resistant to her intended assimilation as an aspect of player subjectivity" (p. 491). Whatever the reason, the main audience for *Tomb Raider* is indeed male.

This raises questions about whether male players identify with the female avatar. Although Mikula (2003) argues that the male players like "looking after" Lara (p. 81), which distances them from pure control of the character, Rehak (2003) believes that *Tomb Raider* "encourages players to 'possess' Croft as an object, while they 'become' her through avatarial identification" (p. 490). Rehak also sees the process of male player identification with Lara as a complex one, citing Flanagan's taxonomy of player positions: "making Croft act; watching Croft act on her own; acting *with* Croft 'as a friend or companion'; becoming Croft through identification; reacting *to* Croft" (cited in Rehak, 2003, p. 490, emphasis original). According to Flanagan, then, there are five different positions available to the male player for interacting with Lara Croft. Kennedy (2002) theorizes that, when playing Lara, the male player, who both actively controls and passively watches Lara, can assume a trans-gendered identity: he interacts with the game space as female body (see also Cassell & Jenkins, 1998). On this reading, such gaming becomes a safe utopian space without the usual gender boundaries. At the very least, a momentary enjoyment of being female in such a space does not have any real-world consequences.

Kennedy (2002) is, however, cautious about any empowerment enabled by technology. Although the virtual world of computer games might become a means of transcending one's own body, it also provides "opportunities for the playing out of fantasies of conquest and control of the 'other,'" a premise also emphasized by Sarkeesian. Any male identification with Lara, Kennedy adds, "is disavowed through the production of stories and art that tends to want to securely fix Lara as an object of sexual desire." Rehak (2003) also observes that Croft continues to offer fertile ground to extended male fetishistic involvement "through the creation of erotic pictures and paratexts" (p. 491) that are absent, as noted by Kennedy (2002), in the actual game. Several researchers recognize the role of what is known as *hacking* in the active player manipulation of Croft's character (e.g., Mikula, 2003; Schleiner, 2001). Some point particularly to the hack known as "Nude Raider," which allows the player to strip Lara of her clothing while in action. Schleiner (2001), however, argues that, the Nude Raider aside, hacking can provide "a new range of subject positions...that challenge given gender categories and adapt them to the diverse gender sensibilities of men, women and others" (p. 225). Similarly, although the hyper-feminine image can exclude many women and girls from ballet, the pleasures of actually doing ballet can provide a new range of subject positions.

Kolb and Kalogeropoulou (2012) clearly distinguish between "the pleasures of viewing and aesthetically appreciating ballet and the pleasures of actually practising it" (p. 113). Several other researchers, such as Alter (1997), Clark (2014), and Picard and Bailey (2009), theorize that dancers' lived experiences—the combination of ballet's physical, affective, and social aspects—make ballet particularly enjoyable. Pickard and Bailey report that young ballet dancers find enjoyment in skill mastery, emotional connection to dance, and a sense of belonging. These experiences also translate as positive interpretations of setbacks. In fact, ballet dancers of all ages appear to enjoy the physical challenge provided by ballet. In her study of young recreational ballet dancers in a commercial studio in Canada, Clark (2014) found that practising new skills and executing a demanding ballet move were central aspects of these dancers' enjoyment of dance, even more central than the dance performance. Kolb and Kalogeropoulou (2012), who study the pleasurable experiences of adult recreational ballet dancers (18–67 years old) in the UK, New Zealand, and Germany, have found that ballet's discipline, particularly the discipline of repeating the same exercises over and over in a ballet class, is the most frequently cited source of pleasure. The enjoyment of the physical challenge is "united" with accompanying mental and affective aspects of "the challenge, sense of achievement and/or determination asso-ciated with the art form" (p. 116). Thus, the dance students consider ballet both physically and intellectually challenging. Ballet, for them, provides a harmony of the body and mind not available in other aspects of their lives. Pickard and Bailey (2009) similarly observe that "the majority of the experi-ences that were shared as noteworthy and significant by the dancers were positive and linked to elevated feelings of happiness, excitement and some-times euphoria" (p. 179). Alter (1997) also finds positive responses among ballet students, reporting that the participants in her study defined ballet as an outlet for self-expression, an emotional release, an opportunity to be creative, and a way to feel alive, full, and joyful. For participants in Kolb and Kalogeropoulou's study (2012), these experiences provided an escape and rest from their everyday lives and an opportunity to socialize with other female dancers.

These ballet dancers also talked positively about their performance experiences. For young dancers interviewed by Pickard and Bailey (2009), performance is a major stimulation that facilitates a continual engagement in ballet. Kolb and Karogeropoulou (2012) found that, during performance, some ballet dancers, like some gamers, enjoy transforming themselves into other characters. For example, one participant explains, "'When I disguise myself [for a performance] then I'm not me, I'm someone else...But somehow that's also very exciting, so tingling, I think that's great, and also when I portray another person that doesn't have to be connected with me'" (p. 120). The researchers conclude that, "While studio classes help participants to find and express their own personalities, performances give them the chance to slip into other characters and explore alternative identities in an entirely different sphere from real life" (p. 121). In their study, the identity of a ballet dancer is often described by highlighting attributes not typically consid-ered feminine, "such as strength, toughness, resilience, and the testing of one's limits, within an almost exclusively female environment" (p. 119). Fisher (2007), a ballet dancer who herself "experienced ballet as a positive force," a means of "learning about personal agency, collaborative effort, and spiritual expansion" (p. 4), endorses a similar view. The ballet dancers she interviewed acknowledge the stereotype of the delicate ultra-feminine, skeletal, and hyper-flexible ballerina, but also perceive the ballerina as a powerful athlete and a liberated, unmarried woman who is glamorous, driven, strong, and successful, although she also (as we have seen in the case of Anna Pavlova) has to conform to standards set by professional ballet companies in order to have a career. Fisher believes that such a dual identity for the ballerina illustrates ballet's "wide-ranging embrace of life" (p. 15). Kolb and Kalogeropoulou (2012) summarize the enjoyment of practising ballet:

> Ballet's codified technique thus seems to usher in a form of expression which is socially cohesive but which still allows the individual dancer a range of personally meaningful movement that is both physically and mentally satisfying. The intricate interplay between a more "generic" rhetoric of affects, culturally shared and understood by all ballet aficionados, and the sense of an individual, self-expressive identity channelled through ballet's codified language is clearly a major stimulus for its practice. (p. 118)

While gaming can also provide the pleasure of cognitive challenges and the positive effects of successfully answering them, the pleasures of movement are less prominent. Some recent technology, however, incorporates bodily movement beyond hand dexterity to enhance the experience of gaming. In her article, Shinkle (2008) highlights the connections between being able to use the kinaesthetic sense and emotions, as in ballet, in gaming and in dance—a connection that comes into play in iGiselle.

Shinkle (2008) begins by observing that video games, due to their special structure and narrative form, are often "situated in relation to visual technologies," such as paintings or cinema (p. 908). Yet games also offer an opportunity for the player to explore the space actively, in real time, as an agent of the game. While playing video games, she continues, it is possible to employ, in addition to hearing and vision, kinesthetic, proprioceptive, and vestibular senses to support "full experiential flow" that links "perceptions, cognitions and emotions with actions, and engaging the broad spectrum of sensory modalities involved in perception" (p. 208). Emotionality created by employing multiple forms of perception constitutes the full meaning of gaming and, thus, influences reason, which is enmeshed with the same body-regulating brain systems. Shinkle summarizes: "Emotionally involving and meaningful gameplay...is a function of the player's physical presence, their actions and gestures at the level of the interface" (910). Therefore, the players' emotional investment, enjoyment, and immersion in the game can be enhanced by including "dynamic and meaningful physical actions" (p. 912). This type of agency allows the players to find their own ways of doing things, instead of following "a set of established protocols and narrative events" (p. 912).

Unfortunately, standard game controllers limit physical and gestural expression. Shinkle (2008) points instead to control systems like the Nintendo Wii and the Sony EyeToy that allow players to control events in the game world by moving their bodies. According to Shinkle, these types of physical interfaces, while not without limitations, "draw on...individuality, supporting a more nuanced kind of proprioceptive engagement with the game" by accommodating the player's unique presence in time and space (p. 912). Like performing ballet, embodied control systems enable the player to assume another identity because they collapse "the distance between self and avatar, and between real and virtual worlds" (p. 913) and, thus, provide a better connection with the character or avatar. With words that recall the dancers' enjoyment of practising ballet, Shinkle cites McGonigal, who extols her experiences with Wii as follows:

> MOVING VIGOROUSLY—shaking, waving, pumping, pointing, and so on—is more fun than pressing buttons. Not because it's a more "realistic analog" of what a game avatar is doing. Just because it's REALLY more fun...You are REALLY doing stuff...REALLY using your body in totally fun, original, happy-making ways. (cited in Shinkle, 2008, p. 912, emphasis original)

In some games, the physical action corresponds exactly to real-world actions, but, based on McGonigal's experience, any type of movement as part of a game can considerably enhance the player's enjoyment. Our game, *iGiselle*, was also designed to solicit player emotions, in part through the use of the

Kinect motion control that detects bodily movement to enable the player to proceed to the next screen in some aspects of the game.

The danger of actual physical action, however, is a possible increase in the socially problematic aspects of gaming, such as violence, that "take on a new significance when violent acts are simulated by means of analogous physical gestures, and presumably accompanied by augmented emotions" (Shinkle, 2008, p. 913). The same point was emphasized by Sarkeesian (2014b), who argues that a player, even when using the standard controller, interacts with game characters that are capable of extreme violent actions. She also asserts that passively witnessing such violence without interference by the playable character constitutes accepting these actions.

Conclusion: Are the "Pink Games" the Answer?

If even strong characters, like Lara Croft, perpetuate sexual difference along the lines established by patriarchal society and, thus, serve to marginalize women and girls, can computer games ever become sites of empowerment?[4] What about Romantic ballet, with its fixed, conventional nineteenth-century representation of gender(s)? Many gaming girls and women remain dissatisfied with the violence embedded in current gaming narratives, even if executed by an action heroine. In addition, although offering multiple possible subject positions, the active female body of such heroines continues to appear primarily as an object of (male) sexual desire. As Kennedy (2002) concludes, "If we are going to encourage more girls into the gaming culture then we need to encourage the production of a broader range of representations of femininity than those currently being offered"—images that do not "reinstate doggedly rigid gender stereotypes" of women or men—the stereotypes also found in the ballet *Giselle*.

At the same time as Lara Croft's first appearance in the UK, the "'girls' games' movement emerged from an unusual and highly unstable alliance between feminist activists (who wanted to change the 'gendering' of digital technology) and industry leaders (who wanted to create a girls' market for their games)" in the US (Cassell & Jenkins, 1998, p. 4). This movement, now described as the first wave of feminist game studies (Kafai, Richard, & Tynes,

2017; Jenkins & Cassell, 2008), advocated separate games designed to appeal to girls by incorporating the following:

- *leading characters who were everyday people that girls can easily relate to*
- *exploration and variable outcomes, rather than fixed goals and hierarchical scoring*
- *emphasis on characters and stories over speed and action*
- *everyday settings*
- *success through social networking, instead of combat and competition* (Jenkins & Cassell, 2008, p. 11).

Other researchers also noted gender differences in preferences for game settings, narratives, and characters. According to these studies, girls and young women appear to favour realistic settings that, nevertheless, encourage appropriate levels of skill, challenge, exploration, communication, and collaboration without violence. They prefer rich narratives that include engaging, positive characters enabled by sophisticated graphic and sound design (de Castell & Bryson, 1998; Dickey, 2006; Kafai, 1998).

Although *iGiselle* was not originally designed as a specifically girls' computer game, similar preferences influenced the design, narrative, and character development of our video game. The lead characters resemble real dance students wearing training clothes rather than willowy ballerinas in tutus. The relatively complex story of *Giselle* is also relocated to an everyday dance environment, although we acknowledge that being cast in the lead role in a ballet would be an unrealistic goal for most girls. The characters operate generally through social networking rather than fierce combat. While the traditional gender roles of ballet are largely retained, there are opportunities to explore variable outcomes.

On the other hand, designing specifically *feminine* games does not necessarily challenge (hyper)masculinity as the norm for video and computer games. Some researchers caution against perpetuating existing gender divisions by isolating specific girls' games from mainstream games. Dickey (2006) proposes, for instance, that such a strategy potentially perpetuates gender inequality based on binary constructs of naturally occurring differences between male and female (games). It is also important to note that the views based on quantifiable survey research on girls' leanings towards so-called pink games do not necessarily represent all girls' and women's ideal gaming experience. As Dickey summarizes, "The main problem with developing games targeted specifically for girls and women is the question of whose notion of 'female' is being portrayed in the game" (p. 789). This research, that Kafai, Richard, and Tynes (2017) now characterize as the second wave of feminist game studies, promotes the so-called "purple games" that focus on "'real life' issues and social realities that would interest female players" (p. 5). While some feminist gaming scholars continue to track the differences between men and women's gaming preferences, Kafai, Richard and Tynes (2017) find the current research entering its third wave with an interest in more nuanced understanding of gendered gaming experiences that also intersect with sexuality, ethnicity, race, and class differences.

Meanwhile, games' designs and selections continue to diversify; there are now many types of games with many types of characters, yet feminist readings of sexism in existing computer games remain unpopular among gamers, as the recent controversy around Sarkeesian, who has received death threats from some members of the gaming community, demonstrates (see also Kafai, Richard & Tynes, 2017). Nevertheless, feminist criticism continues to ask whether such features as reduced violence, increased challenge, everyday characters, exploration, and complex narrative lines could come to characterize all computer games, not to mention ballet. There is evidence, after all, that reducing stereotypical representations of men and women can improve characteristics, features, actions, and ethics in the virtual worlds of digital computer games and in the material world of ballet—and, in so doing, potentially improve the quality of all lives.

Notes

1. While it is difficult to find recent research articles on the number of women playing video games, an online survey in 2015 by Pew Research Center in the US found that, of those surveyed, 48% of women and 50% of men played video games. Interestingly, 38% of women aged 50 or older reported playing video games compared to 29% of men in the same age bracket (Duggan, 2015). In a 2016 survey, Statista established that 59% of men and 41% of women (up from 38% in 2006), played video games in the US (Distribution, 2018). Furthermore, Campbell (2017) reports that women prefer mobile match-3 and farming games over sports and shooting games. This finding is based on an online survey of 270,000 gamers, of whom only 18.5% identified as female. Jayanth (2014) notes that, in the UK, 52% of gamers are women who prefer mobile games, free-to-play games and social games: games generally considered inferior to traditional games by the industry. In Canada, Wilson (2016) reports that 48% of gamers are women who prefer educational games such as puzzles and word games.

2. Barlett and Harris (2008) found that college-aged males who played a video game featuring hypermuscular characters for fifteen minutes had significantly lower body esteem than did males who did not play a body-emphasizing game.

3. Mulvey's (1975) original theory focused on different representations of men and women in Hollywood films. She demonstrated that films are structured based on active male characters and female characters who provide "to-be-looked-at-ness" to these males. Therefore, the viewers are invited to see the film through the gaze of the male who can identify with the active male character and who sees the female only as an object to gaze at. The female audience members can, therefore, only identify with the objectified female and come to understand themselves as such. According to Mulvey, this structure replicates the unequal power structure of the patriarchal society that exists, according to Lacanian psychoanalysis, because women have been placed in passive positions due to the male fear of castration and their resolution of this complex. Women lack a penis, and they are, therefore, frightening for men, in that they signal the possible loss of active phallic power. Consequently, men turn women into fetishized objects. Therefore Mulvey, like Lacan, defines women based on what they lack, namely the phallus.

4. According to Dickey (2006), the first games designed for girls included *Barbie Fashion Designer* (1997) by Mattel and *Cosmopolitan Virtual Makeover* (1997) by Sega. More sophisticated games included *American Girl* by the Learning Company, the *Rockett* series by Purple Moon, and *McKenzie & Co.* and *Nancy Drew* (not designed particularly for girls) by Her Interactive.

References

Adair, C. (1992). *Women and dance: Sylphs and sirens*. Basingstoke: Macmillan.

Anderson, C., & Bushman, B. (2001). Effects of violent video games on aggressive behavior, aggressive cognition, aggressive affect, physiological arousal, and prosocial behavior: A meta-analytic review of the scientific literature. *Psychological Science, 12,* 353–59.

Anderson, C.A., & Dill, K.E. (2000). Video games and aggressive thoughts, feelings, and behavior in the laboratory and life. *Journal of Personality and Social Psychology, 78,* 772–90.

Alter, J. (1997). Why dance students pursue dance: Studies of dance students from 1953 to 1993. *Dance Research Journal, 29*(2), 70–89.

Banes, S. (1998). *Dancing women: Female bodies on stage*. London and New York: Routledge.

Barlett, C.P., & Harris, R.J. (2008). The impact of body emphasizing video games on body image concerns in men and women. *Sex Roles, 59,* 586–601.

Beasley, B., & Collins Standley, T. (2002). Shirts vs skins: Clothing as an indicator of gender role stereotyping in video games. *Mass Communication and Society, 5*(3), 279–93.

Campbell, C. (2017, January 20). Which games are women and girls playing? *Polygon.* www.polygon.com/2017/1/20.

Cassell, J., & Jenkins, H. (1998). "Chess for girls: Feminism and computer games. In J. Cassell & H. Jenkins (Eds.), *From Barbie to Mortal Kombat: Gender and computer games* (1–41). Cambridge, MA: MIT Press.

Clark, M. (2014). *Dancing the self: How girls who dance in commercial dance studios construct a self through the dancing body* (Doctoral dissertation, University of Alberta, Edmonton, AB).

Cooper Albright, A. (1997). *Choreographing difference: The body and identity in contemporary dance*. Hanover, NH: Wesleyan University Press.

Daly, A. (1987). The Balanchine woman: Of hummingbirds and channel swimmers. *Drama Review, 31*(1), 8–21.

de Castell, S., & Bryson, M. (1998). Retooling play: Dystopia, disphoria, and difference. In J. Cassell & H. Jenkins (Eds.), *From Barbie to Mortal Kombat: Gender and computer games* (231–61). Cambridge, MA: MIT Press.

Dempster, E. (1988). Women writing the body: Let's watch a little how she dances. In S. Sheridan (Ed.), *Grafts: Feminist cultural criticism* (35–54). London: Verso.

Dickey, M. (2006). Girl gamers: The controversy of girl games and the relevance of female-oriented game design for instructional design. *British Journal of Educational Technology, 37*(5), 785–93.

Dietz, T. (1998). An examination of violence and gender role portrayal in video games: Implications for gender socialization and aggressive behavior. *Sex Roles, 38*(5/6), 425–41.

Distribution of computer and video gamers in the United States from 2006 to 2018, by gender (2018, July 12). www.statista.com/statistics.

Duggan, M. (2015, December 15). Who plays video games and identifies as a "gamer." www.pewinternet.org.

Ekos Research Associates (2014, July 21). *Findings from Yes I Dance: Survey of who dances in Canada*. Canada Council for the Arts. canadacouncil.ca/-/media/Files/CCA/ Research/2014/07/Yes_I_Dance_Final_Report_EN.pdf.

Fisher, J. (2007). Tulle as tool: Embracing the conflict of the ballerina as powerhouse. *Dance Research Journal, 39*, 2–24.

Fisher, J. (2012). The swan brand: Reframing the legacy of Anna Pavlova. *Dance Research Journal, 44*, 50–67.

Flanagan, M. (1999). Mobile identities, digital stars, and post-cinematic selves. *Wide Angle, 21*, 76–93.

Foster, S.L. (1996a). The ballerina's phallic point. In S.L. Foster (Ed.), *Corporealities: Dancing knowledge, culture and power* (17–24). London: Routledge.

———. (1996b). *Choreography & narrative: Ballet's staging of story and desire*. Bloomington, IN: Indiana University Press.

Irvine, M. (2018, July 16). Survey: Nearly every American kid plays videogames. *A B C News*. abcnews.go.com/Technology/story?id=5817835.

Ivory, J. (2006). Still a man's game: Gender representation in online reviews of video games. *Journal of Mass Communication & Society, 9*, 103–14.

Jenkins, H., & Cassell, J. (2008). From Quake Grrls to Desperate Housewives: A decade of gender and computer games. In Y.B. Kafai, C. Heeter, J. Denner, & J.Y. Sun (Eds.), *Beyond Barbie and Mortal Kombat: New pespectives on gender and gaming* (5–20). Cambridge, MA: M I T Press.

Jayanth, M. (2014, September 18). 52% of gamers are women—but the industry doesn't know it yet. *The Guardian*. www.theguardian.com.

Kafai, Y.B. (1998). Video game designs by girls and boys: Variability and consistency of gender differences. In J. Cassell & H. Jenkins (Eds.), *From Barbie to Mortal Kombat: Gender and computer games* (90–114). Cambridge, MA: M I T Press.

Kafai, Y.B., Richard, G.T., & Tynes, B.M. (2017). The need for international perspectives and inclusive designs in gaming. *Diversifying Barbie and Mortal Kombat: Intersectional perspectives and inclusive designs in gaming* (1–20). Pittsburgh, PA: E T C Press.

Kennedy, H. (2002). Lara Croft: Feminist icon or cyberbimbo? On the limits of textual analysis. *Game Studies, 2*(2). www.gamestudies.org.

Kirsch, S. (1998). Seeing the world through "Mortal Kombat" colored glasses: Violent video games and the development of a short-term hostile attribution bias. *Childhood, 5,* 177–84.

Kolb, A., & Kalogeropoulou, S. (2012). In defence of ballet: Women, agency and the philosophy of pleasure. *Dance Research, 30*(2), 107–25.

"Lara Croft." *Wikipedia.* en.wikipedia.org/wiki/Lara_Croft.

Martins, N., Williams, D.C., Ratan, R. A., & Harrison, K. (2011). Virtual muscularity: A content analysis of male video game characters. *Body Image, 8,* 43–51.

Mikula, M. (2003). Gender and videogames: The political valency of Lara Croft. *Continuum: Journal of Media & Cultural Studies, 17*(1), 79–87.

Miller, M., & Summers, A. (2007). Gender differences in video game characters' roles, appearances, and attire as portrayed in video game magazines. *Sex Roles, 57,* 733–42.

Mulvey, L. (1975). Visual pleasure and narrative cinema. *Screen, 16*(3), 6–18.

Pickard, A., & Bailey, R. (2009). Crystallising experiences among young elite dancers. *Sport, Education & Society, 14,* 165–81.

Rehak, B. (2003). Mapping the bit girl: Lara Croft and new media fandom. *Information, Communication & Society, 6*(4), 477–496.

Sarkeesian, A. (Writer and Presenter). (2013, March 7). Damsel in distress: Part 1 [YouTube video series episode 1]. In Sarkeesian (Producer), *Tropes vs women in video games.* Feminist Frequency. www.youtube.com.

———. (2013, May 28). Damsel in distress: Part 2 [YouTube video series episode 2]. In Sarkeesian (Producer), *Tropes vs women in video games.* Feminist Frequency. www.youtube.com.

———. (2013, August 1). Damsel in distress: Part 3 [YouTube video series episode 3]. In Sarkeesian (Producer), *Tropes vs women in video games.* Feminist Frequency. www.youtube.com.

———. (2013, November 11). Ms. male character [YouTube video series episode 4] In Sarkeesian (Producer), *Tropes vs women in video games.* Feminist Frequency. www.youtube.com.

———. (2014, June 16). Women as background decoration: Part 1. [YouTube video series episode 5] In Sarkeesian (Producer), *Tropes vs women in video games.* Feminist Frequency. www.youtube.com.

———. (2014, August 25). Women as background decoration: Part 2. [YouTube video series episode 6] In Sarkeesian (Producer), *Tropes vs women in video games.* Feminist Frequency. www.youtube.com.

Schleiner, A.-M. (2001). Does Lara Croft wear fake polygons: Gender and gender role subversion in computer adventure games. *Leonardo, 34*(3), 221–26.

Scharrer, E. (2004). Virtual violence: Gender and aggression in video game advertisements. *Mass Communication and Society*, 7(4), 393–412.

Sherlock, J. (1993). Dance and the culture of the body. In S. Scott & D. Morgan (Eds.), *Body matters: Essays on sociology of the body* (35–48). London: Routledge.

Sherry, J. (2001). The effects of violent video games on aggression: A meta-analysis. *Human Communication Research*, 27, 409–31.

Shinkle, E. (2008). Video games, emotion and the six senses. *Media Culture Society*, 30(7), 907–15.

Taylor, T.L. (2003). Multiple pleasures: Women and online gaming. *Convergence*, 9(1), 21–46.

Wack, E., & Tantleff-Dunn, S. (2008). Cyber sexy: Electronic game play and perceptions of attractiveness among college-aged men. *Body Image*, 5, 365–74.

Wilson, J. (2016, January 15). Women are almost half of the gamers population in Canada. *Global News*. globalnews.ca/news.

Wulff, H. (1998). *Ballet across borders: Career and culture in the world of dancers*. Oxford, UK: Berg.

Contributors

VADIM BULITKO is Professor of Computing Science at the University of Alberta. He received his PHD in computer science from the University of Illinois at Urbana-Champaign in 1999. He is interested in building artificial general intelligence, as well as understanding intelligence and cognition in humans and animals.

WAYNE DEFEHR earned his PHD from the University of Alberta, where he completed a dissertation that drew on a philosophy of geometry to sketch out an approach to two cyber-punk films, *Bladerunner* and *Brazil*. The themes of this research continue to inform his work as instructor, author, and experimental interactive performer, re-drawing the lines between the boundary markers of audience expectations. Taking the textual authority of the tabloid and the ocular precision of the fish-eye lens as points of reference, his projects playfully tease out the underlying metaphors of our relentless entertainment media, and perturb them into the re-mash and mix-up of strange new hybrid forms.

CHRISTINA GIER is Associate Professor of Musicology at the University of Alberta. She received her PHD from Duke University (2003), and she researches gender and music in European and American twentieth-century music. She has published *Singing, Soldiering, and Sheet Music in America During the First World War* (2016) and articles on Alban Berg, Hollywood film music, and songs from the First World War in the journals *Women and Music*, the *Journal of Musicological Research*, and *Musica Humana*, and in the collections *Anxiety Muted* and *Musik bezieht Stellung*.

PIRKKO MARKULA is a professor of socio-cultural studies of physical activity at the University of Alberta. Her research interests include social analyses of dance, exercise, and sport in which she has employed several theoretical lenses ranging from critical, cultural studies research to Foucault and Deleuze. She is also a contemporary dancer and choreographer. She is the co-author, with Michael Silk, of *Qualitative Research for Physical Culture* (2011), co-author, with Richard Pringle, of *Foucault, Sport and Exercise: Power, Knowledge and Transforming the Self* (2006), editor of *Feminist Sport Studies: Sharing Joy, Sharing Pain* (2005) and *Olympic Women and the Media: International perspectives* (2009), co-editor of *The Evolving Feminine Ballet Body* (2018), co-editor of *Endurance Running: A Socio-Cultural Examination* (2016), co-editor of *Women and Exercise: Body, Health and Consumerism* (2011), co-editor of *Critical Bodies: Representations, Identities and Practices of Weight and Body Management* (2007), and co-editor of *Moving Writing: Crafting Movement in Sport Research* (2003).

MARK MORRIS is a writer, photographer, music critic, and award-winning librettist. He has written widely on music and opera, including several years as the Wales Correspondent of *Classical Music Fortnightly* in the UK, and has regularly broadcast on music, notably a series of intermission essays for CBC's *Saturday Night at the Opera*. He is currently the classical music critic for the *Edmonton Journal*. As librettist, he has written thirteen operas that have been performed in eight countries and broadcast by CBC and SkyTV. He has directed and designed stage works from Shakespeare and Goethe to Verdi and Auden and Isherwood. He is the author of *Domesday Revisited* (1987), a

Historical Book Club Choice, and his *Guide to 20th Century Composers* (1996) was described as "one of the four indispensable surveys of the music of the last century." He currently teaches English at the University of Alberta.

SERGIO POO HERNANDEZ completed his Bachelor's degree in computer engineering from Instituto Tecnologico de Estudios Superiores de Monterrey Campus Guadalajara. He completed his MSC in Computing Science at the University of Alberta under the supervision of Vadim Bulitko. He is currently a doctoral candidate at the University of Alberta.

EMILIE ST. HILAIRE is an interdisciplinary artist currently pursuing doctoral studies in the Humanities PHD program at Concordia University in Montreal. She completed her Bachelor of Fine Arts at the University of Manitoba and her Master of Fine Arts at the University of Alberta. Her FRQSC-funded doctoral research examines the sub-cultural phenomenon of reborn dolls. She has participated in several research-creation projects at Canadian universities and has presented conference papers on research in the arts. She has been published in the journal RACAR and has exhibited her artwork at galleries and festivals nationally and internationally. She has received grants and awards from organizations including the Canada Council for the Arts, the Alberta Foundation for the Arts, and the Edmonton Arts Council.

NORA FOSTER STOVEL is Professor Emerita at the University of Alberta, where she taught in the Department of English and Film Studies from 1985 to 2014. She received her Honours BA, Honours MA, and PHD degrees from McGill, Cambridge, and Dalhousie Universities, respectively, followed by SSHRC and University of Calgary Postdoctoral Fellowships. She is a member of the Canadian Dance Teachers' Association and the British Imperial Society of Teachers of Dance. She has taught ballet for twenty years at three universities: Yale, Dalhousie, and Alberta. She has published books and articles on Jane Austen, D.H. Lawrence, Margaret Laurence, Margaret Drabble, and Carol Shields, including *Divining Margaret Laurence: A Study of*

Her Complete Writings (2008). She has edited Margaret Laurence's *Long Drums and Cannons: Nigerian Dramatists and Novelists* (2001) and *Heart of a Stranger* (2003), plus *Jane Austen Sings the Blues* (2009) and *Jane Austen and Company* (2011). She is composing *"Sparkling Subversion": Carol Shields's Vision and Voice* and editing *"Recognition and Revelation": Margaret Laurence's Short Non-fiction Writings* and *"My Miniature Art": The Poetry of Carol Shields*, while planning *Women with Wings: The Romantic and Classical Ballerina*.

LAURA SYDORA is a doctoral candidate in English and Film Studies at the University of Alberta. She completed her BA in Honors English and Communications at the University of California, Davis and Trinity College Dublin before pursuing her MA in English at the University of Alberta. Her dissertation focuses on second-wave feminist periodicals in the Republic of Ireland and the intersection of media forms and social movements. Her research interests include twentieth-century Irish literature, specifically women's print culture, archival research, discourses of feminism, and theories of nationalism. She has published in *Irish Studies Review* and *Women's Studies: An Interdisciplinary Journal*.

Index

Gündüz, Zeynep, 140–41
Gutierrez, Hayna, 19

habitus, 137–38
hacking, 176
Half-Life 2 (video game), 112
Hamlet (Thomas), 51
Hansen, Mark, 135–36, 137
haptic creativity, 134, 138–39
Haraway, Donna, 130, 141–42
harmonic motion, 37
Harris, R.J., 183n2
Harrison, K., 162, 164
Hart, Evelyn, viii, 30, 31, 32n10
Hayles, N. Katherine, 136–37, 138,
    144n5
Heine, Heinrich, 9–10, 11, 32n7, 71,
    81, 92
Heppenstall, Rayner, 5
Hoffman, E.T.A., 151
Homans, Jennifer, 31n3, 31n5
Hugo, Victor, 11, 12, 92
human-computer interaction
    (HCI), 134–35. *See also* body,
    in technology

I, Giselle (Early and Lansley), xxii, 95
Ibsen, Henrik
    A Doll's House, 92
iGiselle (video game)
    about, xix–xx, xxv, 90, 129–30,
        159–60
    comparison to original *Giselle*,
        103–4

comparison to similar video
    games, xiii–xiv
control via dance positions,
    104n1, 121, 133
as cyborg, 142
development of multimedia
    content, xiv–xv, 99, 122–23,
    132–33
development of narrative, x–xii,
    97–99, 130–31, 132
development team, x, xix, 124n2
enjoyment through physical
    movement, 179–80
game interface, 121
"girls' games" movement and,
    181
inspiration for, vii–viii
interactive aspect, xiii, xiv
launch of, xv
narrative, 100, 131–32, 143n2
potential endings and
    protagonist-player agency,
    102–3, 144n3
Wilis, 101–2
See also music (*iGiselle*); Player
    Appraisal Controlling
    Emotions (PACE)
Illica, Luigi, 83
Imagine: Ballet Star (video game),
    xiii
improvisation, 140–41
interdisciplinary collaboration,
    xxiii–xxiv, 140, 141–42, 142–43,
    144n6

Taglioni, Marie, 3, 5, 7, 8, 31n4, 35
Tantleff-Dunn, S., 162
technology, *see* body, in technology
Temperley, Nicholas, 58, 64, 85n12
Tennant, Veronica, viii
Thomas, Ambroise
    Hamlet, 51
Thoms, William J., 53
Thuringia, 18, 32n11
Titanfall (video game), 111
Tomb Raider (video game), *see* Lara
    Croft (*Tomb Raider* heroine)
tonal harmonic theory, 37, 48n5
tone poems (symphonic poems),
    147–48
transdisciplinary collaboration,
    142, 144n6. *See also*
    interdisciplinary
    collaboration
Troika Ranch, xiv
tutu, 7–8
Tynes, B.M., 182

Ulanova, Galina, viii
United Kingdom, *see* British theatre

Vera, Dayron, 29
Verdi, Giuseppe, 65–66, 78, 86n16
Verga, Giovanni, 68, 82
verismo, 82, 84
Vestris, Auguste, 8
Victoria (queen), 58
video games

Artificial Intelligence for player-
    experience management,
    112–13
critiques and scholarship,
    160–61, 182
"damsel in distress" characters,
    162–63
emotional connection via
    narrative, 111–12
enjoyment from physical
    movement, 178–79
exercise-oriented, 123
female consumption and
    participation, 161, 180
gendered popularity of, 159,
    183n1
gesture consoles, 104n1
"girls' games" movement,
    180–82, 183n4
hacking, 176
introduction of *iGiselle's* team
    to, xi
Lara Croft (*Tomb Raider*
    heroine), 169–73, 174–76
"Ms. male character" characters,
    163
music in, 153–54
narratives in, 89–90, 93, 94
objectification vs. identification
    with characters, 174–76
racial homogenizing and
    stereotyping, 105n9

representations of men, 162,
183n2

representations of women, 101,
131, 161–64

sexualization of women in,
163–64

software for music composition,
155–56

violence concerns, 160–61, 164,
180

See also Artificial Intelligence
(AI), and emotional
responses in video games;
iGiselle (video game); Player
Appraisal Controlling
Emotions (PACE)

Villella, Edward, 33n22

violence, in video games, 160–61,
164, 180

virtual reality (VR), 98, 134–35

Wack, E., 162

Wagner, Richard, 65, 67, 69, 71, 134

Walburg (Walpurga), St., 54–55,
85n5

Wallace, William, 57, 85n7

Weber, Carl Maria von
Der Freischütz, 36, 71
Oberon, 58, 64

Wechsler, Robert, xiv

White Act (*ballet blanc*), ix, 6

White Goddess, *see* ballerina

whiteness, 95–96

Wii (Nintendo), 179

Wilis, 9–10, 11, 32n17, 51, 53–54,
85n3, 101–2

Williams, D.C., 162, 164

Williams, Peter, 16

Wilson, J., 183n1

wings, 7, 31n3

The Wizard of Oz, 65

women, *see* ballerina; gender; video
games

Wulff, H., 166

Zuelli, Guglielmo, 73